The Village Atlas

The Growth of Derbyshire,
Nottinghamshire and Leicestershire
1834 - 1904

The Village Atlas

The Growth of Derbyshire, Nottinghamshire and Leicestershire
1834 - 1904

The Alderman Press

Published by The Village Press Limited
7d Keats Parade, Church Street, Edmonton, N9 9DP.

June 1990

© The Village Press 1990

British Library Cataloguing in Publication Data

The village atlas : Derbyshire, Nottinghamshire & Leicestershire
    1834-1904

    1. England. Midlands. East Midlands, history. Maps, atlases
    I. Bruff, Barry Robson, 1926-
    911'. 425

ISBN 1-85540-026-X

Typesetting by Haworth Associates, Winchmore Hill.
Artwork by Active Art, Winchmore Hill.
Printed and bound in Gt. Britain
by The Bath Press, Bath, Avon.

Acknowledgements.

The maps in this book are reproduced with the kind permission of The British Library.

The publishers would like to thank the staff of the Map Library and Photographic Department of the British Library for their help during the preparation of this Atlas.

The staff of the Reference Library Enfield Middlesex.

Introduction

Derbyshire, in common with other industrial areas, had an enormous growth in population during the nineteenth century, from 161,567 in 1801 to 621,636 by 1901, purely because of the development of already established industries such as textiles, chiefly cotton, silk, hosiery and lace-making; coal and iron mining and agriculture. In the early years of the century the last was the principal occupation, employing 18,616 people in 1841. (Of the others, textiles employed 11,141, hosiery and lace-making 8,219, mining 6,784 and iron trades 5,092, at the same date). However, by 1901 mining and engineering had long overtaken it in importance; though the numbers employed then were only 3,000 fewer, this was of course an enormous percentage decrease in terms of the whole working population. Those working in the textiles and hosiery trades and in lace-making numbered 12,620 and 8,963 respectively. Mining, however, employed 45,062 - almost all of them coal miners, the iron miners having gone and the lead miners much declined. The iron trades employed 19,723 workers.

The cotton industry in Derbyshire received a boost when Richard Arkwright removed to **Cromford** in 1771. By 1803 there were thirty-seven mills in the county when steam power began to replace water power, although at the Masson Mill at **Matlock** power was still supplied by water at the end of the century. By 1861 nearly 16,000 cotton workers were employed. The numbers dropped after this because of the introduction of improved machinery, although production increased considerably.

Pottery has been Derby's speciality for centuries because of the wealth of raw materials found in the surrounding area and since the eighteenth century, when the Chelsea and Bow factories were removed to Derby, it has enjoyed a world-wide reputation for its porcelain. However, in terms of numbers employed, it played a minor part in Derby's industrial base.

Chesterfield in the Rother valley is one of the centres of Derbyshire's coal and iron mining. In 1801 the population was 7,330; by 1851 it had nearly doubled to around 13,000 but by 1901 had risen to an astonishing 39,995 people. George Stephenson came here to supervise the building of the Midland

Railway and it was the railway which encouraged the growth in population and brought its prosperity.

Alfreton, a mining town dating back to the Middle Ages, with a population of 2,301 in 1801, witnessed a seven-fold plus increase to 17,505 people, an amazing increase.

Heanor, a busy market town with coal mining, hosiery and engineering and pottery works, also had notable growth in population during the century, 2,322 inhabitants in 1851, 5,982 in 1851 and 16,906 by 1901.

Not far away is **Ilkeston**, which had one of the biggest percentage increases of all the towns in the county due to its textile manufacturing and collieries. A small market town in 1801, with a population of 2,422 people, it saw this gradually rise to 9,662 by 1871 and from then until the end of the century an increase of some four to five thousand each decade, until by 1901 it had reached 25,384.

Pentrich grew from 1,761 inhabitants in 1801 to 10,402 by 1901. Here, in 1817, during the industrial unrest in the hosiery and weaving trades, due to the new machinery, a man called Jeremiah Brandreth hatched a plot at the White Horse Inn to march on London to overthrow the government. It failed miserably and Brandreth and two others were hanged, drawn and quartered at Derby; they were perhaps the last in England to suffer such a fate.

Ripley, a market and industrial town in a mining area, saw its population grow steadily throughout the century from 1,091 to 9,239. The Butterfly Iron Works furnished St. Pancras station with its magnificent roof.

Church Gresley, another mining town, had a rapid increase in population during the latter half of the century. A mere 1,180 in 1801, it had reached 3,300 by 1851 and this latter figure had multiplied almost five times by 1901 to 16,458.

Normanton was once, in 1801, a tiny hamlet of 214 people living on some 1,390 acres and it still had only 638 inhabitants in 1871. During the century it was swallowed up by the city and by 1901 its population was 11,792; over 6,000 of that increase was in the last ten years.

North Wingfield, centre of a coal and iron mining district, like all the Derbyshire industrial towns, has the good fortune to be near one of the county's areas of great, natural beauty. Here again the population showed its greatest increase during the latter half of the century; though it had quadrupled from 1715 to 4,351, after that it quadrupled again by 1901 to 16,000.

Belper was already a populous town in 1801 thanks to the river Derwent which supplied water-power for its cotton mills. Its population had risen from 4,500 in 1801 to 10,934 by 1901. It was also fortunate in one of its sons, Jedediah Strutt. Not only had he revolutionised the knitting industry with his own inventions but he also financed Arkwright's new spinning machine, which brought new factories to both Derby and Nottingham. While there were great increases in the population of Derby and the other industrial or semi-industrial towns and villages, in the great majority of villages and hamlets the figures hardly changed over the century, perhaps only by a few percent. In many cases there was a considerable reduction in population. There are some curious anomalies. In **Markeaton** the population almost quadrupled between 1871 and 1891, from 237 to 1,124. This turns out to be due to the building of the Derby Union Work House and Sanatorium. Similarly in **Mickleover** there was an increase between 1851 and 1861 of 300 to 400 when the County Lunatic asylum was built. In Pentrich, mentioned earlier, there was a drop in population after 1821, when the Duke of Devonshire's agents destroyed houses following the Brandreth riots. In **Repton** in 1841 there was a sudden increase caused by attendance at a village wake, as there was at **Kirk Ireton** in the same year for a feast. Over a hundred strangers must have attended. Other places showed increases due to peripatetic railway workers.

Unfortunately the Village Atlas format has meant that a large part of eastern Derbyshire has had to be excluded and we have tried to concentrate on the industrial areas where most changes took place. This has meant that **Glossop**, **Buxton** and **Chapel-en-le-Frith**, where there were also great changes, have been omitted. Glossop, for example, had its population quadrupled over the century from 8,883 to 36,985.

Nottinghamshire, like Leicestershire, had three main trades during the nineteenth century apart from agriculture: hosiery, lace-making and coal mining. Hosiery and lace-making were particularly subject to changes in fashion during the nineteenth century. This resulted in severe depressions at times and although, as elsewhere, there were great increases in population, at times the number of people employed actually fell and in **Nottingham** and surrounding villages, such as **Basford**, **Beeston** and **Radford**, where lace-making was the staple

industry, the suffering was intense.

Thousands of families were unemployed and for those that were in work wages fell by 50% or more between 1820 and 1840. Unfortunately, for reasons of space we were unable to include the area of Newark in the atlas but here the stocking weavers were as badly affected as the lace-makers.

Eventually, around 1870, steam power came to the factories and migration to the towns, especially Nottingham, commenced in earnest. Between 1861 and 1891 the population of the county had increased by some 30% but the population of Nottingham had trebled from 74,531 to 213,877. Villages were either absorbed into the town or, if they lay further out, were deserted. For many years lace was the single most important factor in the life of Nottingham. The story of the town and the decline of the lace trade, the emergence of Jesse Boot, the tobacco industry and Raleigh, plus the dozens of other trades that took the place of lace, belongs to the twentieth century.

By the end of the century coal mining was playing an increasing part in the economics of the county. In 1800 there were some twelve areas where mining was taking place: **Beggarlee**, **Bilborough**, **Brinsley**, **Dunshill**, **Eastwood**, **Greasley**, **Hucknall**, **Limes**, **Shilo**, **Skegby**, **Trowell Moor** and **Wollaton**. By mid-century, with the advent of the railways, the pace of mining increased dramatically. By 1860 there were twenty-one collieries and by 1869, twenty-six and output had more than doubled and the Mansfield district was rapidly developed. By 1899 nearly 7,000,000 tons were being raised in the county and by 1907 that figure had risen to 11,728,886 tons and 35,415 men and boys were employed. The population of **Mansfield** itself, nearly 6,000 in 1801, increased steadily over the century to 21,445 by 1901.

In **Weston Parish** the population in 1801 was 246 and only 310 a century later, yet there was a big jump of nearly 100 in 1851. This proved to have been caused by a number of labourers working on the railway. This may also have happened in **Sutton on Trent** and many other places during these years. In the main, the population of towns and villages where industry settled grew steadily, albeit in some cases extraordinarily.

Sutton in Ashfield, an ancient Saxon village now in the centre of a mining community, had a fairly gradual population growth from 2,801 in 1801, although there was a big increase of nearly 9,000 in the last two decades to bring the population to 18,943 in 1901.

Greasley was another quite, large village in 1801, with a population of 2,968 inhabitants. This rose to 11,861 in 1901.

Two villages which by 1901 had just been reached by the advancing tide of the expansion of Nottingham were **Radford** and **Basford**. Basford by this time was divided into New and Old Basford. The new station on the Great Northern Railway no doubt encouraged the expansion. Basford's population in 1801 had been 2,124. By 1901 it was 27,119.

Radford also divided into Old and New Radford. In 1801 the population was 2,269. In 1901 this had become 35,354. The 1891 population of 15,127 had more than doubled in thirty years.

Gedling in 1801 was composed of three small hamlets, Gedling itself, **Carlton Hamlet** and **Stoke Bardolph Township**. Together they had a combined population of 1,530. Stoke Bardolph, nestling in a bend in the River Trent, hardly changed at all, its population of 157 in 1801 having risen to only 213 by 1901. Gedling started the century with 554 inhabitants and ended with 785. Carlton Hamlet, a mile or so nearer the city, started with 819 people. The city advancing along the main road to **Newark** and the railways surrounding it on three sides, changed all that and by 1901 the population was 10,386. Six thousand of these had arrived since 1881 and the hamlet was no more. The city by 1901 was also enveloping **Sneinton**. Here a population of 558 in 1801 had become 3,605 by 1831, 12,237 by 1871 and 23,093 by 1901.

Kirkby in Ashfield, a mining town, had a steady rise in population during the century from 1,002 to 10,392 inhabitants.

Hucknall, a Saxon village once distinguished as Hucknall Torkard from the name of former landowners, had a relatively small population of 1,498 in 1801. This had only reached 4,257 by 1871 but in the following thirty years, as the railways surrounded the town and the mining industry expanded, another 11,000 arrived. Nine or ten thousand of these must have been newcomers.

Eastwood, a mining village to the north-west of Nottingham whose population rose from 735 in 1801 to nearly 5,000 by 1901, was the birth place of D. H. Lawrence and it was also here that the Iron Masters and Coal Owners of the district met at the Sun Inn, to form the Old Midland Railway which did so much in bringing prosperity to this part of the East Midlands.

Leicestershire has, since the eighteenth century, gradually become dominated by its county town and its industries; **Leicester**, situated in the centre of the county as it is, with all the main roads radiating from it, has over the last two hundred years drawn to itself the majority of the population. In 1801, when the population of the county was just over 130,000, Leicester comprised with its outlying parishes roughly a quarter of the total. By 1911, at the end of the period covered by the atlas, Leicester, a county borough since 1896, had almost one half of the population of 434,019.

The county, from an industrial and population viewpoint, can be divided into roughly three areas: the eastern half where, until recently when light industry came to Market Harborough and Melton, the population either stagnated or fell; the south-west, dominated by the hosiery industry and the north-west where mining drew large numbers from inside and outside the county.

Coalville, for example, had a population of 620 in 1851, of which no less than 507, 82%, were immigrants. By 1901 it had grown to 15,281. The construction of the Leicester-Swannington Railway helped in its rapid growth. A large proportion of its newcomers were from Derbyshire.

In the south-west of the county the hosiery trade dominated although it was originally a cottage industry. The invention of the wide-frame machines capable of making many stockings at once and the growth of the "cut-up" industry, as opposed to the fully fashioned, gradually took trade away from the cottagers. At the beginning of the eighteenth century feeling was so strong, as the people saw the new machinery taking away their bread and butter, that the Luddite Rebellion (named after Ned Ludd, an apprentice who smashed his machine because of a disagreement over wages) was born. In the following decade thousands of machines were smashed. In 1816 Heathcoat's factory at **Loughborough** was broken into and fifty-three machines were destroyed. A year later six men were hanged in Leicester for the crime. It took a long time before the Industrial Revolution was accepted in Leicester - or Derby and Nottingham for that matter - but eventually all settled down, until by the eighteen-thirties there were some ten-thousand stocking frames operating. As always, trade gravitated to the towns.

Hinkley, with some fifteen-hundred frames at this time had a population of approximately 7,000 and had roughly doubled in size by the end of the century.

Wigston, or rather its ancient parish of **Wigston Magna**, once the second largest town in the county, had a population of 1,658 in 1801. By 1901 this had risen to nearly 9,000, and Wigston had a thriving hosiery trade.

The ancient parish of Loughborough's population of 4,546 in 1801 had more than doubled by 1851, and in 1901 - by which time Loughborough had become a municipal borough - was 21,508.

Steam-powered machinery arrived about the eighteen-forties but the hosiery trade remained in small units well into the century because of the workers not caring much for the disciplines required in a large factory. The Education Act of 1870, the abolition of the frame-rent system and the strengthening of the trade unions accelerated the growth of the factory system. The factories were often built in villages like **Kegworth**, **Stoke Golding**, **Hathern** and **Rothley**. In Loughborough, Cartwright and Warner's factory employed over a thousand people and names familiar today, like I & R Morley, had appeared. The hand frame was still very slow in dying out and as late as 1892 there were still some 5,000 hand-framework-knitters in the county. Their survival was largely due to the War Office's reluctance to change the old-style "military-pants" which could only be made by hand. In 1844 some four million dozen pairs were being produced on hand frames. By 1907 production had risen to fourteen million dozen pairs and roughly half the people engaged in the United Kingdom trade were Leicester based. By the beginning of World War I the hand-frames had all disappeared.

The footwear industry became more important as the century wore on. The first boot and shoe manufacturer appeared at **Anstey** in 1863 and by 1870 there were three others in the village. As the cottage industry of hand-frame knitting died out, the workers and their children turned to leather work in places such as **Earl Shilton** and **Sileby**. The firm of Cotton & Son was described as the largest in the country at this time (1870) and four girls were sent from Leicester to teach local workers how to use the machines which were housed in three cottages on the main road in Earl Shilton. This was possibly the earliest shoe factory in the county. By 1896 there were some ninety manufacturers in the county, including seventeen at Anstey, fifteen at **Hinkley**, twelve at Earl Shilton and eleven at **Barwell**.

Leicester's population grew from around 40,000 in 1831 to over 60,000 by the middle of the century, and to 68,000 by 1861. In 1840 the railway joined it to Northampton, Derby and London. Other lines were built in 1848 and 1849 to the Midlands and a direct route to London opened in 1857. As elsewhere, the coming of the railway was accompanied by a frantic building programme, at first along the Aylestone and Walford roads and on the large Southfields estate. The best new houses of this time were built along Granby Street and London Road. Conditions of sale on the more distant parts of the estate meant a middle class area growing up in Stoneygates and Knighton and also in Highfields.

Between 1850 and 1860 six hundred houses were built along the Humberstone road. Unlike towns such as Manchester and Birmingham, the coming of the railway did not immediately bring industrial building because the factory system had not really arrived in the hosiery trade. Land in St Mary's was sold piecemeal by the council without stipulations or control on the buildings put up, so workshops for the hosiers and boot and shoe makers were built along Southgate Street and New Walk and the working class district began to expand along Walford Road. In the old city the centuries-old gardens and orchards had disappeared under houses by around 1850.

The older houses were in the main grouped around narrow courts, badly-ventilated and unsatisfactory, 347 courts contained 1,931 houses. Most were overcrowded.

Sanitation was a constant problem in the centre of Leicester. Flooding from the Soar, Grand Union Canal and Willow Brook left mud and sewage behind, bringing disease in its wake.

After 1860 there was a long period of prosperity in Leicester. Population increased from 68,000 in 1861 to 142,000 in 1891. In the first decade of this period there was an increase of nearly 40%. There was a natural increase as public health improved but the vast majority of the increase came from immigrants and between 1851 and 1911 they accounted for nearly 50% of the population. The number of occupied dwellings increased by some 30,000 between 1861 and 1901, although by the end of the century Leicester had lost its place as the largest city of the East Midlands to Nottingham. By 1911 the population of the county borough of Leicester was 227,222 - a five-fold plus increase from 1841.

With three counties such as Derbyshire, Nottinghamshire and Leicestershire, where almost every village has some historical association, this can only be the briefest of introductions but the publishers hope that it will make a useful companion volume to the many books that have been written and, no doubt, will continue to be written about this area. As the present-day cities grow ever outwards, new towns are built and Nottingham and Derby inch closer and closer together. Maps such as these, which preserve the old place names and connections, become even more important.

Barry Bruff
London 1990.

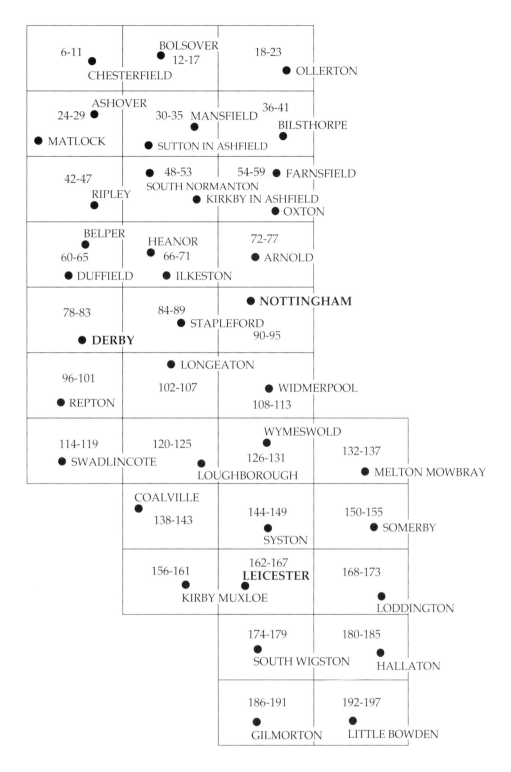

The Maps

Publisher's Note

The maps in this Atlas are based on a scale of two inches to the mile. However, because of the number of different maps involved and the reproduction thereof there may be some minor variations in scale. The age of the maps and the fact that there could be as much as fifteen years difference between the dates of survey of adjoining maps, plus the handling and folding which has taken place over the years, have also meant that there are small differences here and there which are impossible to eradicate.

The publishers have made every effort to minimise these faults and trust the reader will make allowances for any slight imperfections.

1   2

1 mile approx.

24

Published 1840.

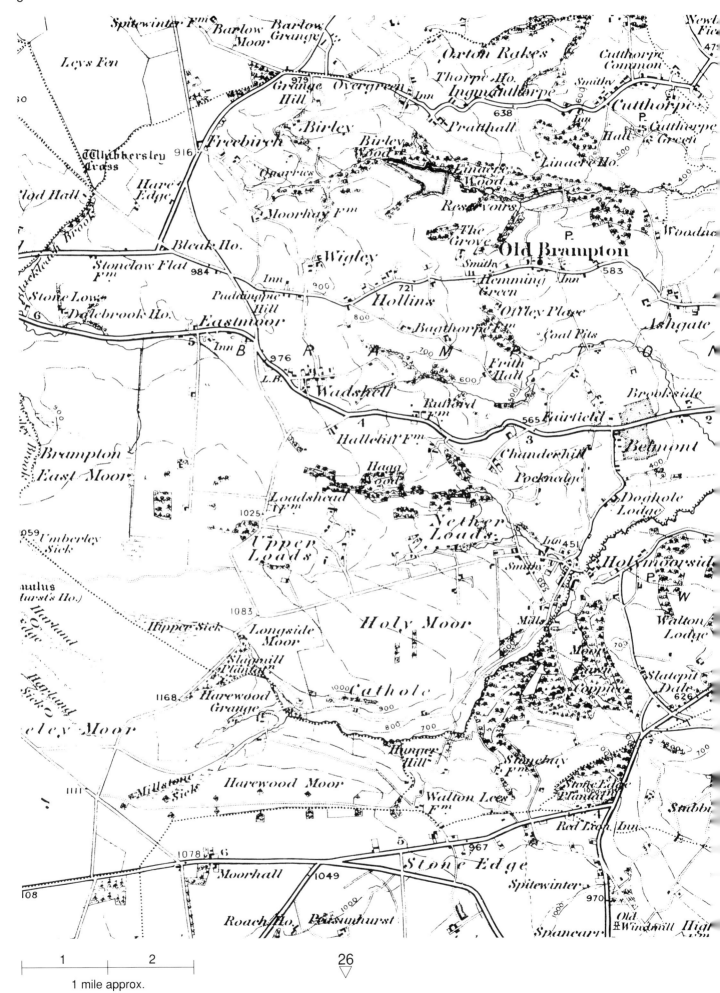

1 mile approx.

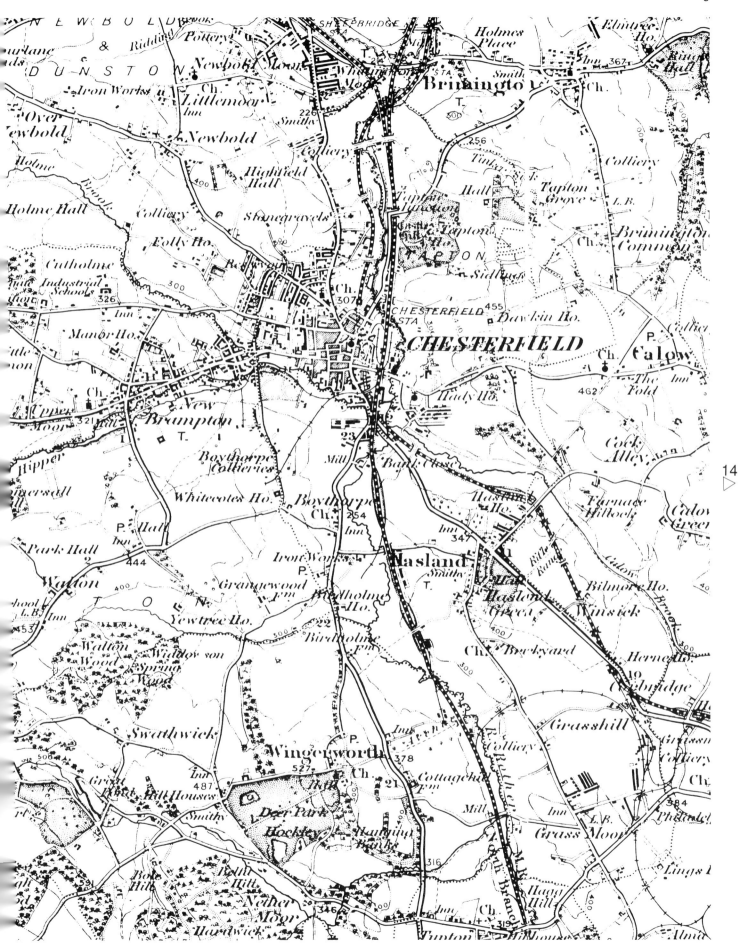

14

Surveyed 1875 - 85. Revised 1895. Published 1897.

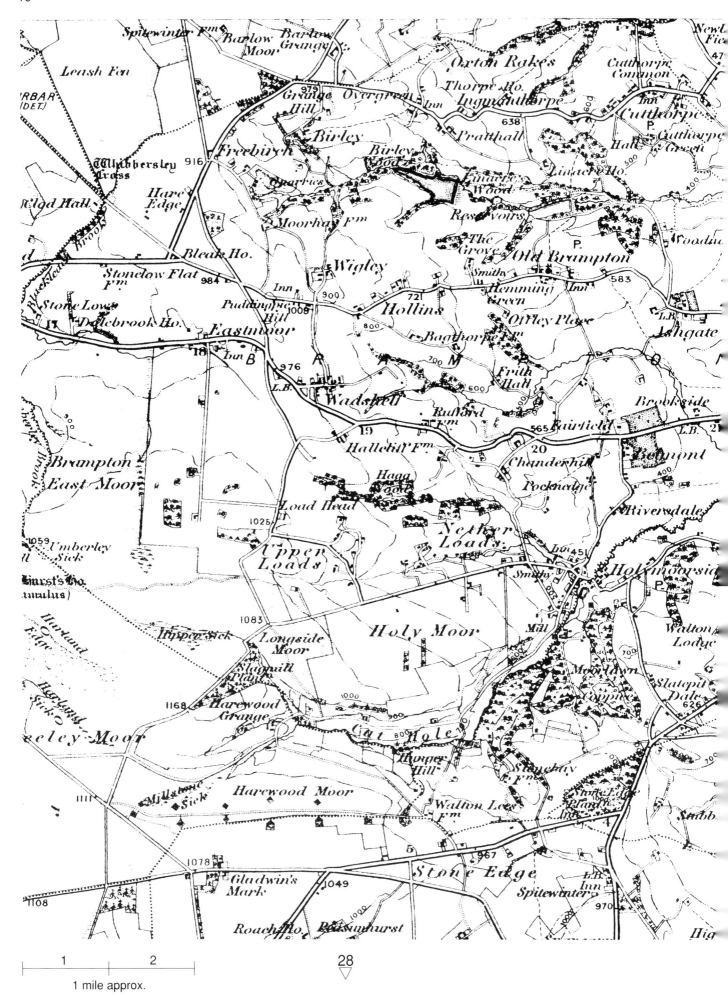

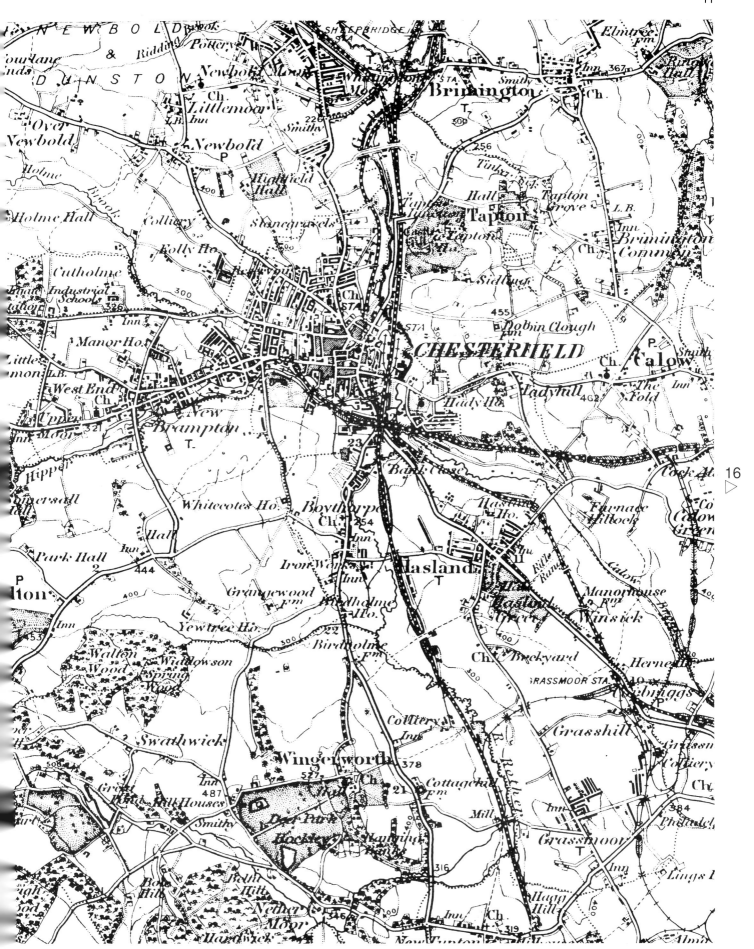

Surveyed 1875 - 85. Revised 1906. Published 1908.

1   2

1 mile approx.

30
▽

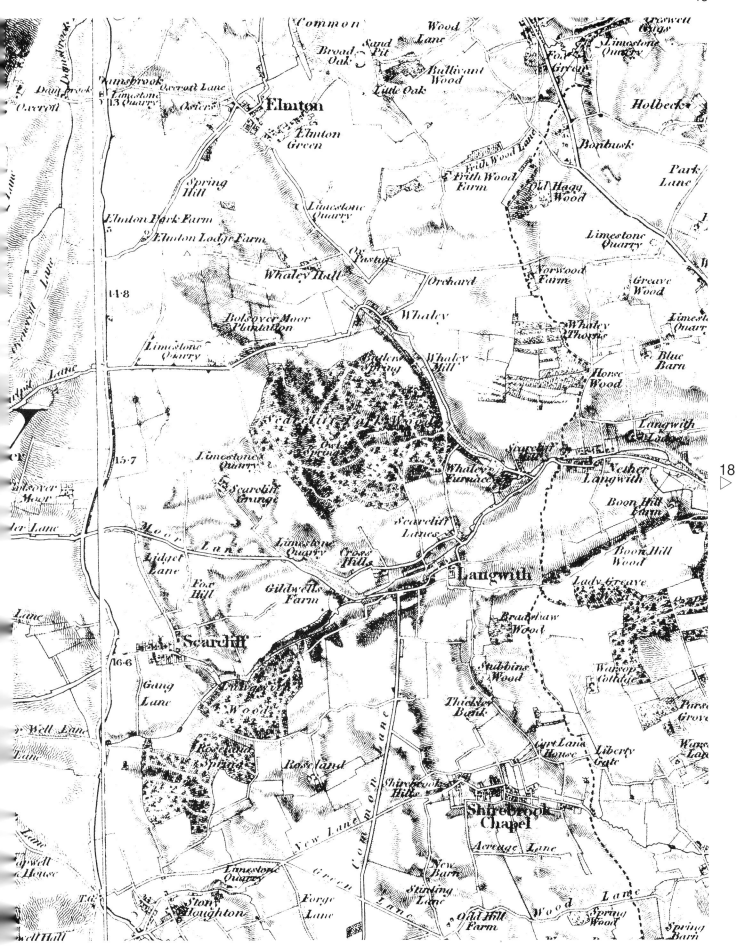

Published 1840.

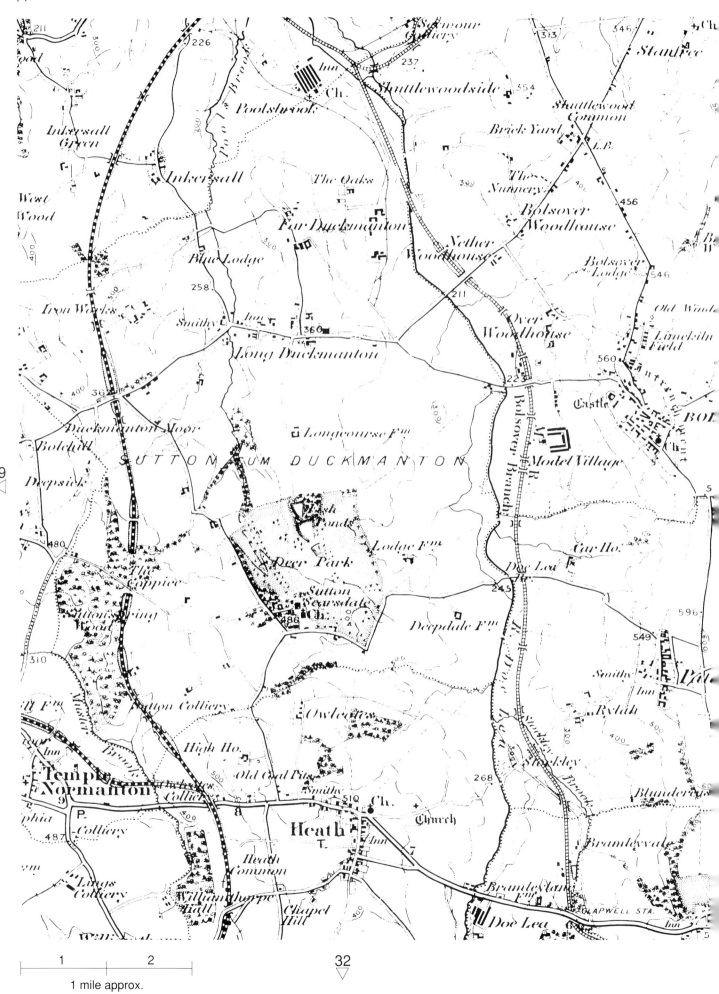

1 mile approx.

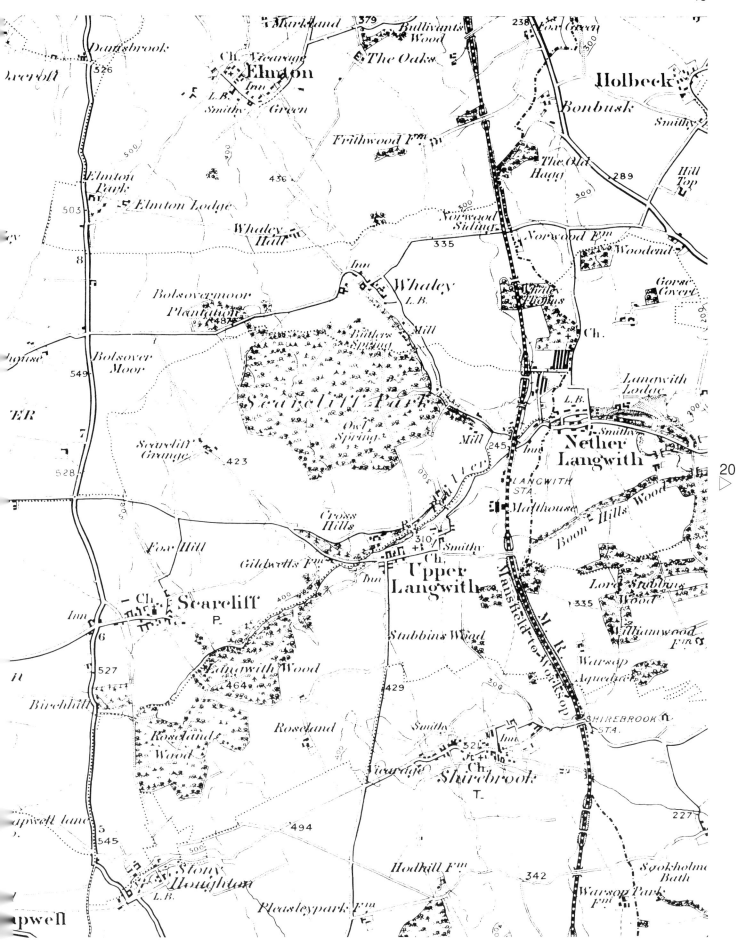

Surveyed 1875 - 85. Revised 1895. Published 1897.

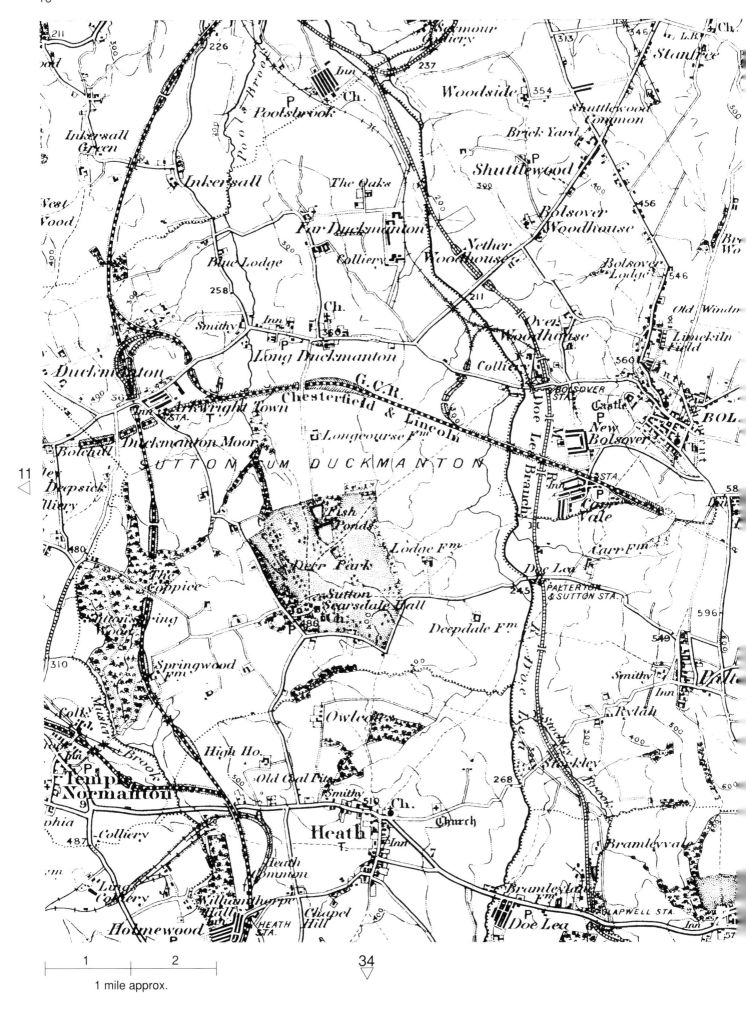

1   2

1 mile approx.

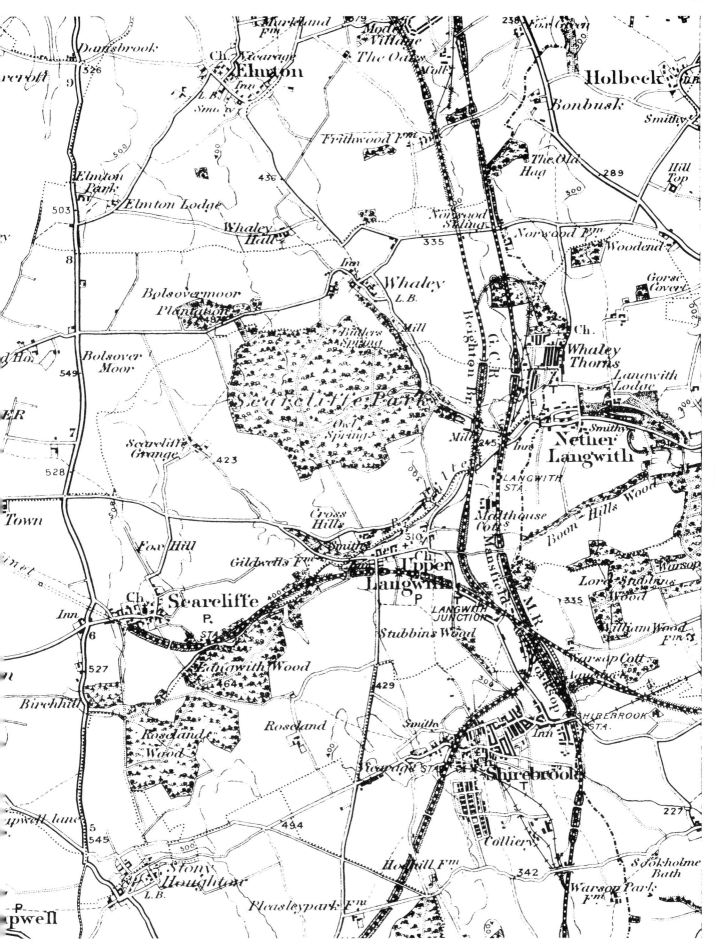

35

Surveyed 1875 - 85. Revised 1906. Published 1908.

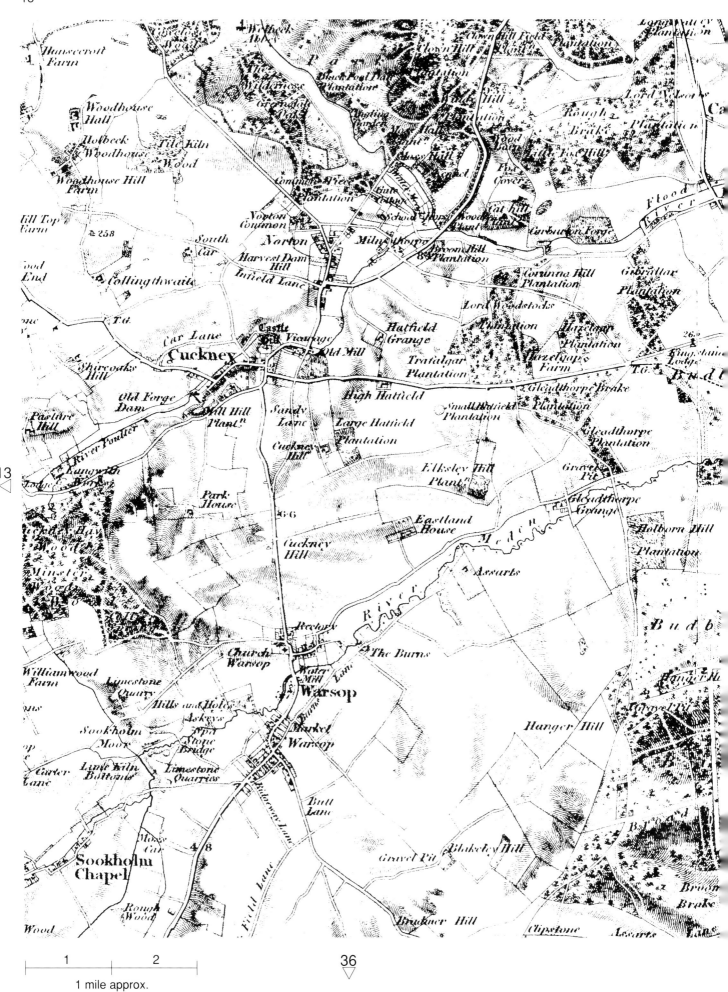

36

1   2

1 mile approx.

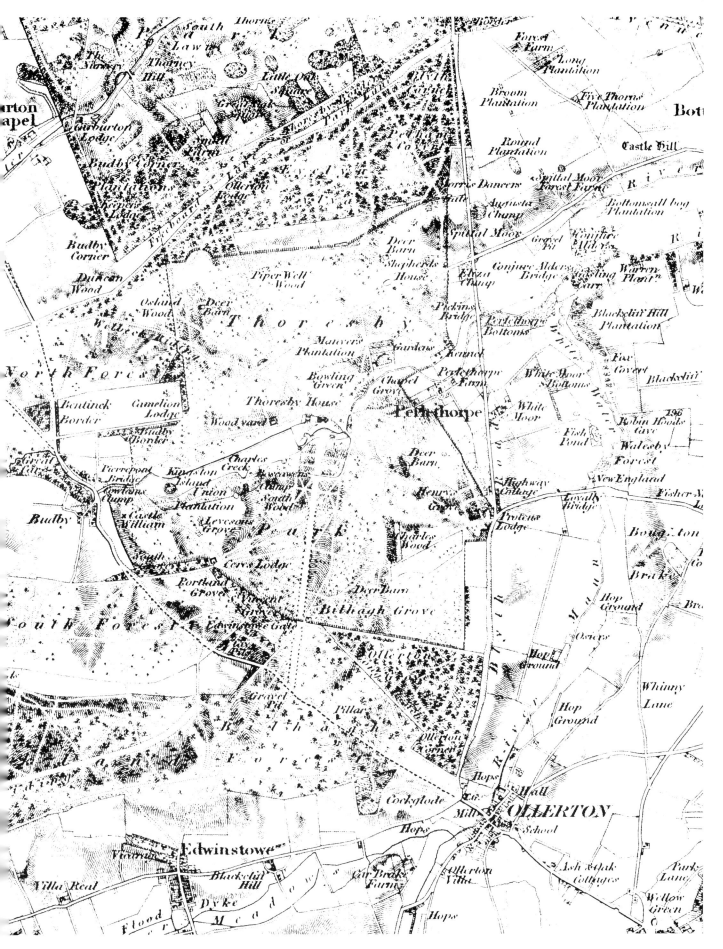

Published 1840.

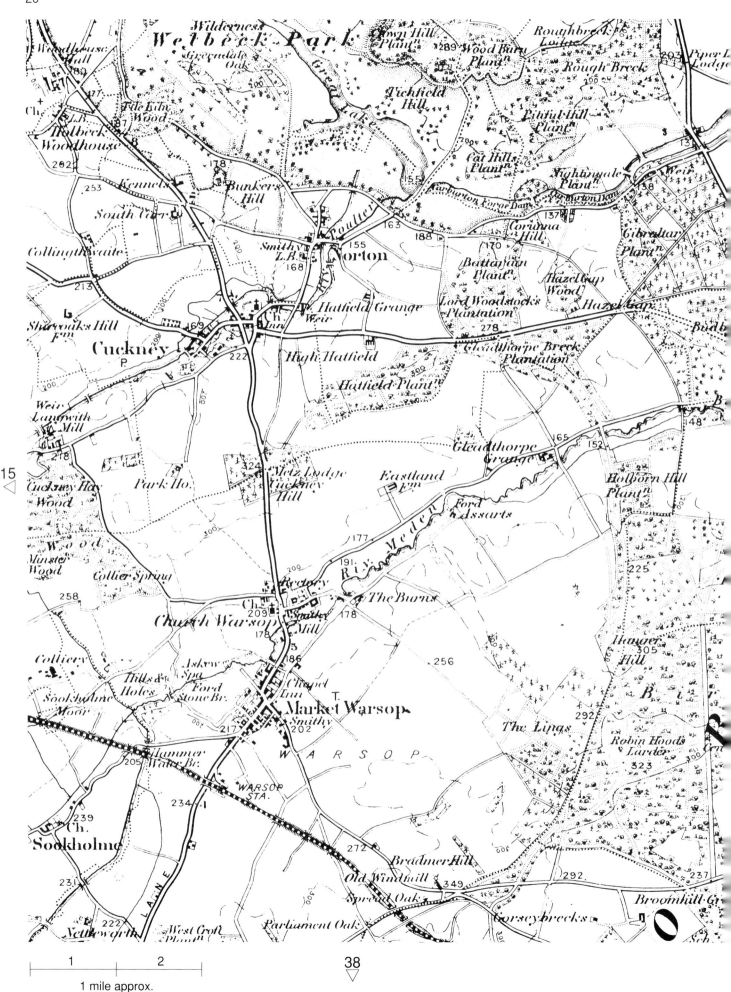

1 mile approx.

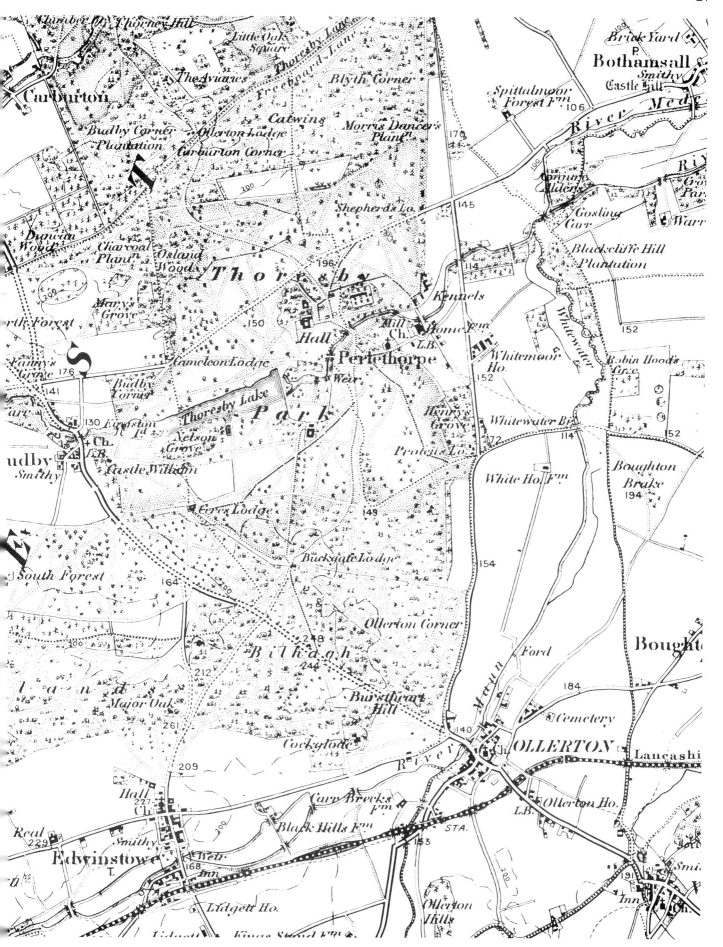

Surveyed 1876 - 84. Revised 1898. Published 1899.

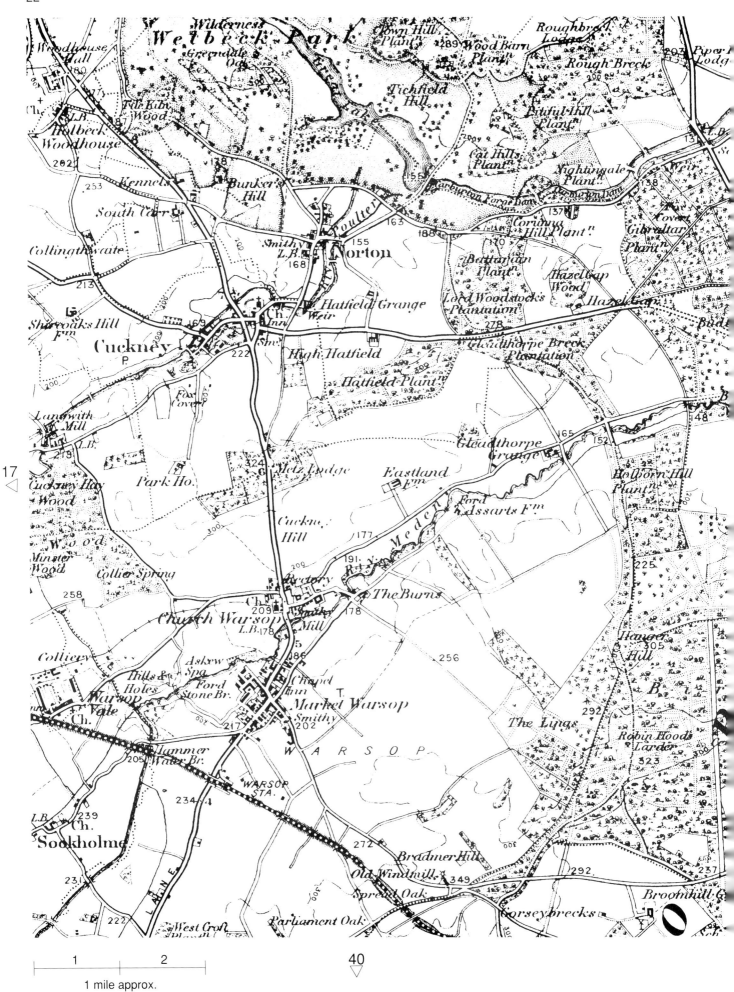

1   2

1 mile approx.

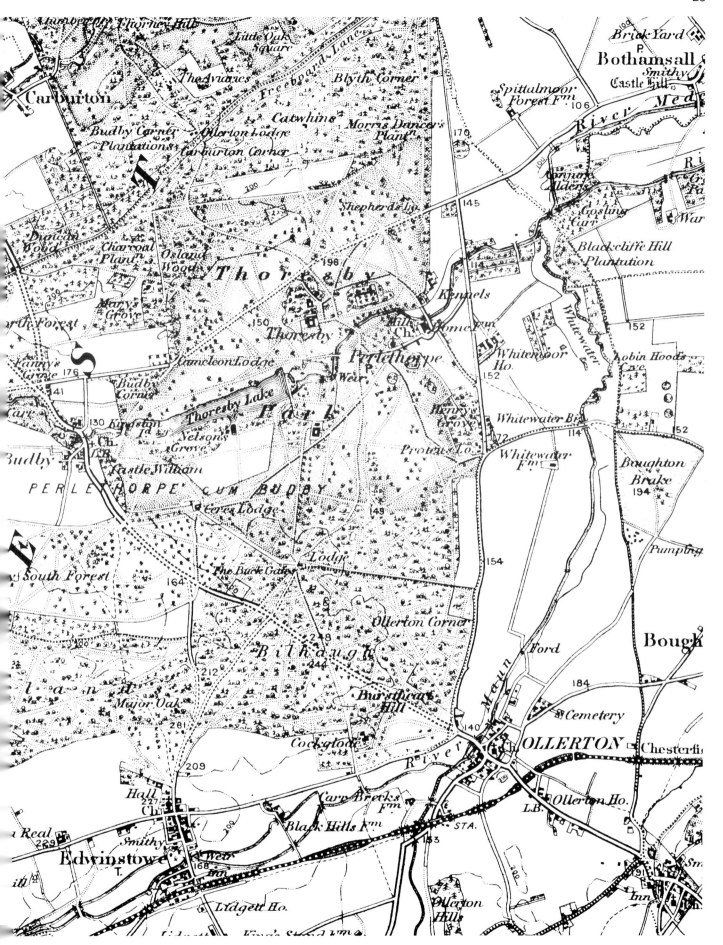

Surveyed 1876 - 84. Revised 1906. Published 1908.

1   2

1 mile approx.

Published 1840.

Jaggers

Lot

sh Ho.

Wilkin Ho.

Buntingfield

Amber Ho.

Dryhurst

Spring Ho.

1044

North Britain

862

864

Sheep

Flash Plantation

Charlestown

Shooterslea

Uppertown

Hardwick

Moor

Flash Dam

Overend

Brockhurst Mill

817

Hilltop

846

900

Rushley Ho.

Robridding

700

Kelstedge

Smithy

Rattle

Nor

Hope Hall

Inn

6

Mawstone

900

Mill

Westedge

As

Sydnope Stand

1038

Ware Stone

Edlestow

577

Butts

Ch

D a r l e y

Matlockmoor Fm

1000

Slack

Tax Fm.

M a t l o c k

955

Goshall

M o o r

Amber Hill

Overton Hall

Hanging Holes

Cuckoostone Ho.

Turning Stone

Cocking Tor

Fall

838

Cuckoo Stone

Lant Lodge

1000

Hurker Hall

900

Holestone

Ravensnest

Farley

800

687

Carolina

Ra Ho

Upper Hackney

8

Bentley Br.

T a n s l e y M o o r

841

The Wolds

700

Foxholes

Red Ho.

Matlock

Blakelow Hill

Dimple

Bank

Paint Hill

Ch.

Lumsdale

T

Tansley wood Mill

Tansley Knoll

Mooredge

900

Butterley

866

BRIDGE STA

312

Ch.

Mill

Inn

Ch.

Scotland Nursery

800

Matlock Bridge

T

Matlock Cliff

Smithy Inn

Tansley

P

Stag Hills

Matlock

Smithy

Riber Hill

Riber

863

700

Dethick Common

Matlock Dale

Castle

High Tor

Hall

600

Starkholmes

Inn

The Bank

Littlemoor

Dethick

Doe

MATLOCK BATH STA

Harston

Hotels ferry

Littlemoor

Lindway

1 2

1 mile approx.

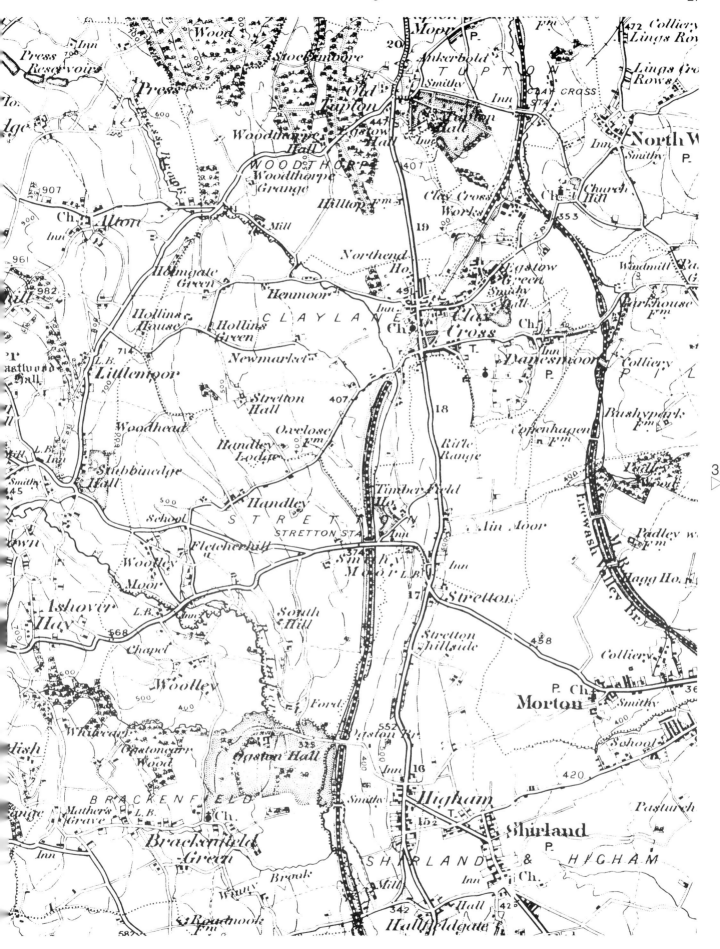

Surveyed 1875 - 85. Revised 1895. Published 1897.

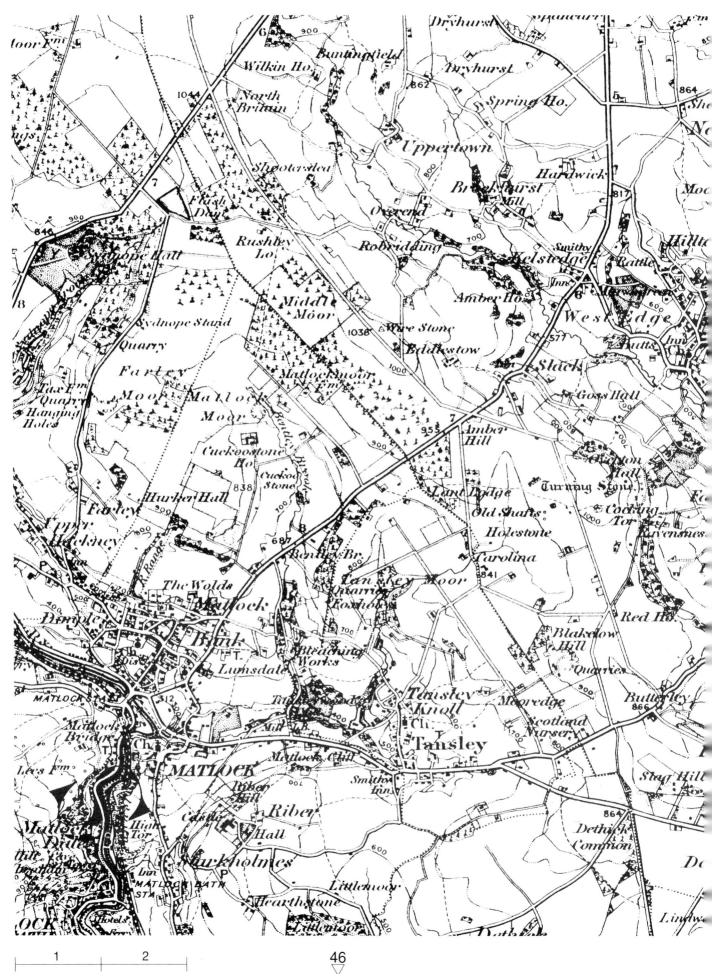

1 mile approx.

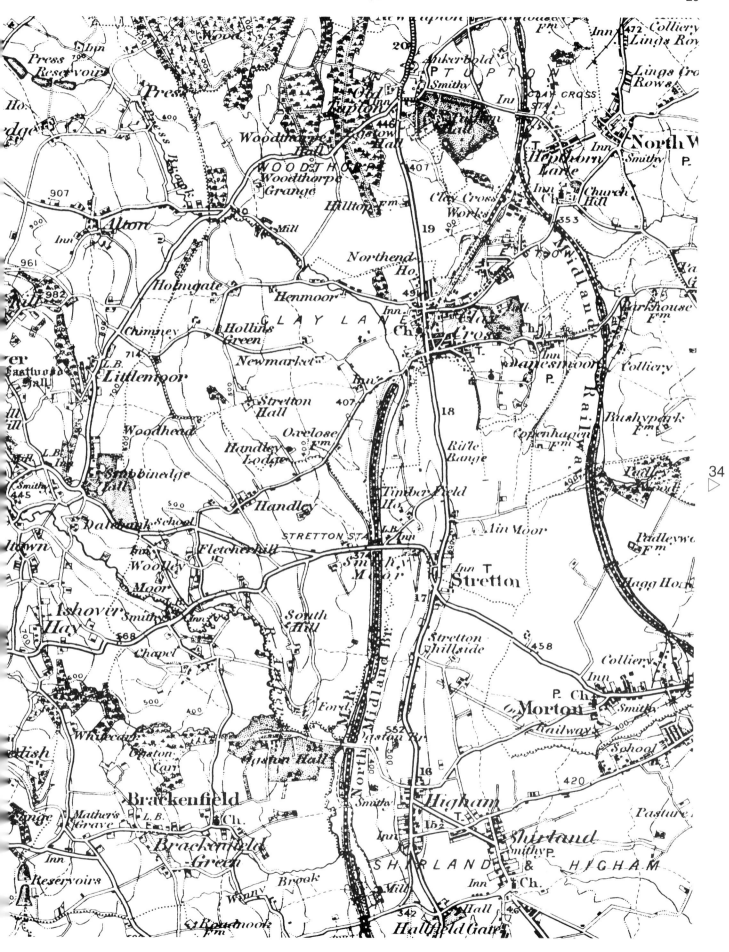

Surveyed 1875 - 85. Revised 1906. Published 1908.

1 mile approx.

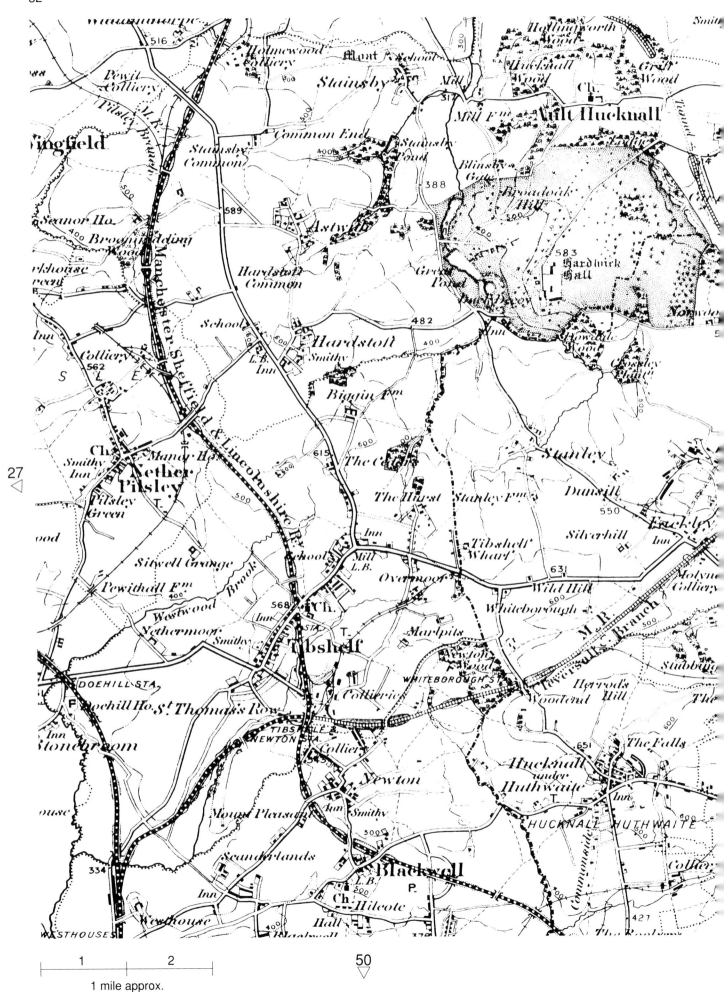

1 mile approx.

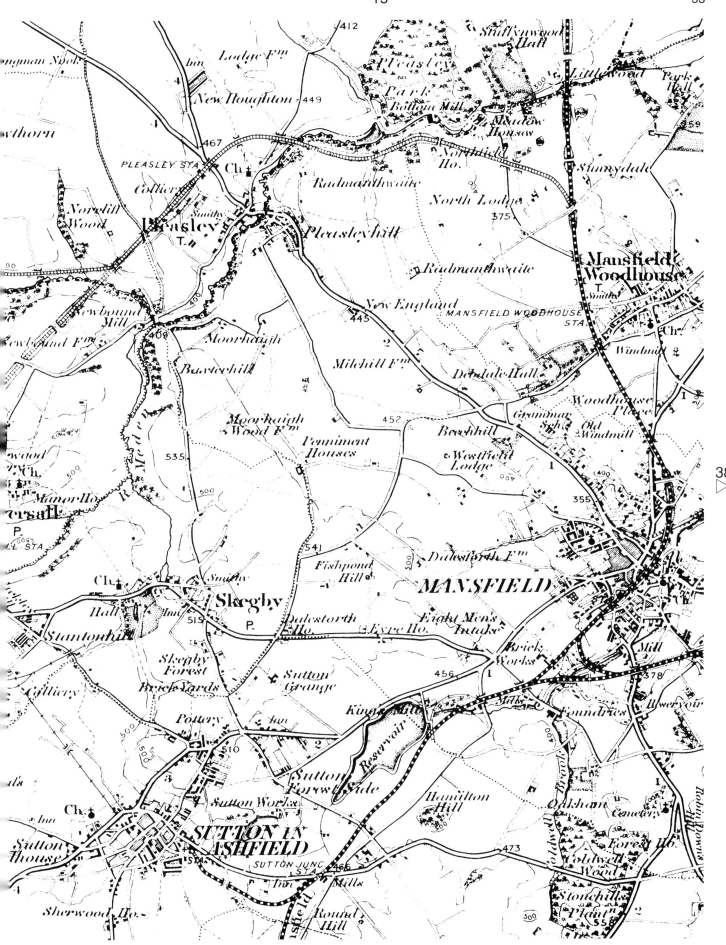

Surveyed 1875 - 85. Revised 1895. Published 1897.

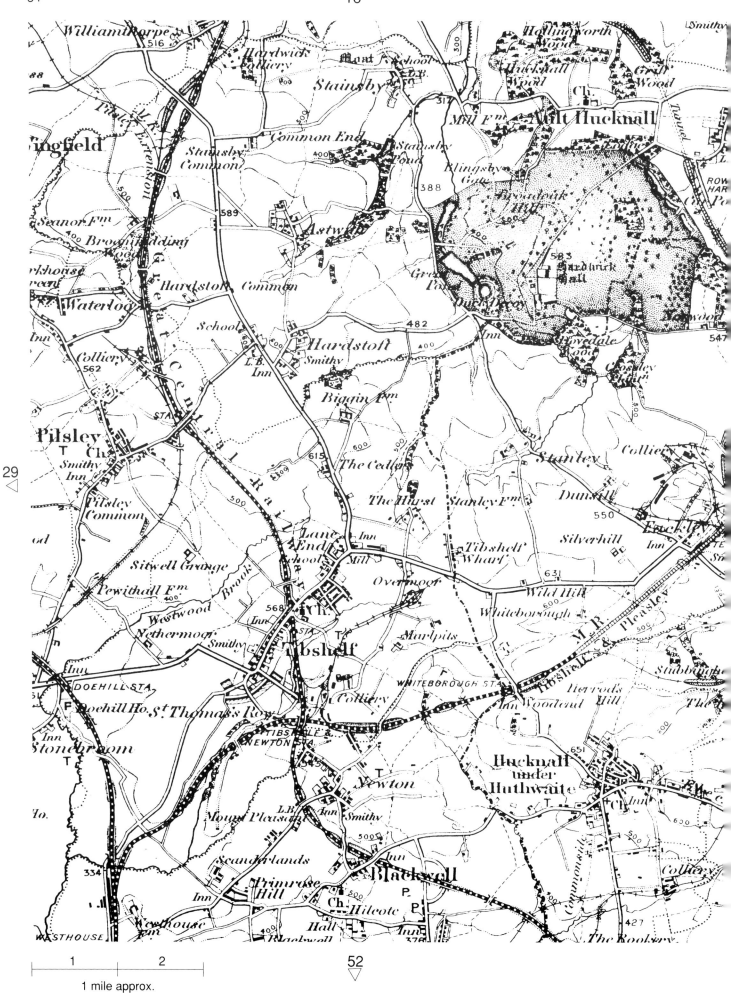

1 mile approx.

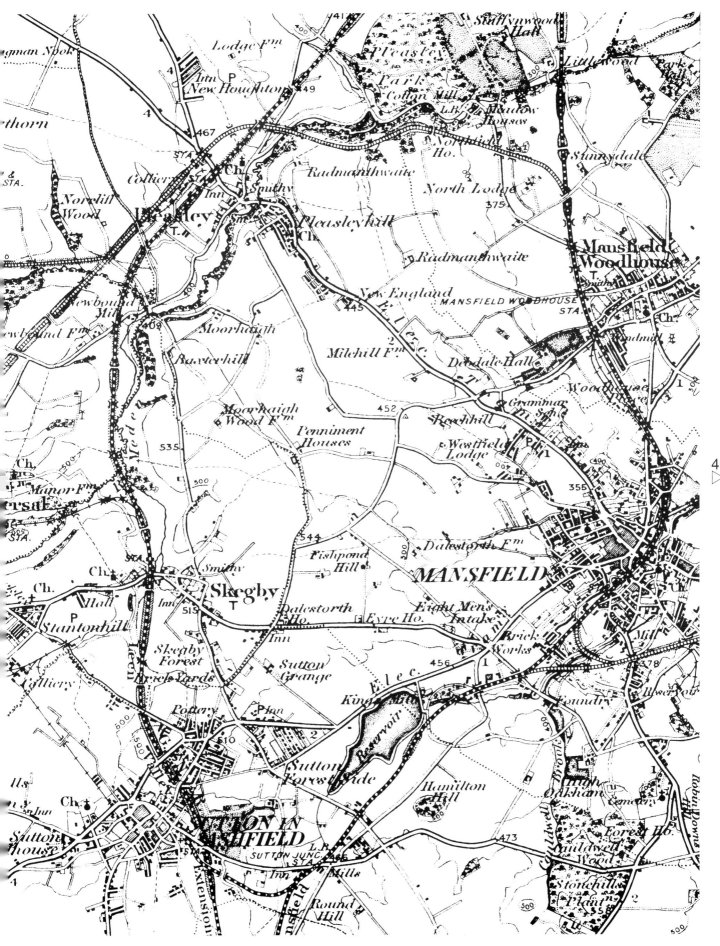

Surveyed 1876 - 84. Revised 1906. Published 1908.

1   2

1 mile approx.

Published 1840.

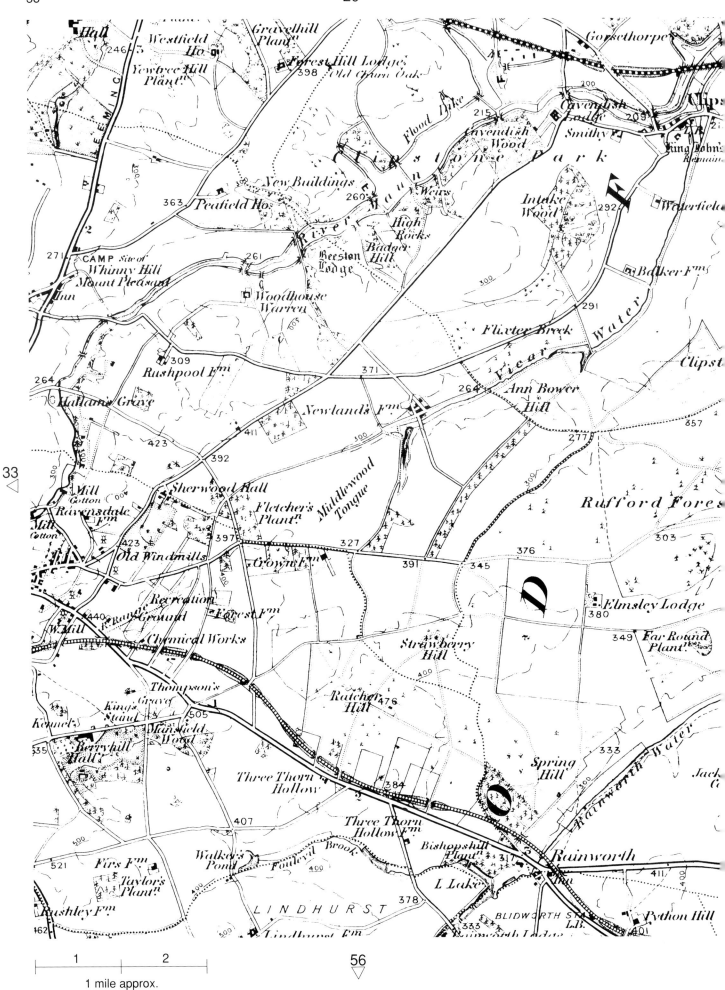

Hall
Westfield Ho.
246·3
Yewtree Hill Plant.n
Gravelhill Plant.n
Forest Hill Lodge
398 Old Churn Oak
Gorsethorpe

LEEMING

Cavendish Lodge
215
200
Cavendish Wood
Smithy
209
King John's Remains
Clipst

300

New Buildings
Weirs
260
292
Intake Wood
Waterfield

363 Peatfield Ho.
261
High Rocks
Badger Hill
Beeston Lodge
300
Balker F.m

271 CAMP Site of
Whinny Hill
Mount Pleasant
Inn
Woodhouse Warren
Flixter Brock
291
Vicar Water
Clipst

309
264
Rushpool F.m
300
371
264
Ann Bower Hill
277
857

Hallam's Grave
Newlands F.m
300

411
392
Middlewood Tongue
Rufford Fores
303

423
Sherwood Hall
Fletcher's Plant.n
327
300
376
380 Elmsley Lodge

Mill Cotton
Ravensdale F.m
423
397
Old Windmills
Crown F.m
391
345
349 Far Round Plant.n

Mill Cotton
440
Ray Ground
Recreation
Forest F.m
Chemical Works
Strawberry Hill
400

W. Mill
Thompson's Grave
King's Stand
Mansfield Wood
505
Ratcher Hill 476
333 Rainworth Water
Spring Hill
Jack G.

Kennels
Berryhill Hall
335
Three Thorn Hollow
384
Rainworth Inn

407
Three Thorn Hollow F.m
Bishopshill Plant.n
311
Rainworth
411

Firs F.m
521
Walker's Pond
Foulevil Brook
400
L Lake
378
Python Hill 401

Taylor's Plant.n
Rushley F.m
462
500
LINDHURST
Lindhurst F.m
BLIDWORTH STA
L.B.
333 Rainworth Lodge

1   2
1 mile approx.

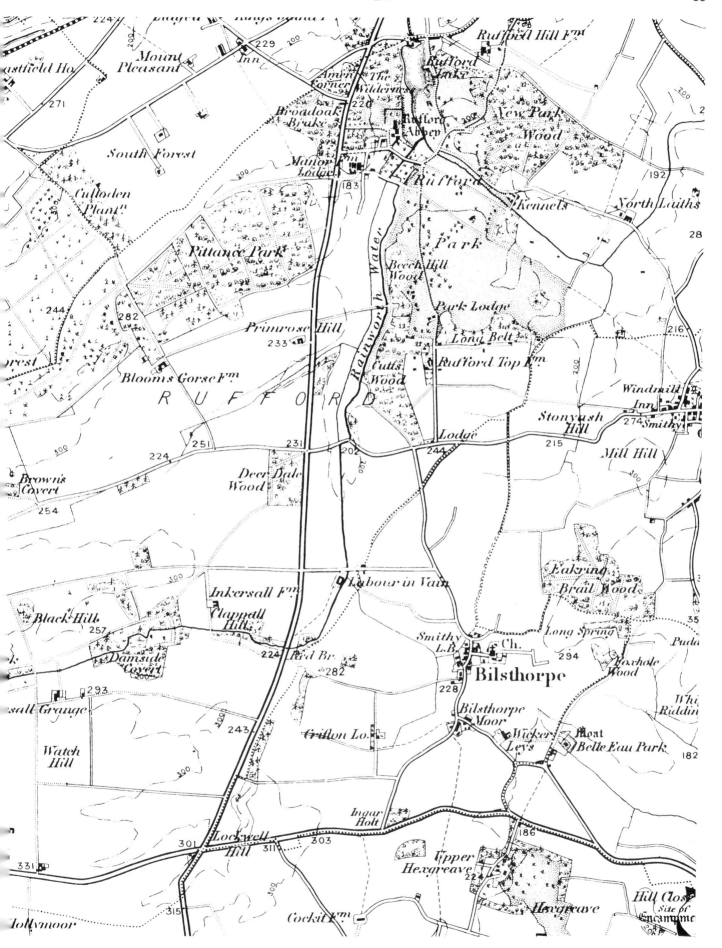

Surveyed 1876 - 84. Revised 1898. Published 1899.

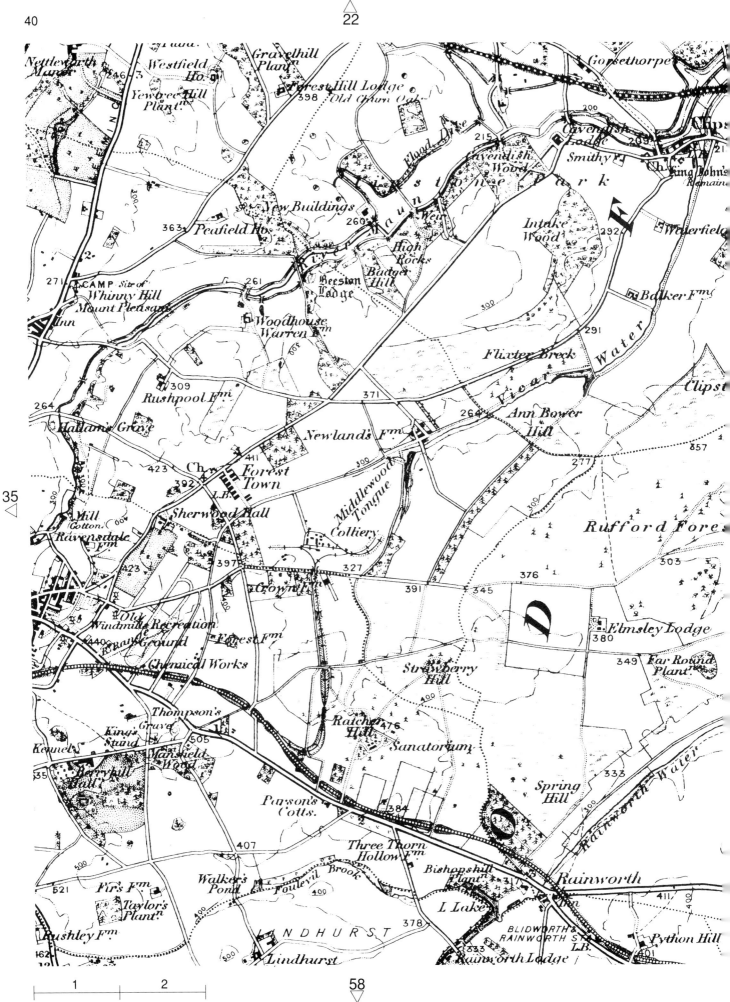

1   2

1 mile approx.

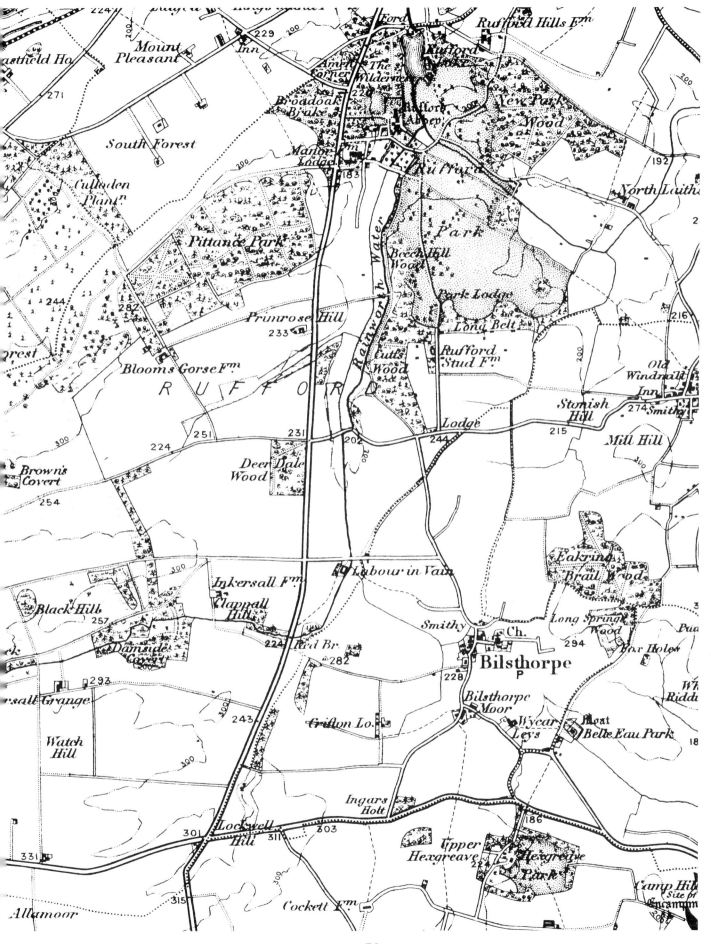

Surveyed 1876 - 84. Revised 1906. Published 1908.

1   2

1 mile approx.

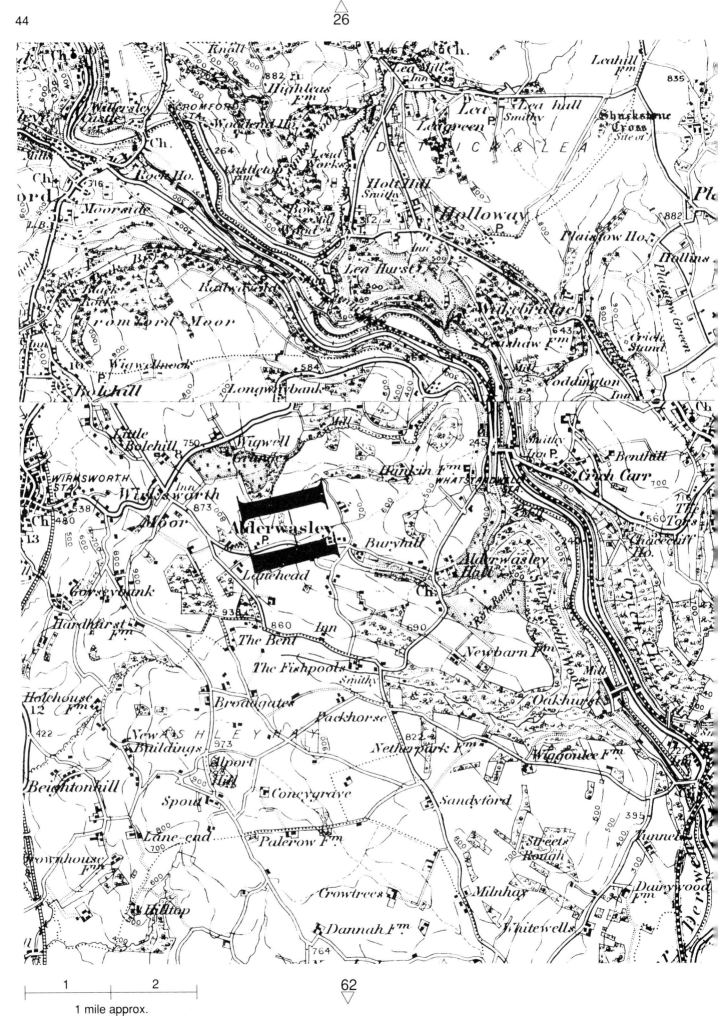

1 mile approx.

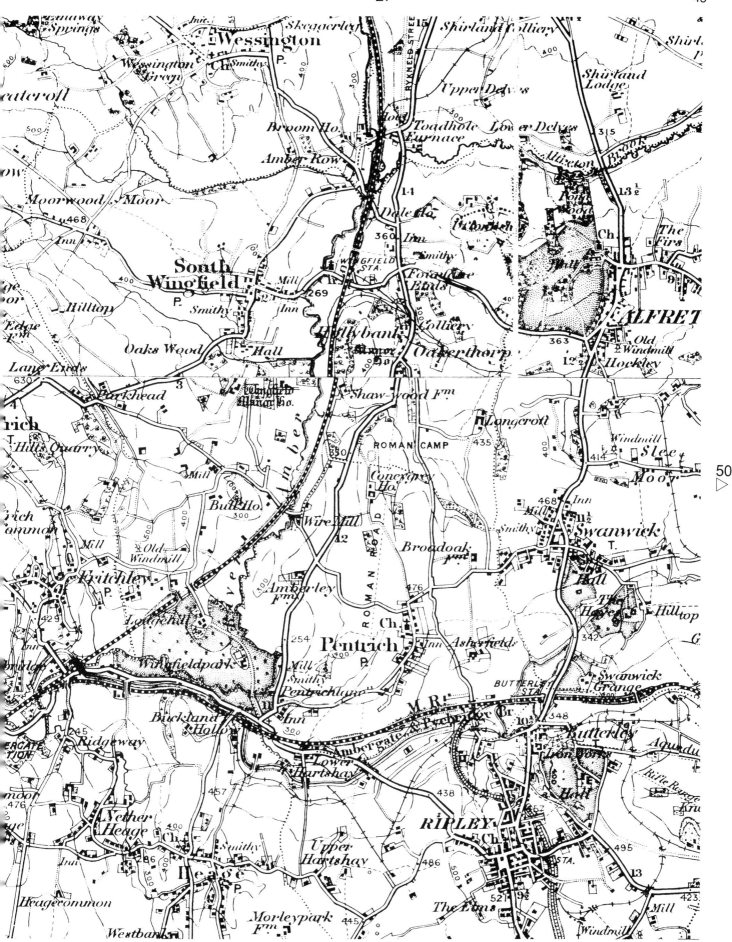

Surveyed 1875 - 85. Revised 1895. Published 1897.

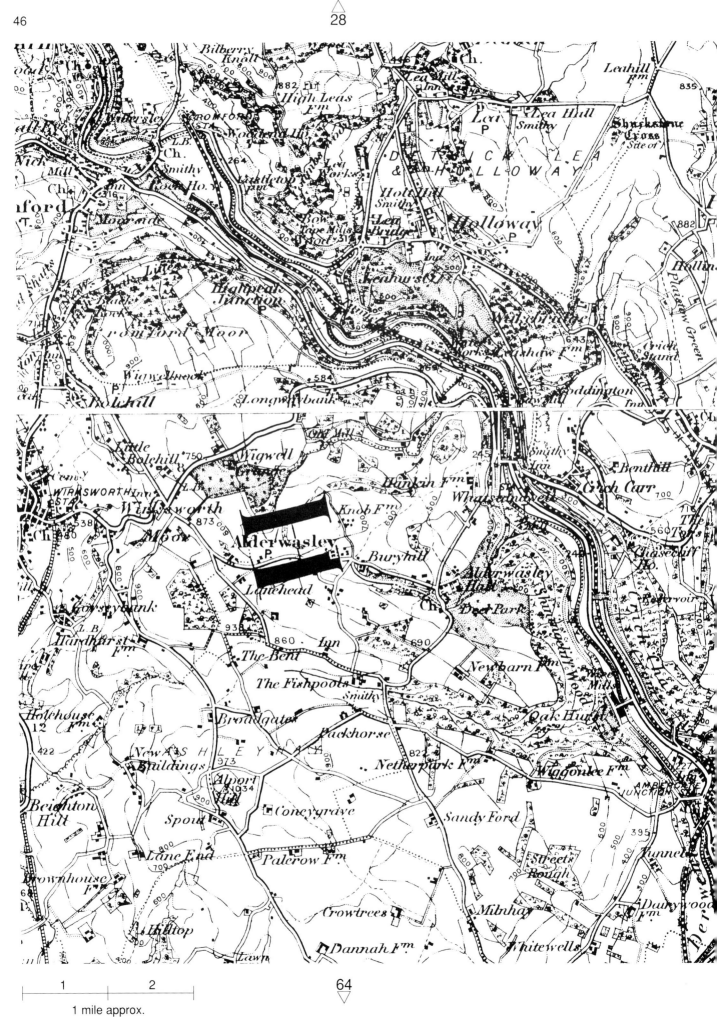

1   2

1 mile approx.

Landway Springs

Wessington

Wessington Green

Ch Smithy

P.

Shirland Colliery

14 2

Wes

Upper Dykes

Shirland Lodge

Broom Ho.

Inn

Toadhole Furnace

Shirland Dykes

Alfreton Brook

Amber Row

Dale Ho.

14

13 1/2

Poll Wood

Moorwood Moor

360

Inn

Smithy

Uttonlieys

Ch

The Firs

468

Inn

South Wingfield

WINGFIELD STA.

Fourlane Ends

Hall

ALFRE

Hilltop

Mill

269

Inn

Hollybank Inn

Colliery

Oakerthorpe

363

Old Windmill

Hockley

Oaks Wood

Hall

13

Edge Moor

Edge Fm

Lane Ends

630

Parkhead

3

Shaw Wood Fm

Longcroft

435

Collieries

Alfreton Com

Windmill

rich

Hills Quarry

Woollen Mill

L.B.

ROMAN CAMP

350

468

Inn

414

Sleet Moor

52 ▷

Wingfield Park

300

Conergrey Ho.

Grich Common

Mill

Old Windmill

Wire Mill

12

Broadoak Inn

Smithy

Swanwick

T.

Fritchley

400

Amberley Fm

476

Hall

The Hayes

342

Lower Hill

254

Ch

Pentrich

Asherfield

Sawmills

Wingfield Park

Mill

Inn

BUTTERLEY

Butterley Grange

Inn

11

Pentrichlane end

M.R.

BUTTERLEY STA.

Buckland Hollow

Ambergate

Bridge

103

348

Butterley

Aque

Ridgeway

245

T.B.

Lower Hartshay

Hammersmith

Iron Works

Hall

Gol

Nether Heage

457

438

RIPLEY

Ch

495

476

Smithy

Upper Hartshay

486

Water Works

13

Godr Gate

Heage

P.

52

STA.

Coll?

Heage Common

Manor

445

The Lims

Cem

Coll?

Surveyed 1876 - 82. Revised 1906. Published 1908.

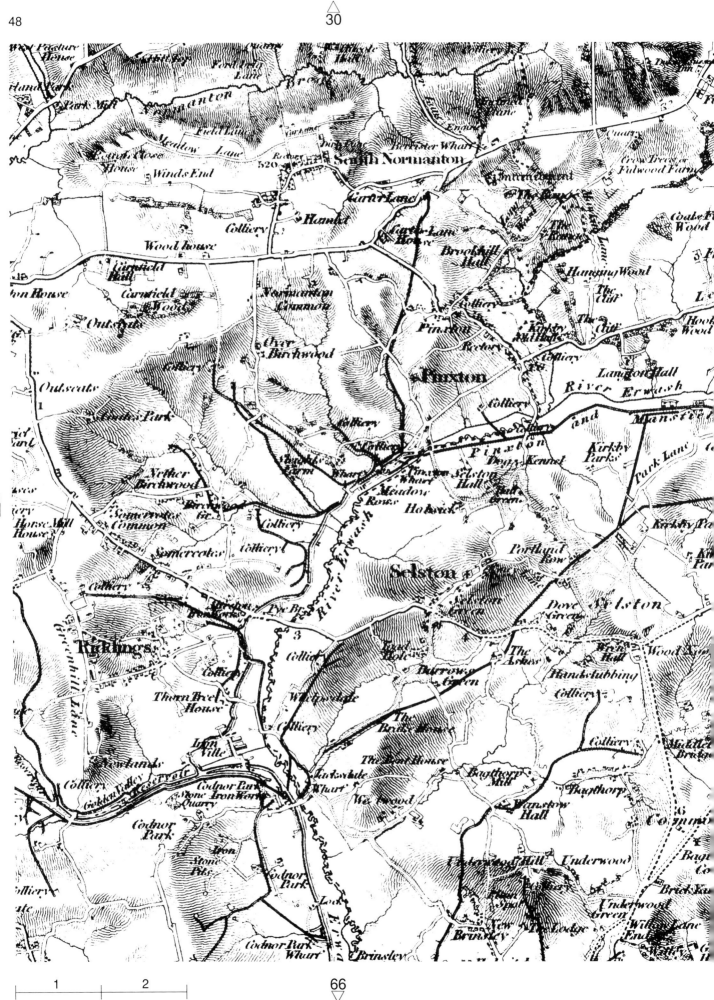

1   2

1 mile approx.

Published 1836.

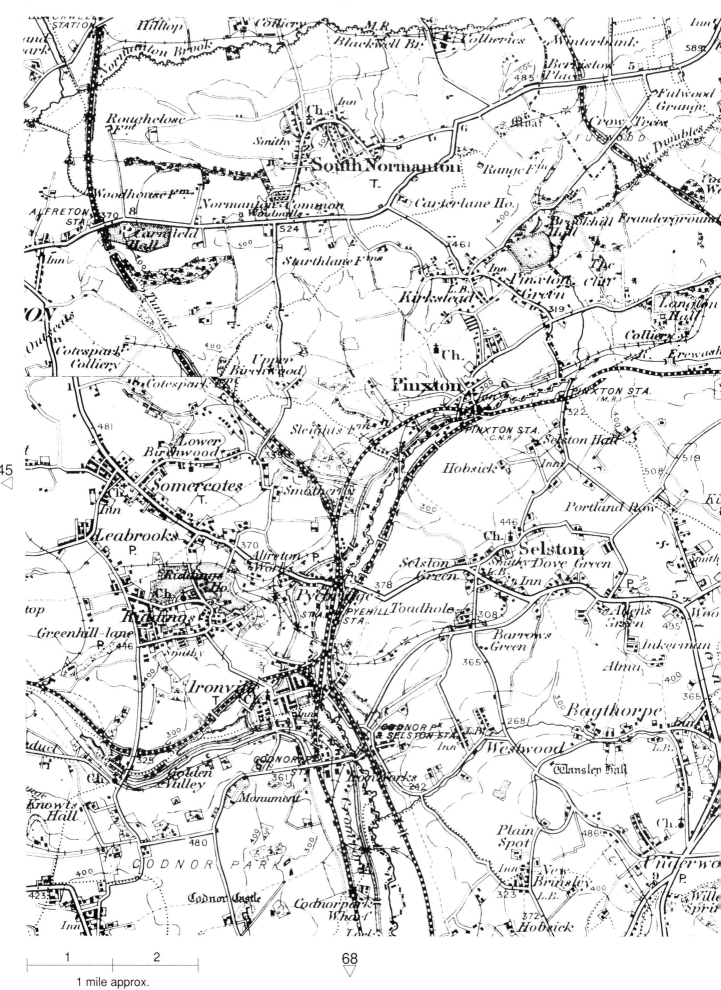

1 mile approx.

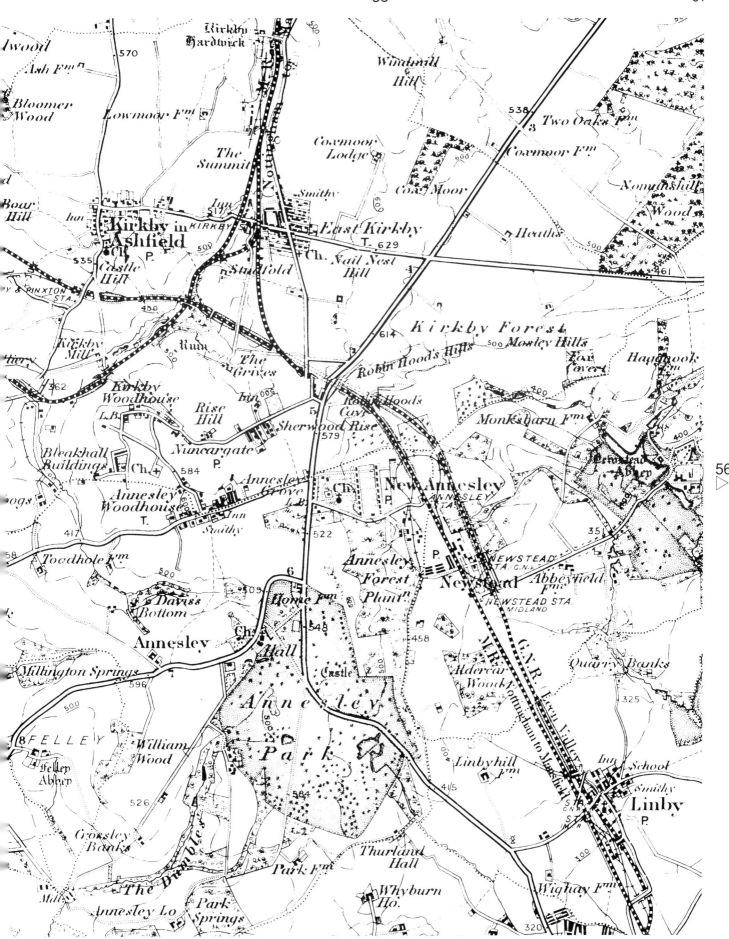

Surveyed 1875 - 85. Revised 1895. Published 1897.

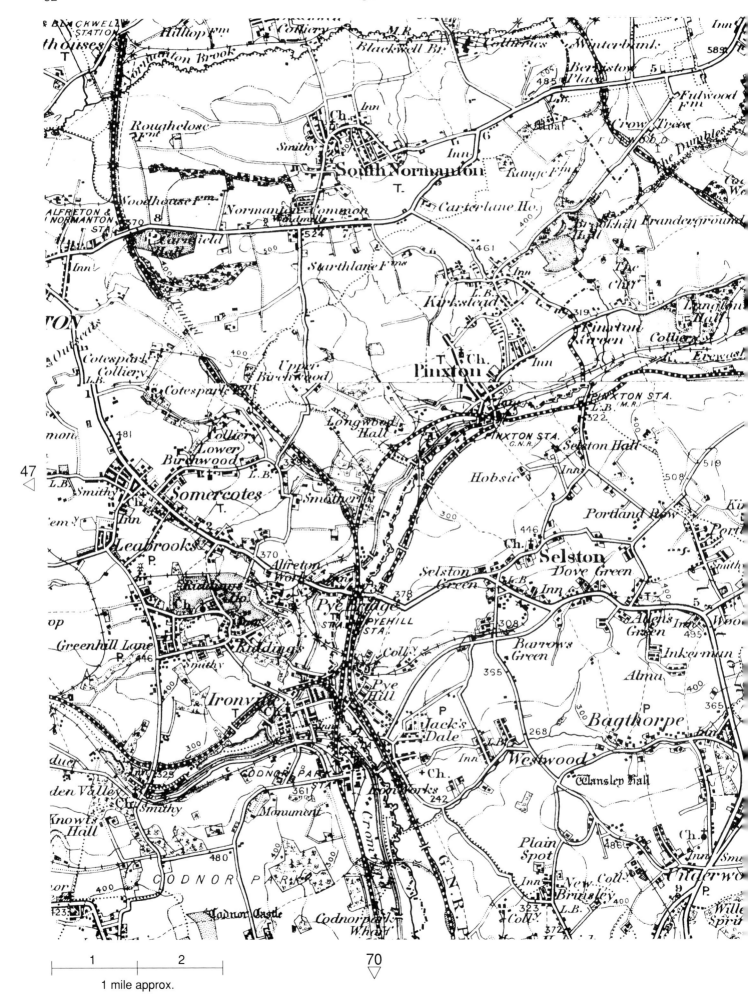

1   2

1 mile approx.

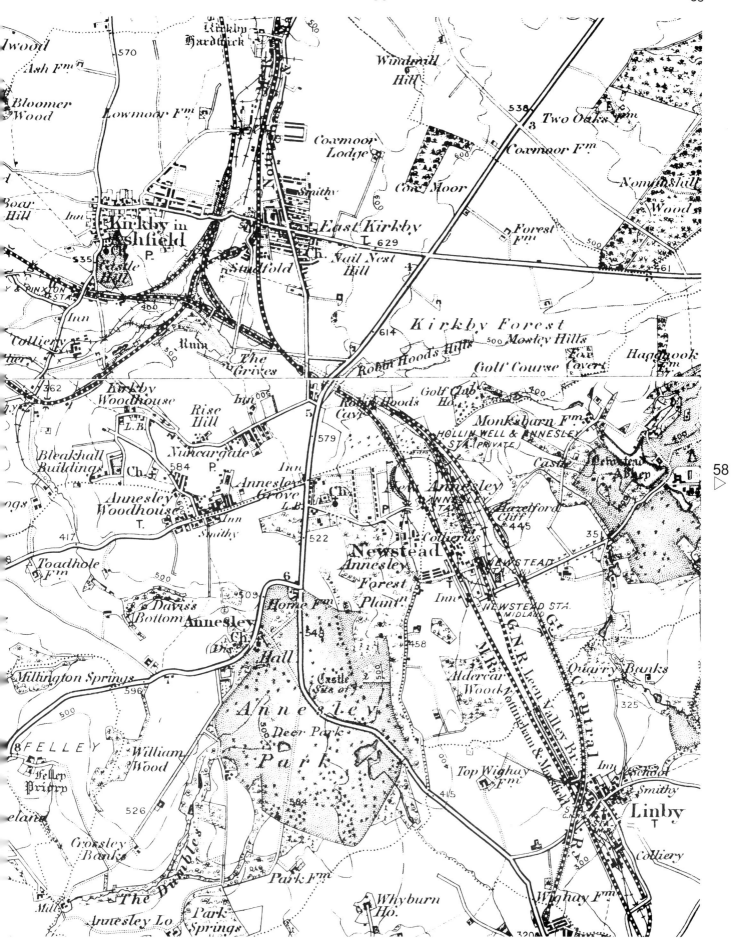

Surveyed 1876 - 82. Revised 1906. Published 1908.

1   2

1 mile approx.

Published 1836.

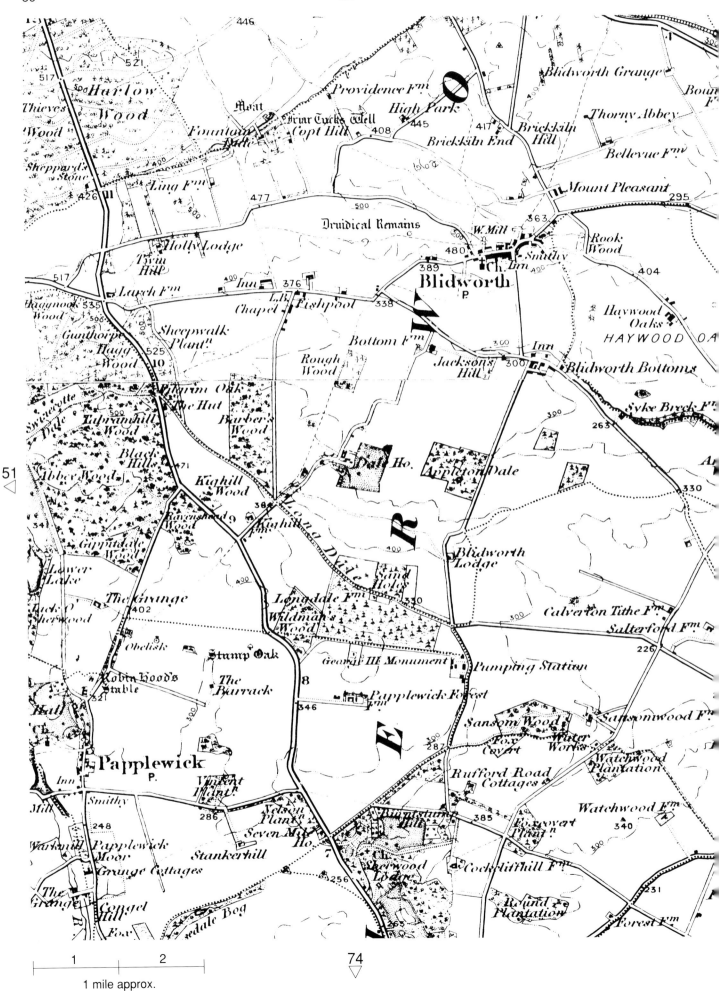

446

517

521

Harlow
Wood

Thieves
Wood

Providence F^m

Meat

High Park

Blidworth Grange

Bou
F^

Thorny Abbey

Brickkiln
Hill

Friar Tucks Well

Fountain
Dale

Copt Hill

408

445

417

Brickkiln End

Bellevue F^m

Sheppard's
Stone

426

Ling F^m

477

500

Mount Pleasant

295

Druidical Remains

W. Mill

363

Rook
Wood

404

Holly Lodge

500

480

Smithy

Ch. Inn

Twin
Hill

389

Blidworth

Haywood
Oaks

HAYWOOD OA

Larch F^m

517

Inn

376

400

Chapel

L.B.

Fishpool

338

400

Haggnook
Wood

535

Sheepwalk
Plant^n

Bottom F^m

300

Inn

Gunthorpe

Hagg
Wood

525

510

Rough
Wood

Jackson's
Hill

300

Blidworth Bottoms

Swinecote
Dale

Pilgrim Oak

The Hut

Barber's
Wood

Dale Ho.

Appleton Dale

Syke Breck F^m

263

Tannanhill
Wood

471

300

330

Black
Hills

547

Abbey Wood

Kighill
Wood

Long Dale

Ravenshead
Wood

36

Kighill
F^m

Blidworth
Lodge

A

Gipptidale
Wood

Sand
Hole

330

330

Lower
Lake

Tuck'O
Sherwood

The Grange

402

Longdale F^m

Wildman's
Wood

300

Calverton Tithe F^m

Salterford F^m

226

Obelisk

Stump Oak

George III Monument

Pumping Station

Hall

Robin Hoods
Stable

32

The
Barrack

346

Papplewick Forest
F^m

Sansom Wood

Sansomwood F^m

Fox
Covert

Water
Works

Watchwood
Plantation

Papplewick

Vincent
Plant^n

Rufford Road
Cottages

Inn

Smithy

286

Nelson
Plant^n

Buristump
Hill

385

Fox Covert
Plant^n

340

Watchwood F^m

Mill

248

Seven Mile
Ho.

Warkhill

Papplewick
Moor

Stankerhill

256

Ch.
Sherwood
Lodge

Cockliffhill F^m

Grange Cottages

The
Grange

Coggil
Hill

365

Round
Plantation

231

Forest F^m

edale Bog

1   2

1 mile approx.

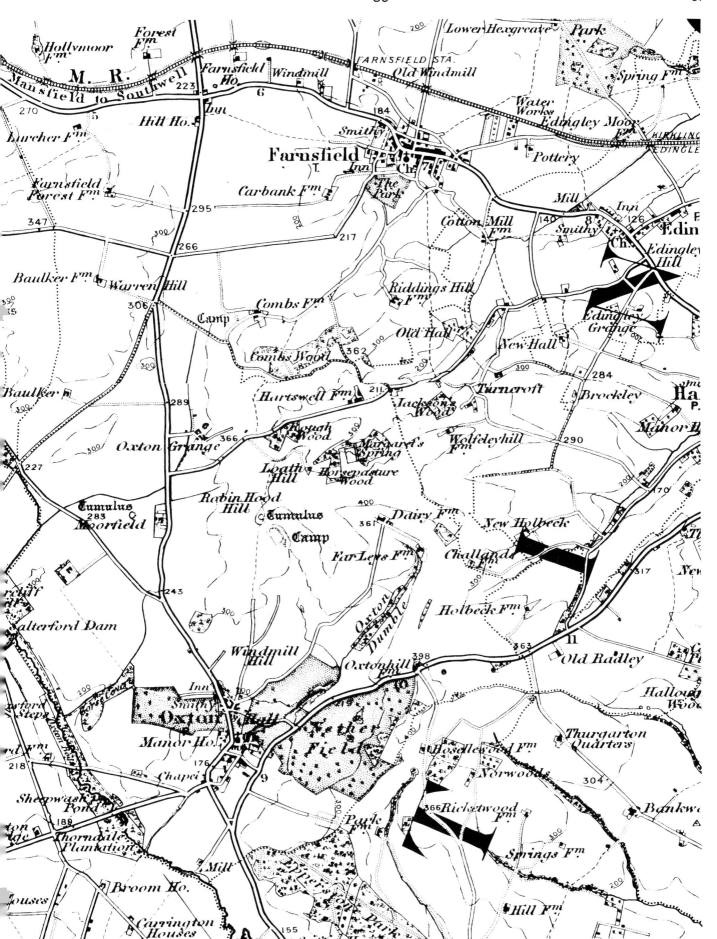

Surveyed 1876 - 87. Revised 1898. Published 1899.

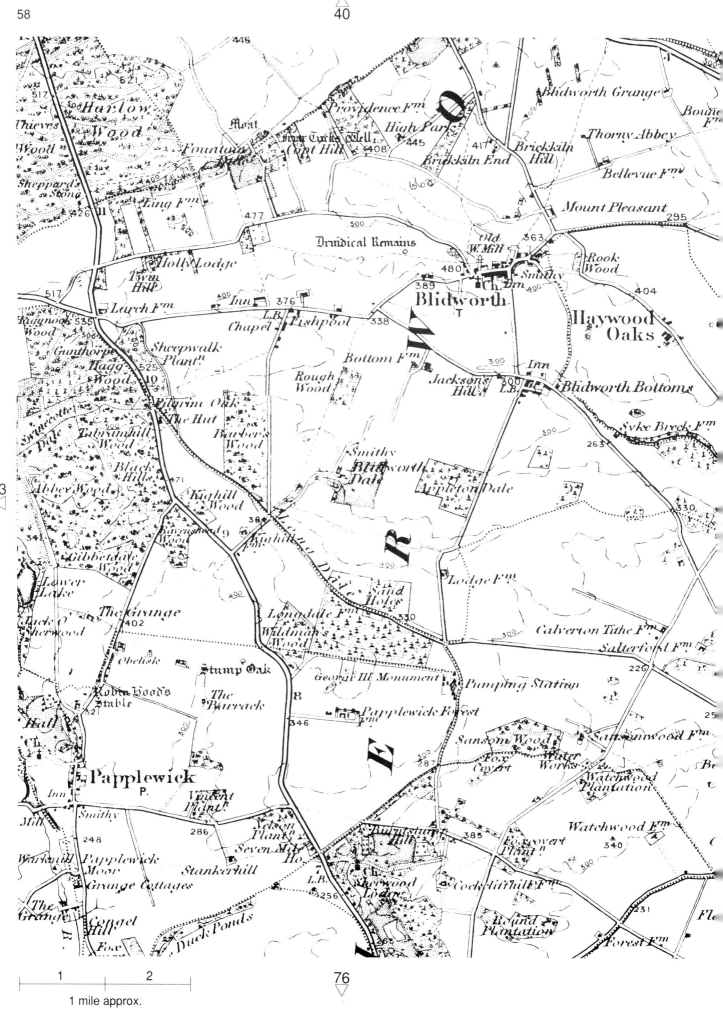

1 mile approx.

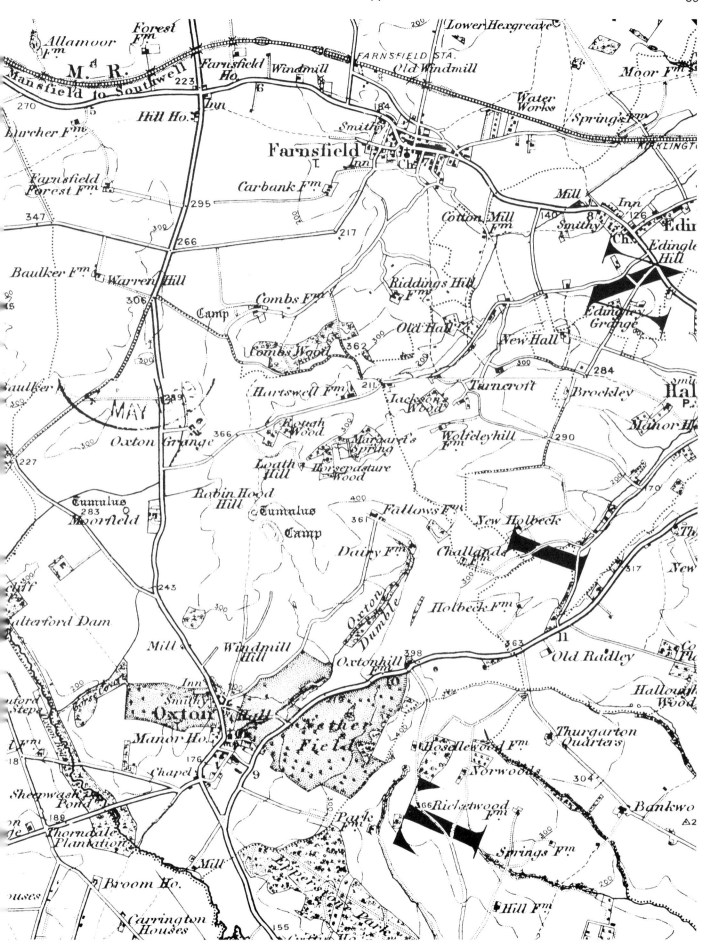

Surveyed 1877 - 87. Revised 1906. Published 1908.

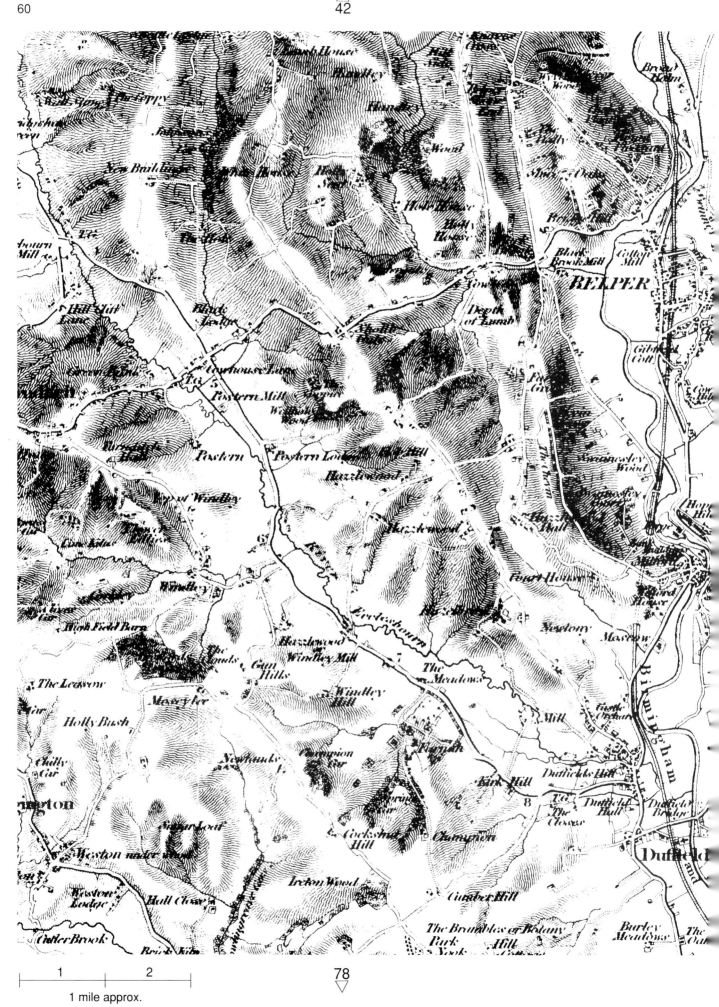

1   2

1 mile approx.

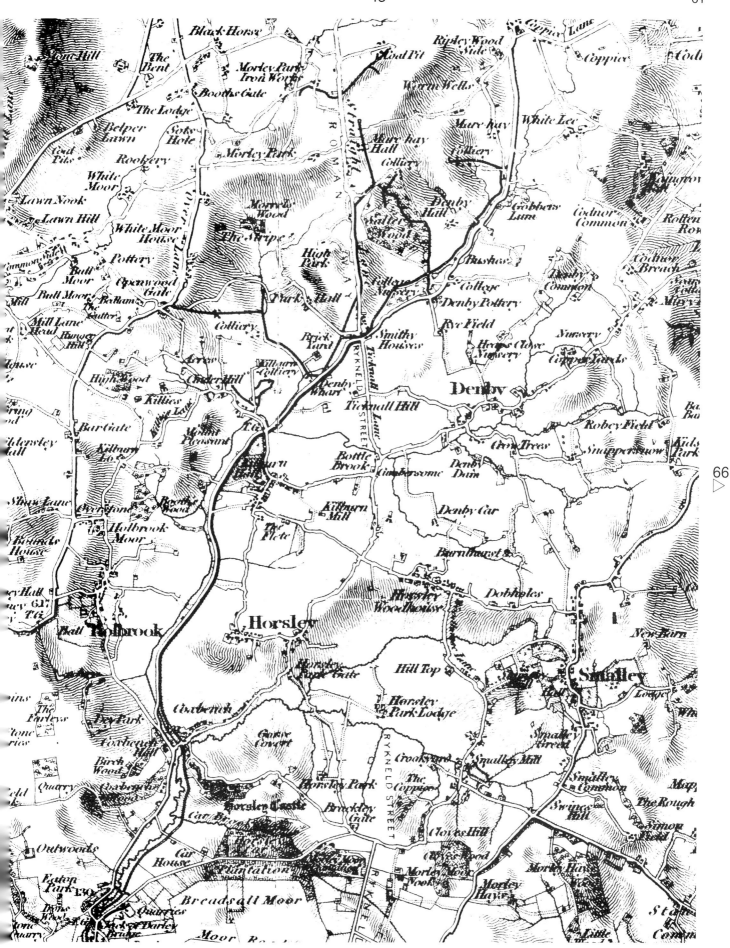

Published 1836.

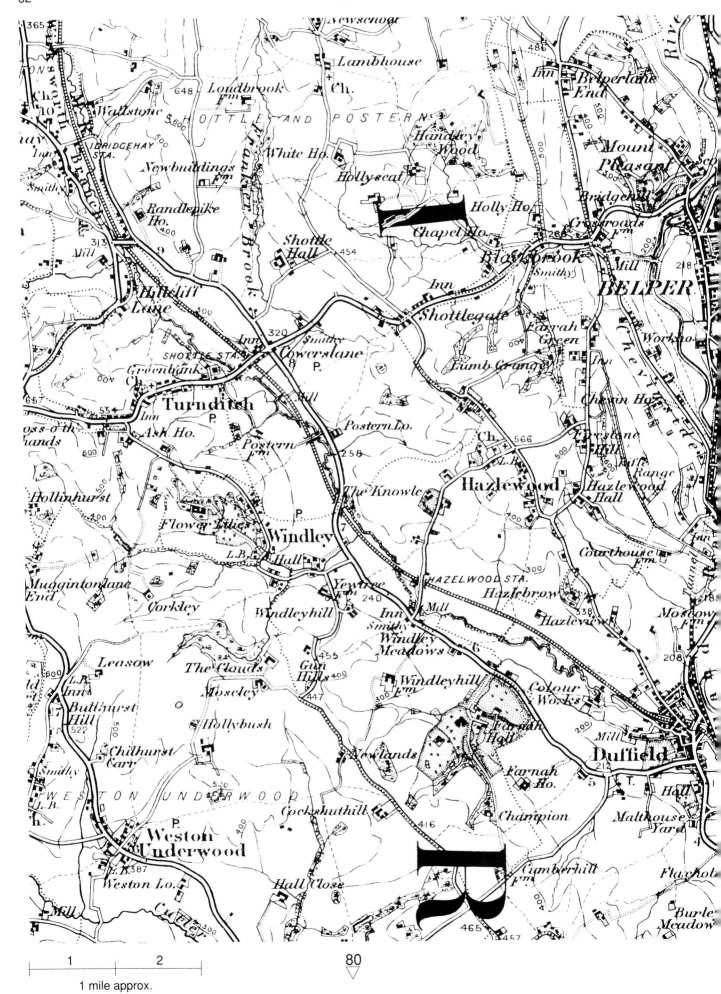

1   2

1 mile approx.

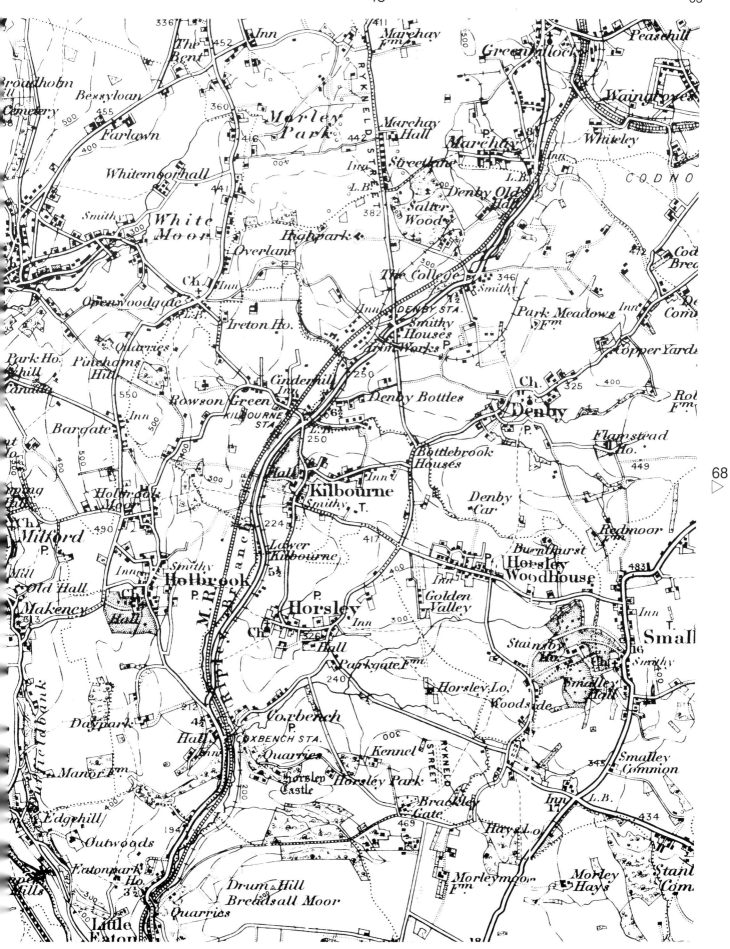

Surveyed 1876 - 82. Revised 1895. Published 1897.

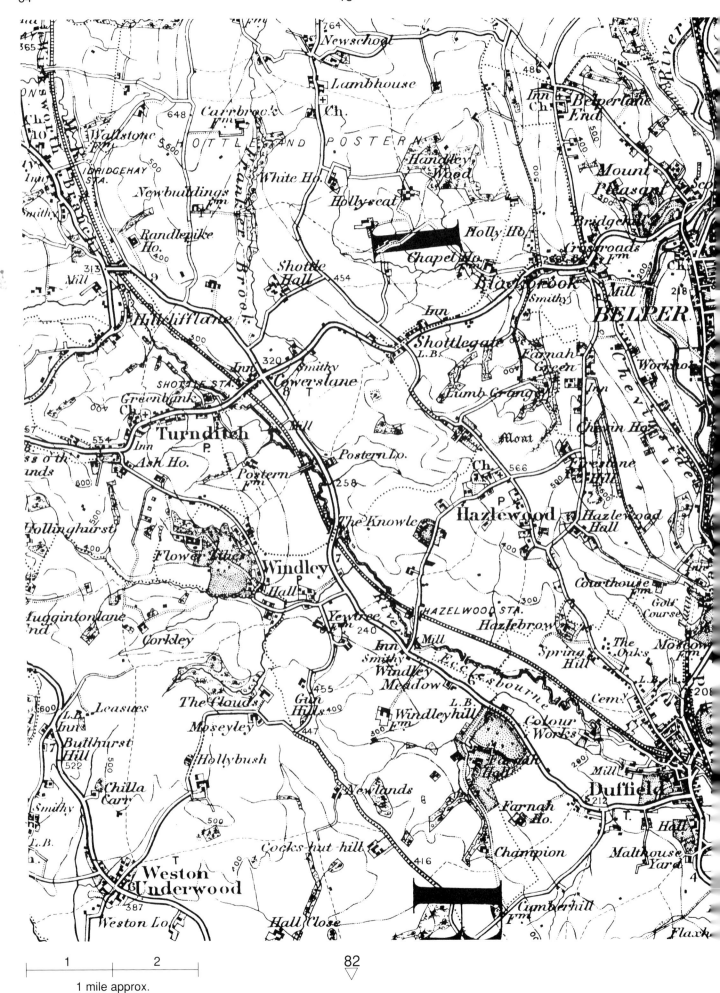

1 ———— 2

1 mile approx.

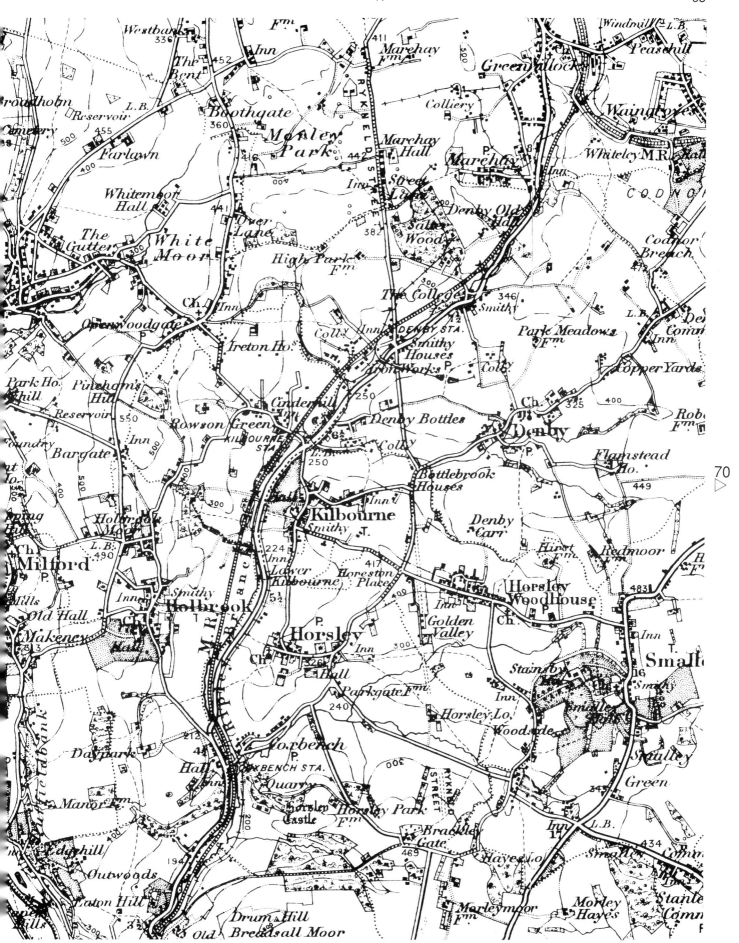

Surveyed 1876 - 82. Revised 1906. Published 1908.

1 mile approx.

Published 1836.

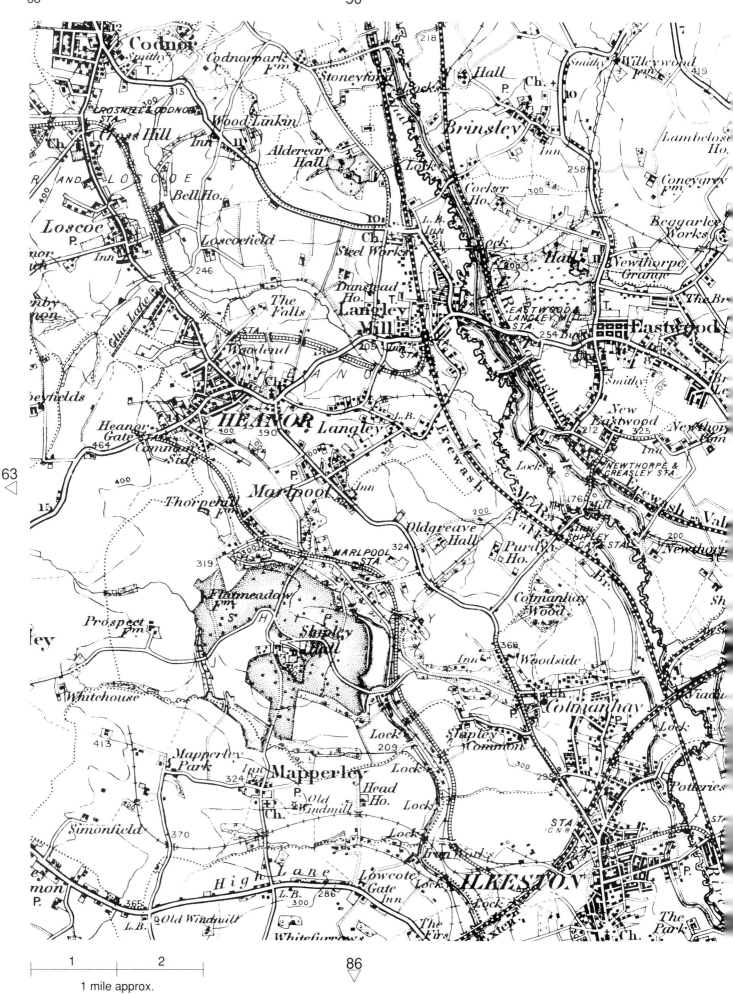

Codnor
Smithy
T.
Codnorpark Fm
Stoneyford
Hall
Ch.
P.
Smithy Willeywood Fm
419
CROSSHILL & CODNOR STA.
Wood Linkin
Brinsley
Inn
Lambcloss Ho.
Cross Hill
Inn
11
258
Coneygrey Fm
R AND LOSCOE
315
400
Aldercar Hall
Cocker Ho.
300
Beggarlee Works
Loscoe
P.
Bell Ho.
Steel Works
Hall
Newthorpe Grange
400
nor
246
Loscoefield
P.
Dunstead Ho.
T.
EASTWOOD & LANGLEY MILL STA.
254
The Br
Eastwood
The Falls
Langley Mill
Woodland
205 Inn
Smithy
8
Br Le
T.
Woodland
New Eastwood
Newthorpe Fm
Heanor Gate Sta.
464
HEANOR
400 390
Langley
Erewash
212
325
NEWTHORPE & GREASLEY STA.
Common Side
400
300
Lock
Erewash Val
Thorpefm
15
Marlpool
Inn
176
Mill
Erewash
200
Newthorpe
Prospect Fm
Oldgreave Hall
Purdy Ho.
SHIPLEY GATE STA.
MARLPOOL STA.
324
Flatmeadow Fm
319
Colmanhay Wood
368
Shipley Hall
Inn
Woodside
Br
Whitehouse
413
Mapperley Park
Inn
324
Mapperley
P.
Old Windmill
Ch.
Head Ho.
Lock
209
Shipley Common
Lock
Colmanhay
P.
Lock
300
295
STA. G.N.R.
Potteries
Simonfield
370
Lock
Lock
High Lane
Lowcote Gate Inn
ILKESTON
The Park
P.
L.B.
365
286
300
L.B.
Old Windmill
Lock
Ch.
L.B.
Whitefurrows
The Firs
xten

1   2
1 mile approx.

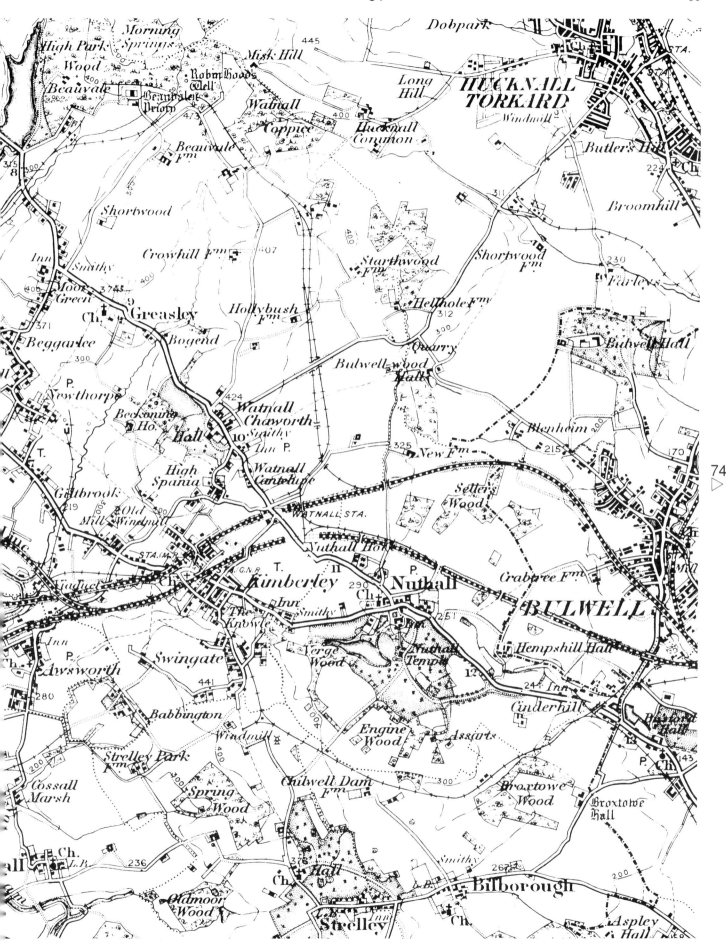

Surveyed 1876 - 82. Revised 1895. Published 1897.

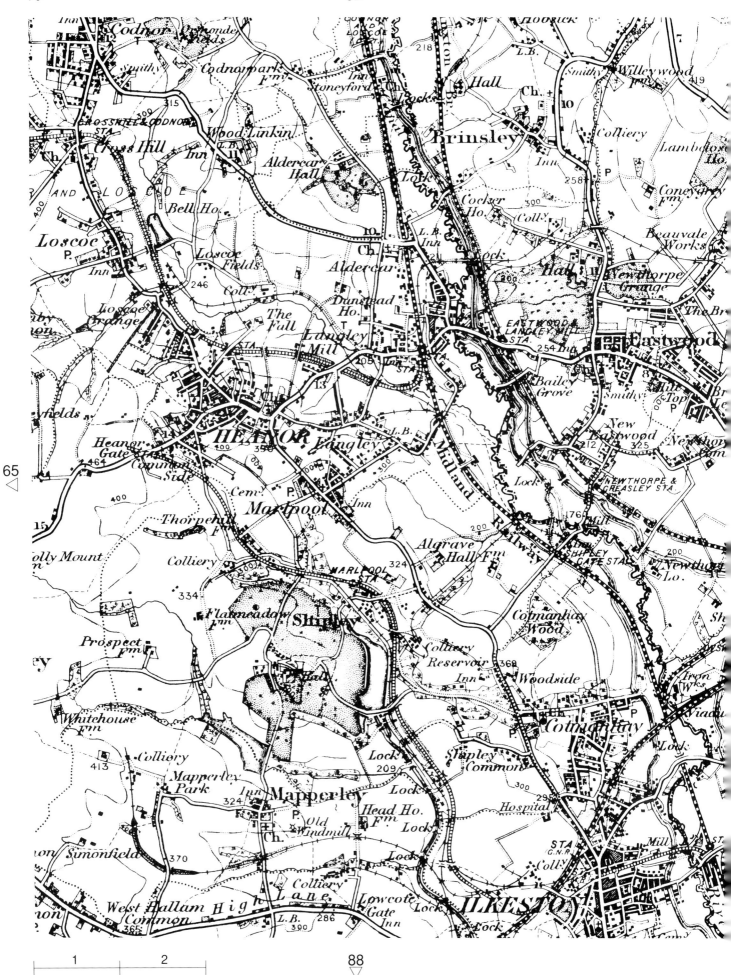

1   2

1 mile approx.

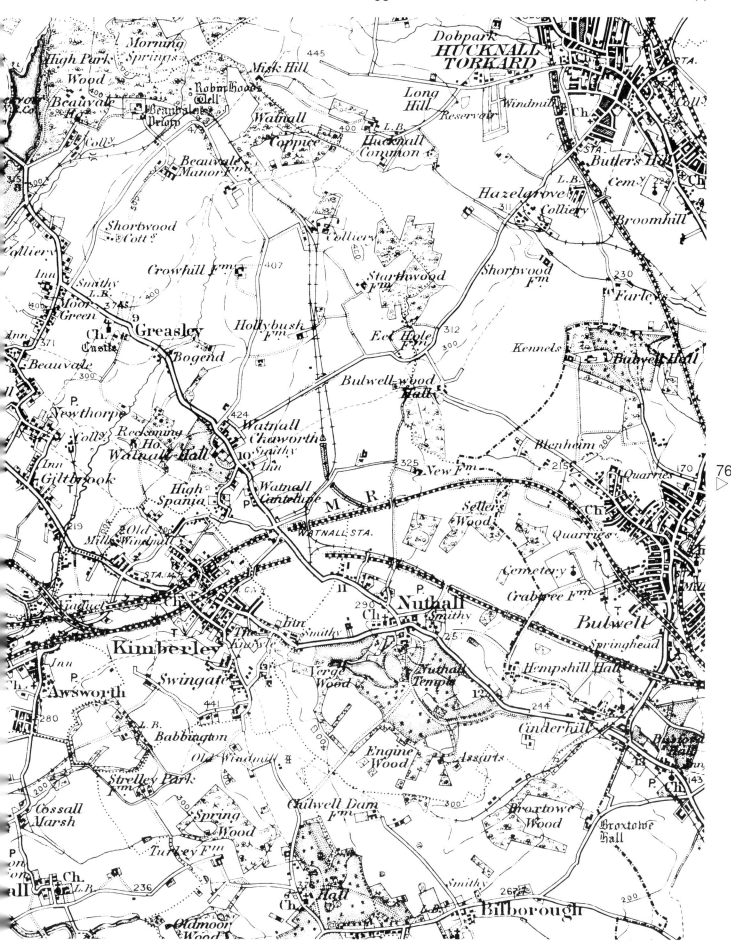

Surveyed 1876 - 82. Revised 1906. Published 1908.

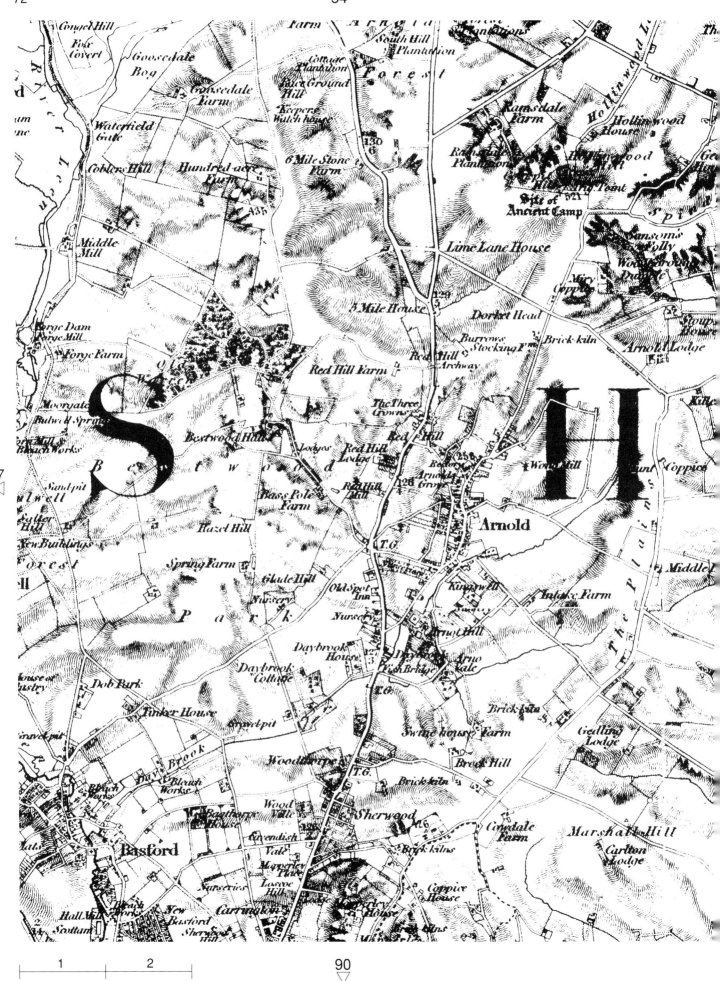

1 mile approx.

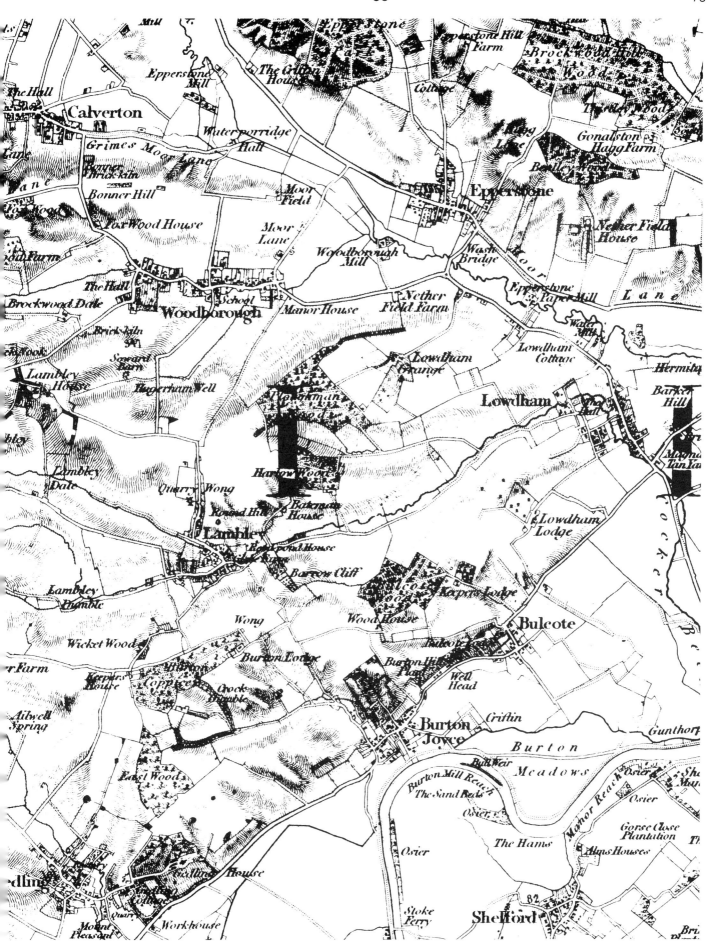

Published 1836.

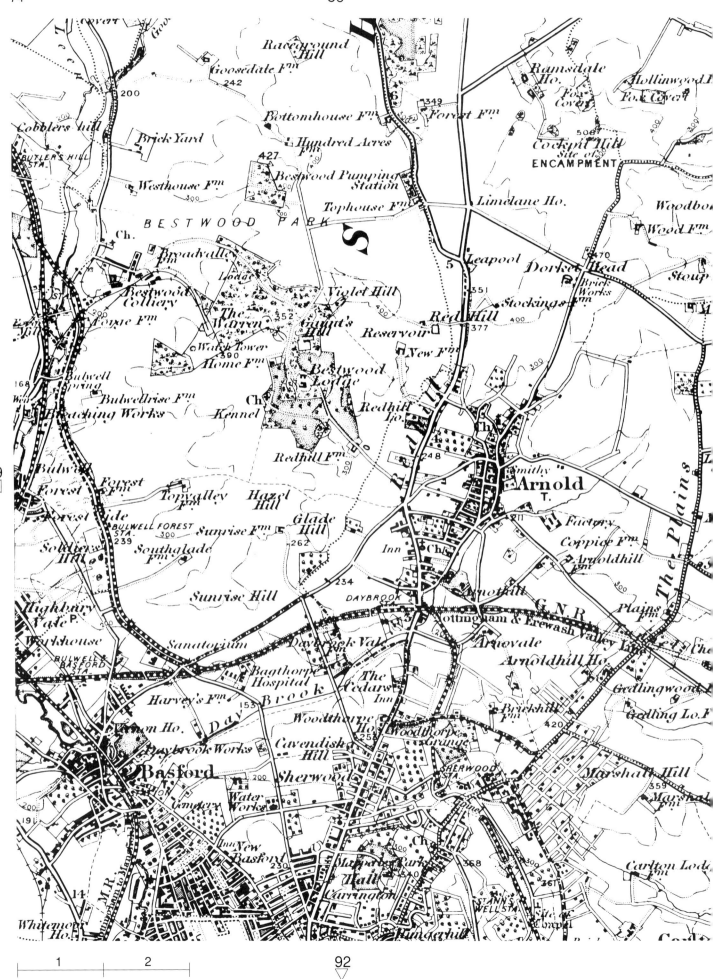

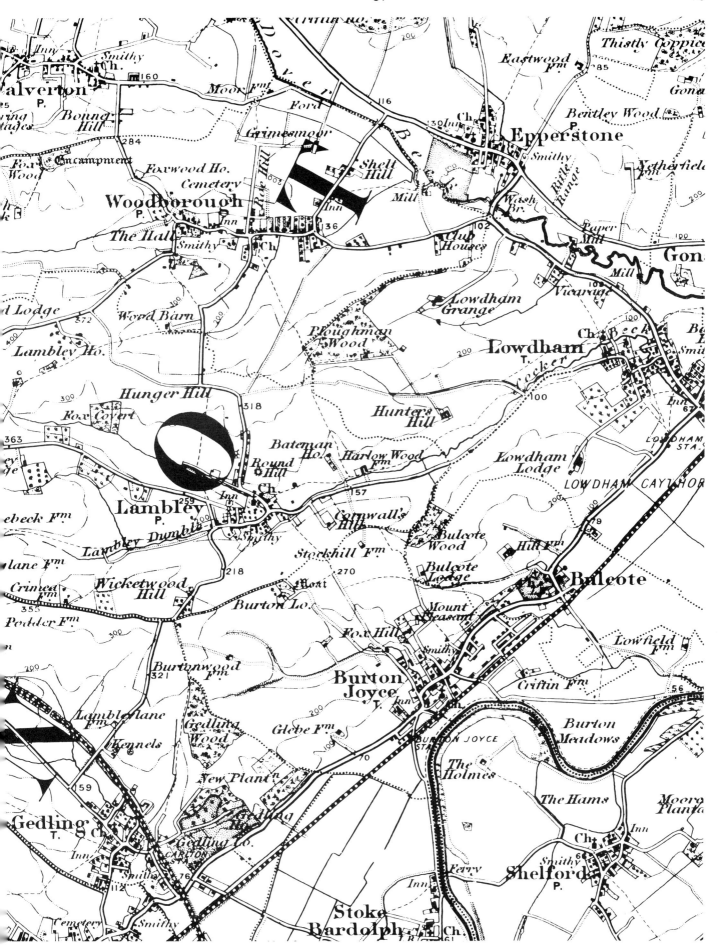

Surveyed 1877 - 87. Revised 1893. Published 1899.

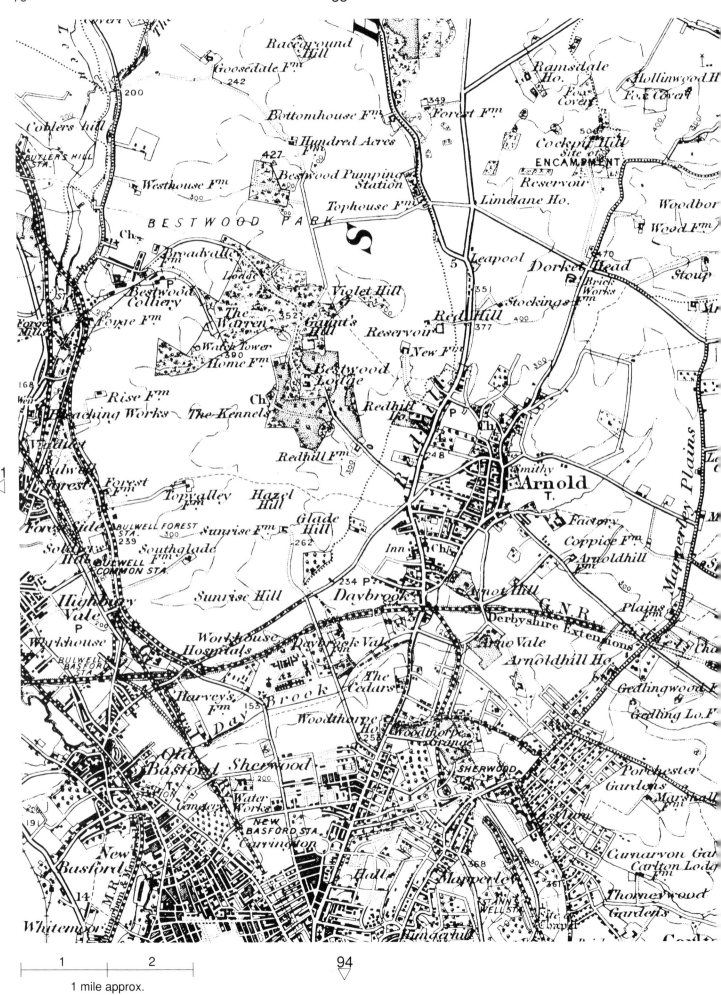

1 mile approx.

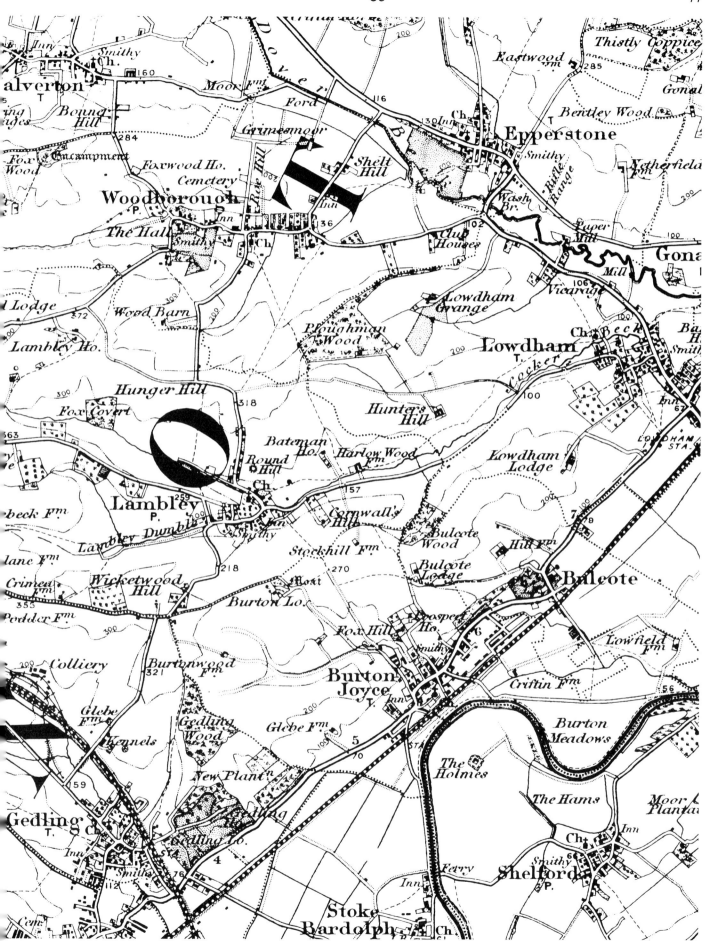

Surveyed 1877 - 87. Revised 1906. Published 1908.

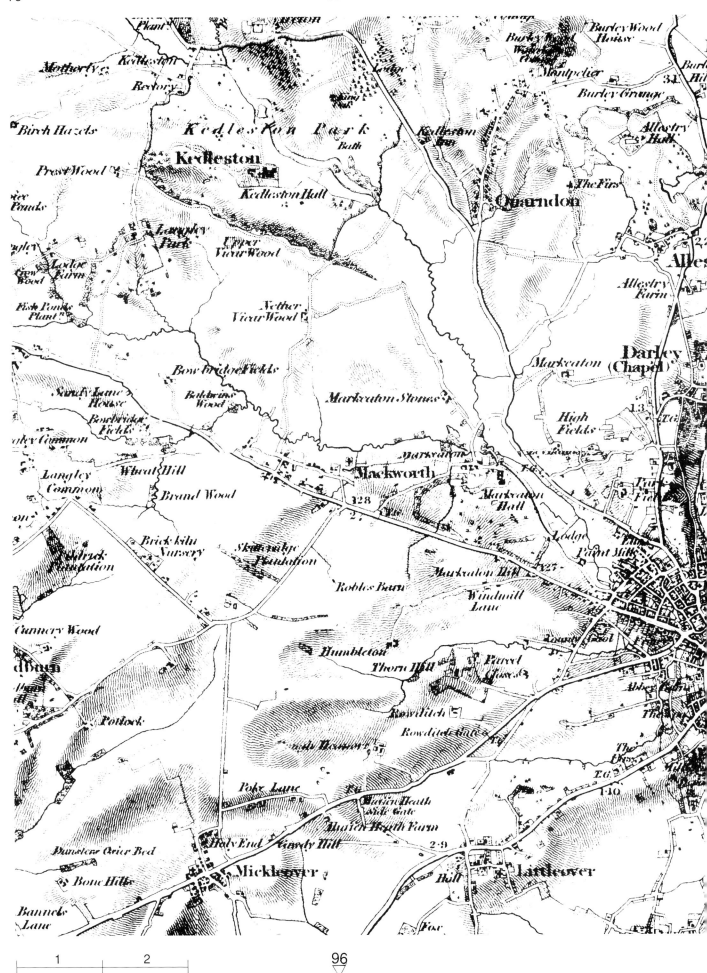

1   2

1 mile approx.

Published 1836.

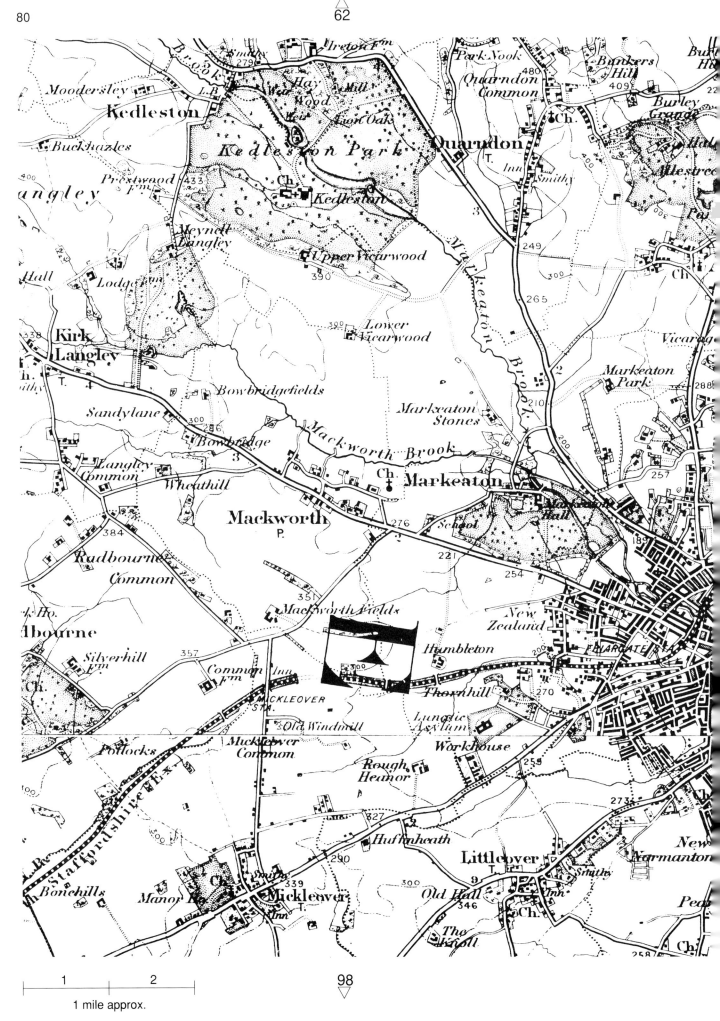

Moodersley

Kedleston

Buckhazles

Prestwood Fm 433

angley

Hall

Kirk Langley

Sandylane

Langley Common

Wheathill

Mackworth

Radbourne Common

384

dbourne

Silverhill Fm

Ch.

Pollocks

Bonehills

Manor Fm

Mickleover

Brook

279

Hay Wood

Mill

Weir

Lion Oak

Kedleston Park

Ch.

Kedleston

Meynell Langley

Upper Vicarwood

390

Lower Vicarwood

Bowbridgefields

Bowbridge

Mackworth Brook

Markeaton Stones

Ch. Markeaton

School

276

Mackworth Fields

Common Fm Inn

300

357

MICKLEOVER STA.

Old Windmill

Mickleover Common

Rough Heanor

327

Huffinheath

290

339

300

Ireton Fm

Park Nook

Quarndon Common

480

Ch.

Quarndon

Inn

Smithy

249

300

265

Walkeaton Brook

210

200

Markeaton Park

257

New Zealand

Humbleton

Thornhill

Lunatic Asylum

Workhouse

255

273

Littleover

Old Hall 346

The Knoll

Bunkers Hill 409

Burley Grange

Allestree

Vicarage

288

18

221

254

Inn

270

New Normanton

Smithy

Ch.

258

1   2

1 mile approx.

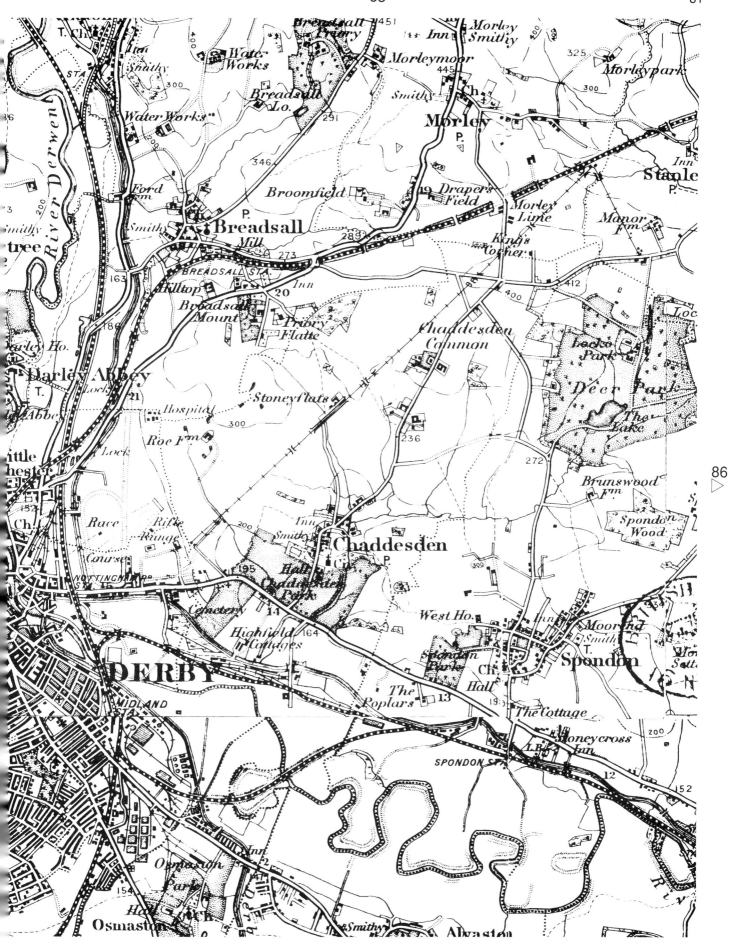

Surveyed 1876 - 83. Revised 1895 - 96. Published 1896 - 97.

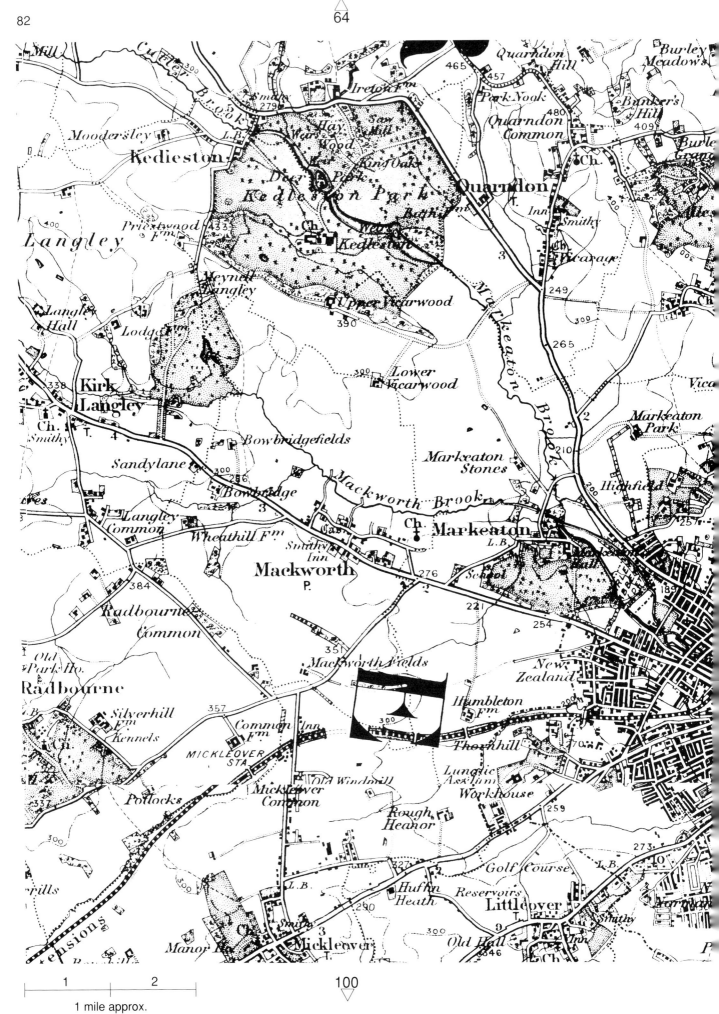

1 mile approx.

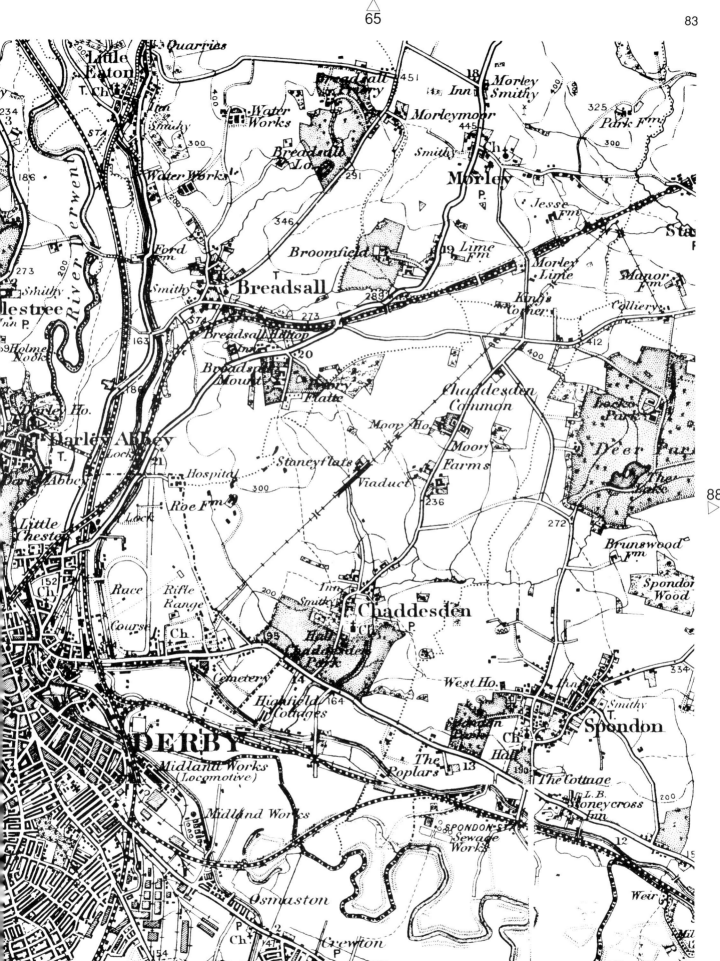

Surveyed 1876 - 83. Revised 1905 - 06. Published 1908.

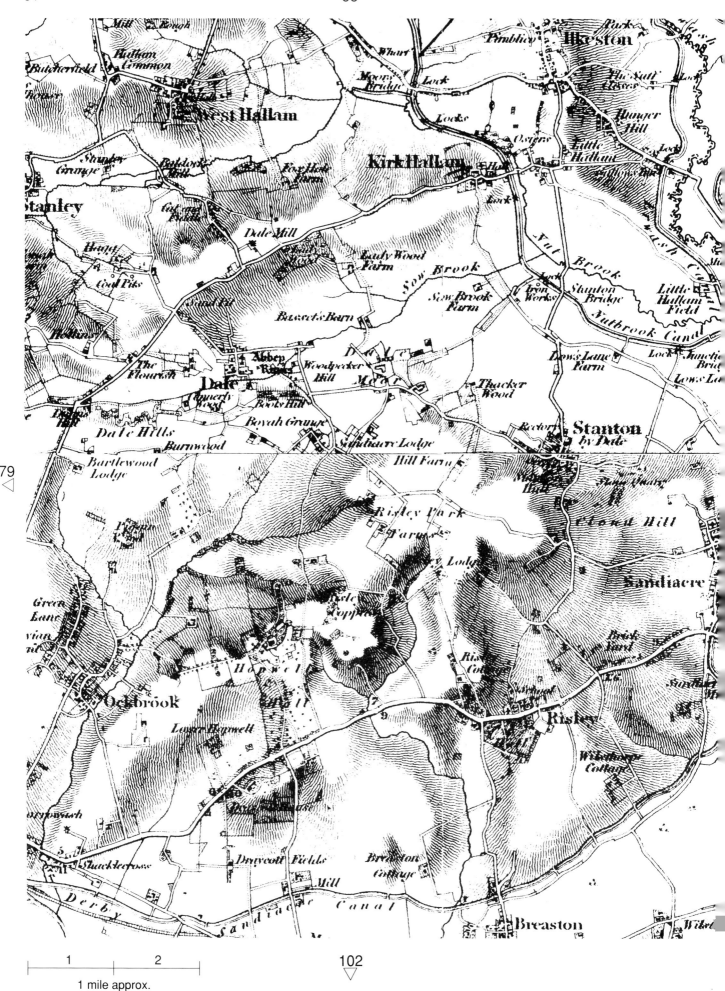

1   2

1 mile approx.

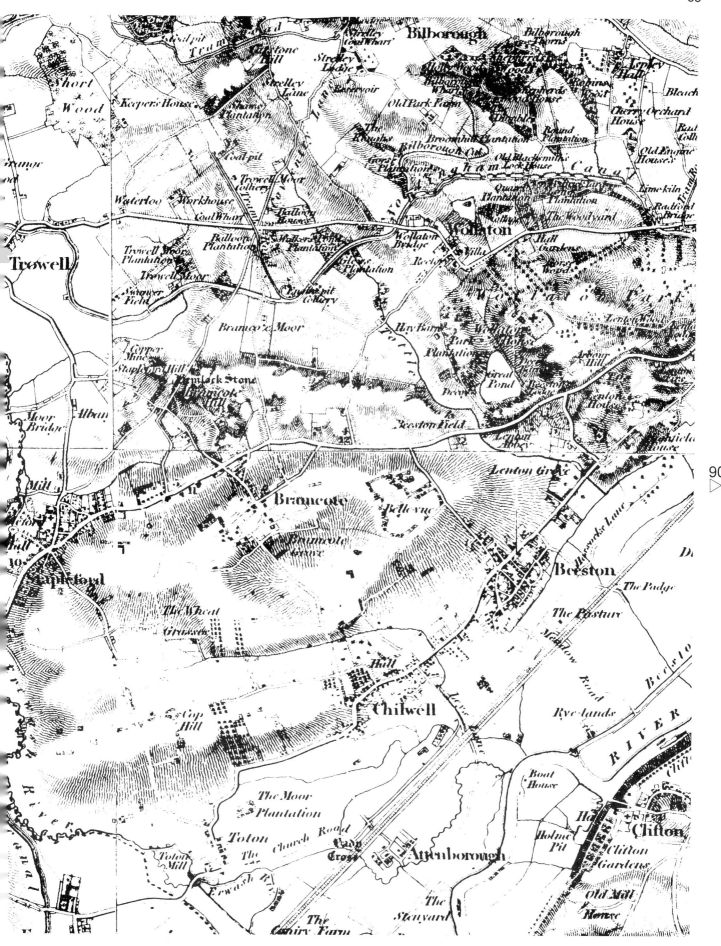

Published 1836.

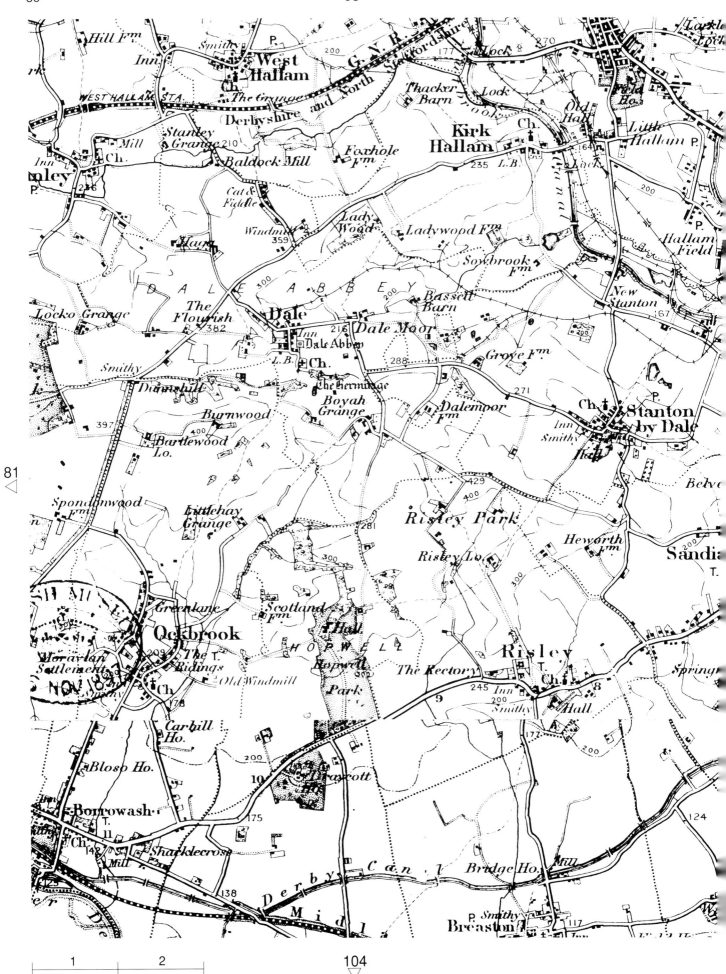

1   2

1 mile approx.

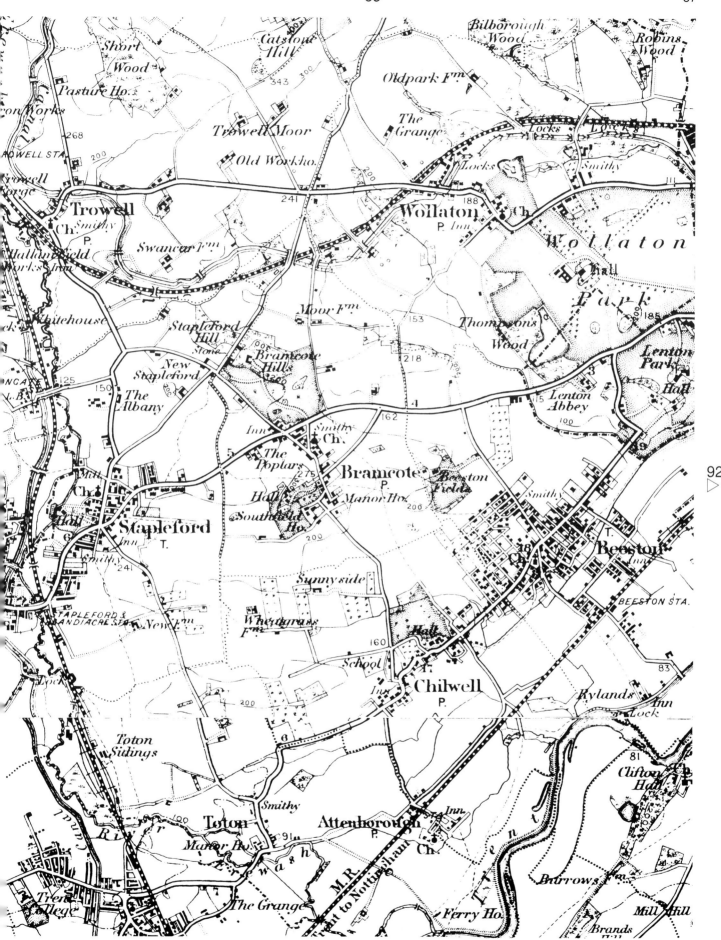

Surveyed 1876 - 83. Revised 1895 - 96. Published 1896 - 97.

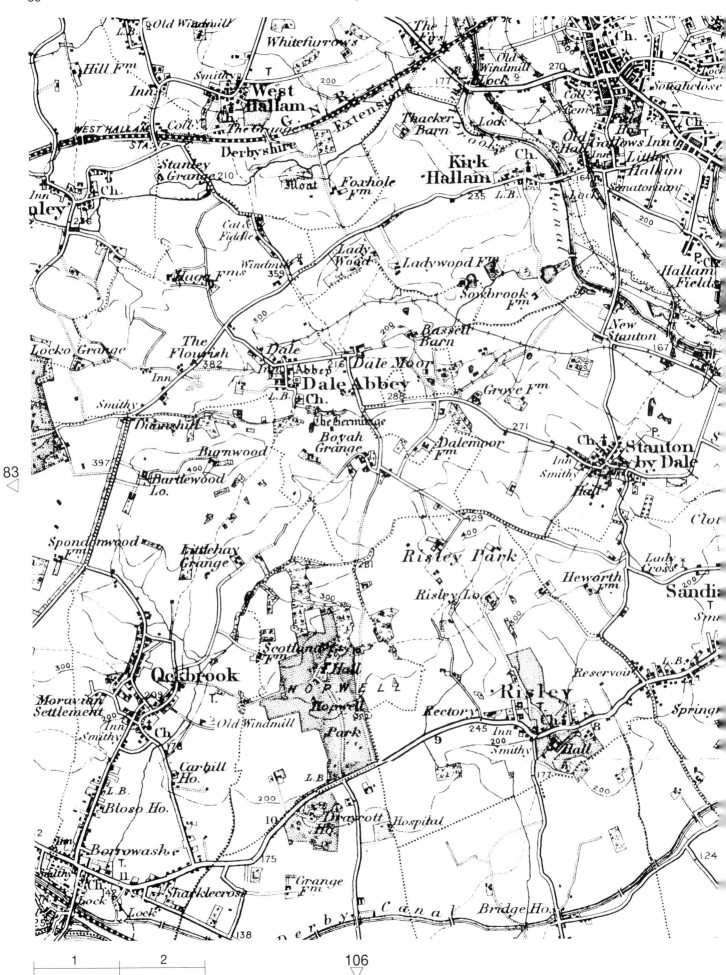

83

Old Windmill
Whitefurrows
Hill Fm
Smithy
Inn
West Hallam
The Grange
Derbyshire
WEST HALLAM STA.
Coll
Stanley Grange
210
Moat
Foxhole Fm
Cat & Fiddle
Lady Wood
Windmill
359
Haga Fms
300
Locko Grange
The Flourish
382
Dale Inn
Abbey
Smithy
Dunnshill
Bignwood
397
Bartlewood Lo.
400
Spondonwood Fm
Littlehay Grange
Ockbrook
300
208
Moravian Settlement
Inn
Smithy
Ch
Carhill Ho.
Blosp Ho.
L.B.
Borrowash
Shacklecross
Grange Fm

Thacker Barn
Lock
Kirk Hallam
235
Sowbrook Fm
Ladywood Fm
Bassett Barn
200
Dale Moor
216
Dale Abbey
Ch.
The Hermitage
Boyah Grange
Dalemor Fm
288
Grove Fm
271
429
400
Risley Park
281
Risley Lo.
300
Scotland Fm
Hall
NORWELL
Hopwell
Park
Hopwell
300
L.B.
200
Dracott Ho.
Hospital
175
138

Old Windmill
Lock
270
177
Old Gallows Inn
Little Hallam
Sanatorium
200
New Stanton
167
Ch.
Stanton by Dale
Inn
Smithy
Hall
Heworth Fm
Lady Cross
Sandi
Reservoir
Risley
Rectory
245 Inn
200
Smithy
Hall
177
200
Bridge Ho.
Derby Canal
124

1   2
1 mile approx.

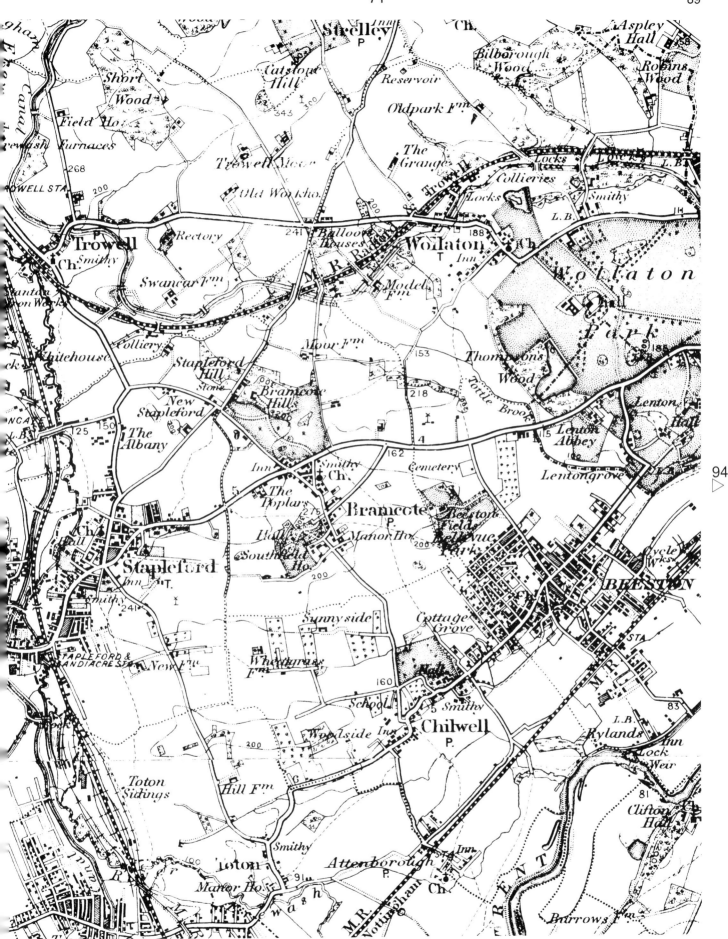

Surveyed 1876 - 83. Revised 1905 - 06. Published 1908.

1   2

1 mile approx.

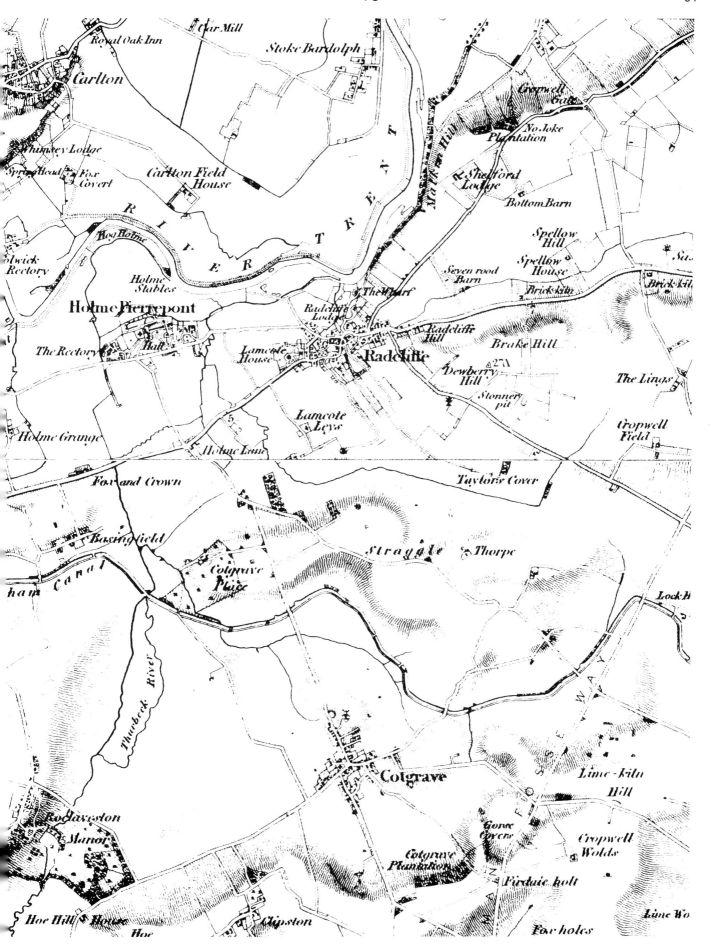

Published 1836.

NOTTINGH

THORNEYWOOD STA.

Radford

Sneinton

RACE

Ch.

Lenton

Smithy Inn

STATIONS

East Croft

The H

NORTH WILFORD

Schools

Old England Ho

Totle Brook

M R

Dunkirk

The Hall

Wilford
P.

West
Bridgford
P. G

Gam

Trent to Nottingham

Beeston Canal

Trentside F^m

Wilford Cot.

SOUTH WILFORD

Bridgford
Covert

Ford

Glebe F^m

Nottingham to Melton Mowbray

C M R

EDWALTON
STA.

Clifton Grove

The Drift

Willwell F^m

Wilford Hill

Clifton
P.

Smithy

Edwalton
T.

Sharp
Hill

Glapton

Ruddington
Grange

Mickleborough
Hill

Glapton
Wood

Fairham Br

CLIFTON WITH GLAPTON

1   2

1 mile approx.

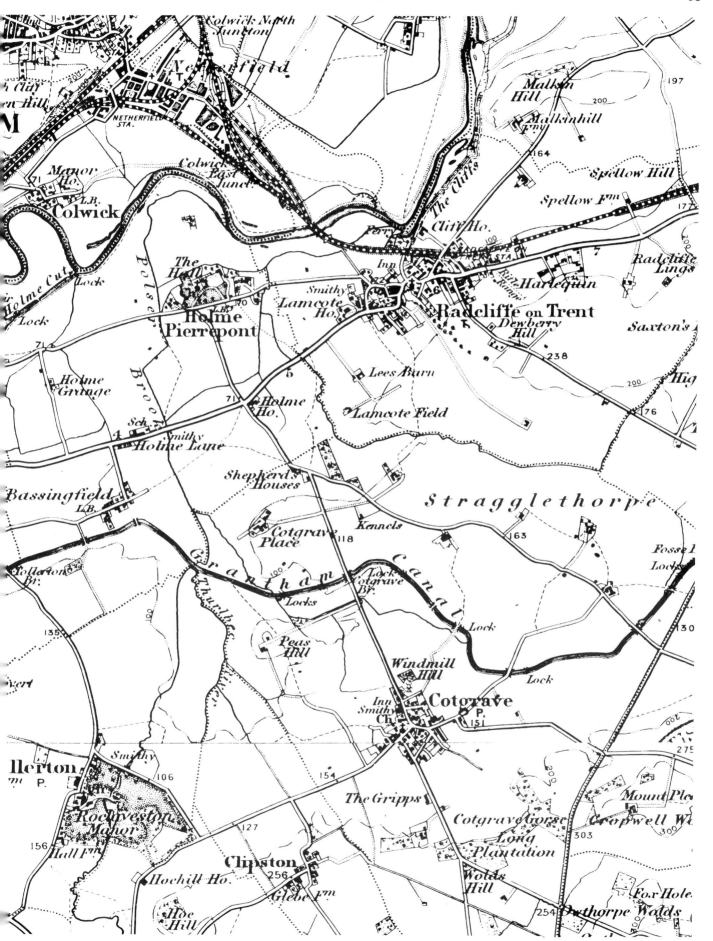

Surveyed 1877 - 87. Revised 1898. Published 1899.

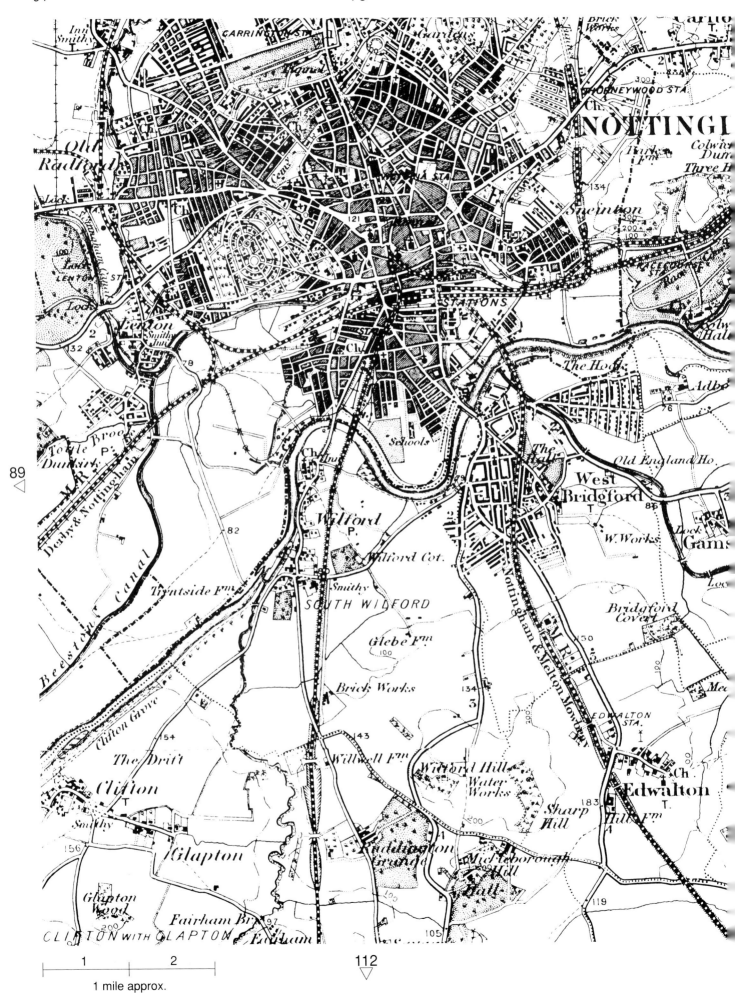

1 mile approx.

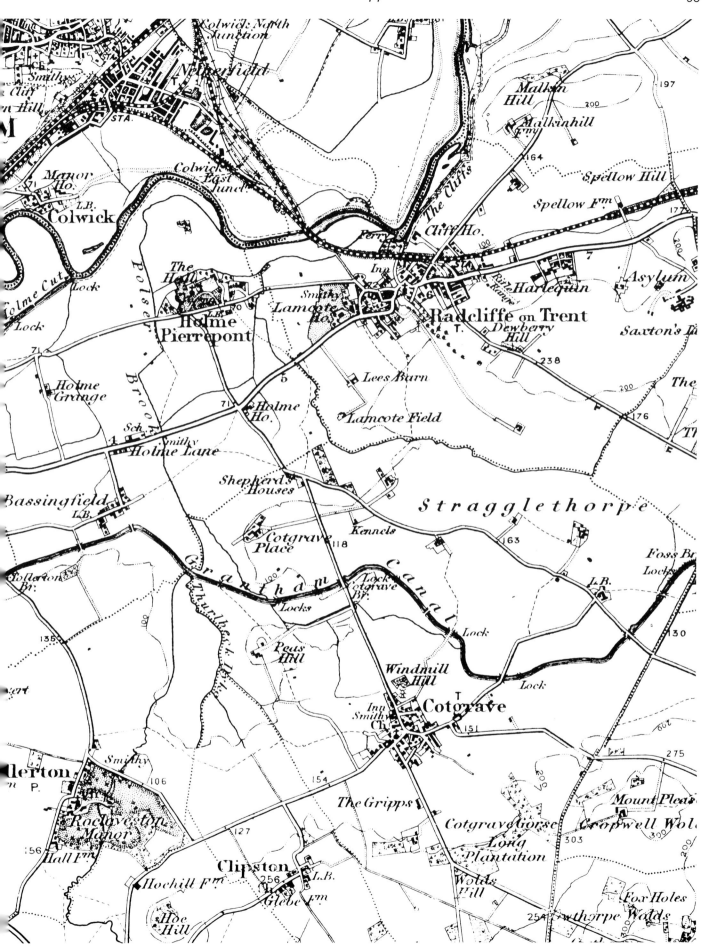

Surveyed 1882 - 87. Revised 1906. Published 1908.

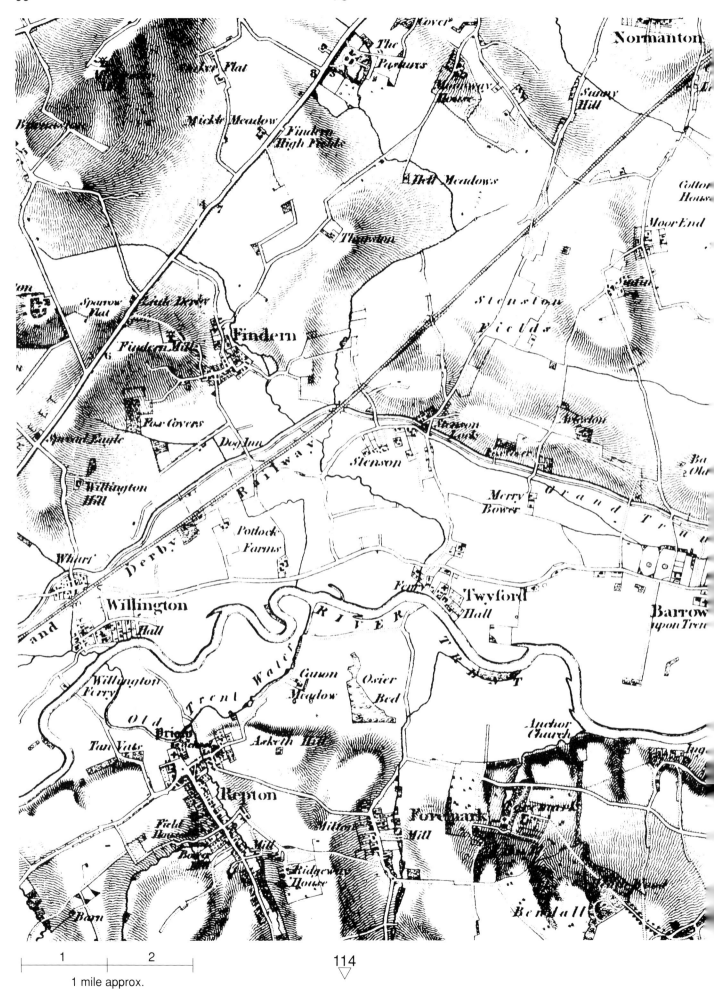

114

1

2

1 mile approx.

Published 1836.

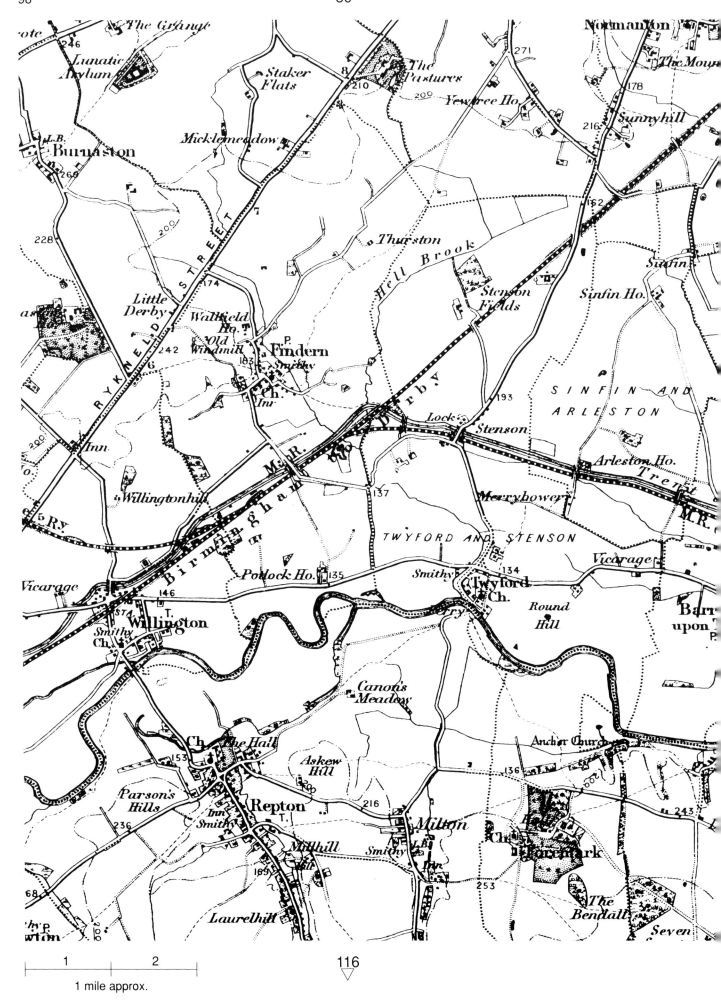

The Grange

Lunatic Asylum

246

L.B.

Burnaston

266

228

Staker Flats

Micklemeadow

200

7

RYKNELD STREET

174

Little Derby

Wallfield Ho.

Old Windmill

242

6

183

Findern

Smithy

P

Ch.

Inr.

The Pastures

8

210

271

200

Yewtree Ho.

Normanton

The Moun

178

216

Sunnyhill

162

Thurston

Hell Brook

Stenson Fields

Sinfin Ho.

Sinfin

Derby

Lock

193

SINFIN AND ARLESTON

Stenson

Arleston Ho.

Trent

M.R.

Inn

200

Ry.

Willingtonhill

M.R.

Birmingham

137

Merrybowen

TWYFORD AND STENSON

Vicarage

134

Vicarage

Podlock Ho.

135

146

ST4

T.

Smithy

Willington

Ch.

Smithy

Twyford Ch.

Round Hill

Barr

upon

P.

Canon's Meadow

Anchor Church

Ch.

The Hall

153

Askew Hill

200

136

243

Parson's Hills

236

Inn

Smithy

Repton

T.

216

Milton

L.B.

Smithy

Ch.

Foremark

253

Inn

68

Millhill

169

Smithy

The Bendall

200

Laurelhill

Seven

ton

1   2

1 mile approx.

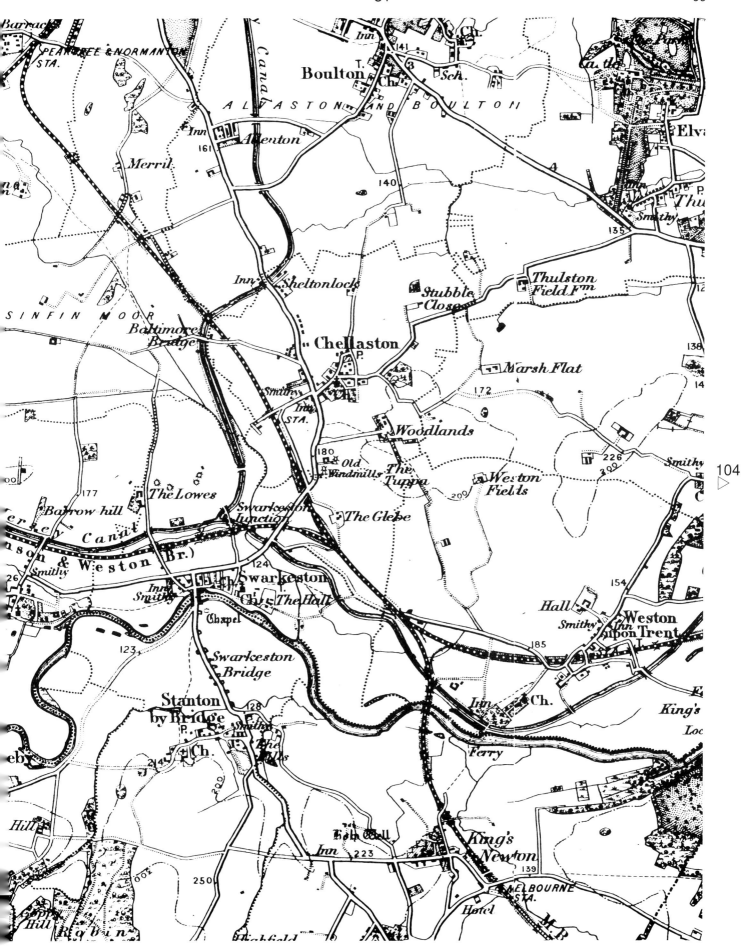

Surveyed 1879 - 83. Revised 1895 - 96. Published 1896.

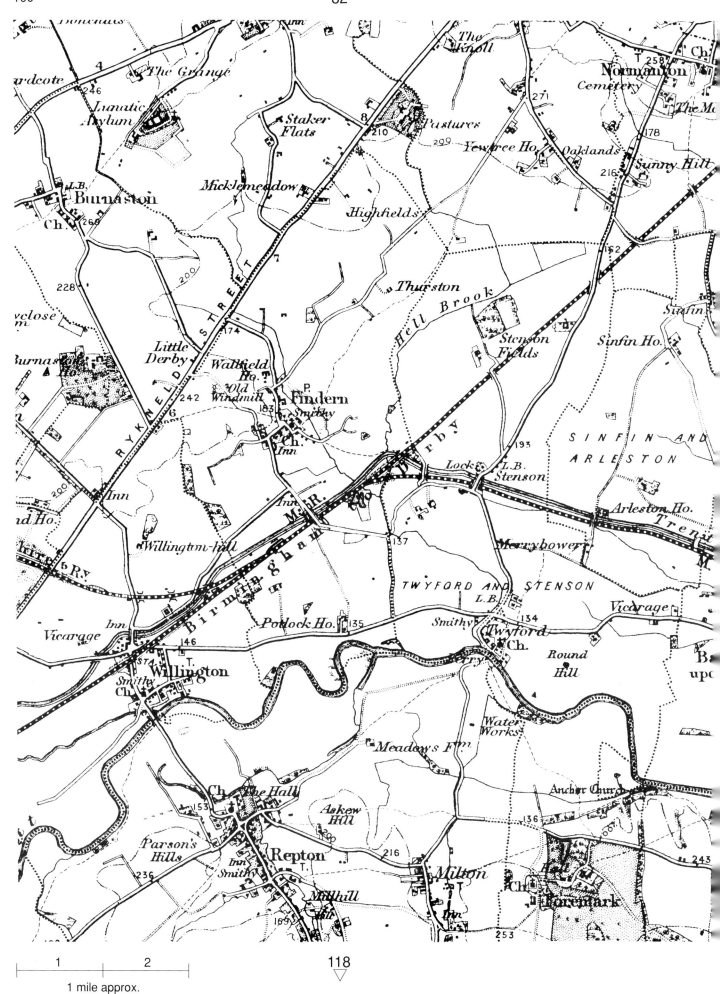

Honehalls

The Grange

4

246

Lunatic
Asylum

Staker
Flats

8

210

The
Knoll

Pastures

271

209

Yewtree Ho.

Oaklands

Normanton

Cemetery

T 258

Ch.

178

The M

216

Sunny Hill

L.B.

Burnaston

Ch. 266

Micklemeadow

Highfields

Thurston

Hell Brook

Stenson
Fields

182

Sinfin Ho.

Sinfin

228

200

174

Little
Derby

Wallfield
Ho.

Old
Windmill

P.

Findern

Smithy

Ch.

Inn

Derby

193

SINFIN AND

ARLESTON

Burnaston
Ho.

242

183

6

200

Inn

Willington-hill

Inn

M. R.

Birmingham

Lock

Stenson

L.B.

157

Merrybower

Arleston Ho.

Trent

M

& R.

TWYFORD AND STENSON

L.B.

Vicarage

Vicarage

Inn

146

Pollock Ho.

135

Smithy

134

Twyford

Ch.

Round
Hill

B

upo

Willington

Smithy

Ch.

374

T.

Water
Works

Meadows F.

Ch.

The Hall

153

Askew
Hill

Anchor Church

136

Parson's
Hills

Inn

Smithy

Repton

T.

216

Milton

T.

253

Foremark

243

236

Millhill

169

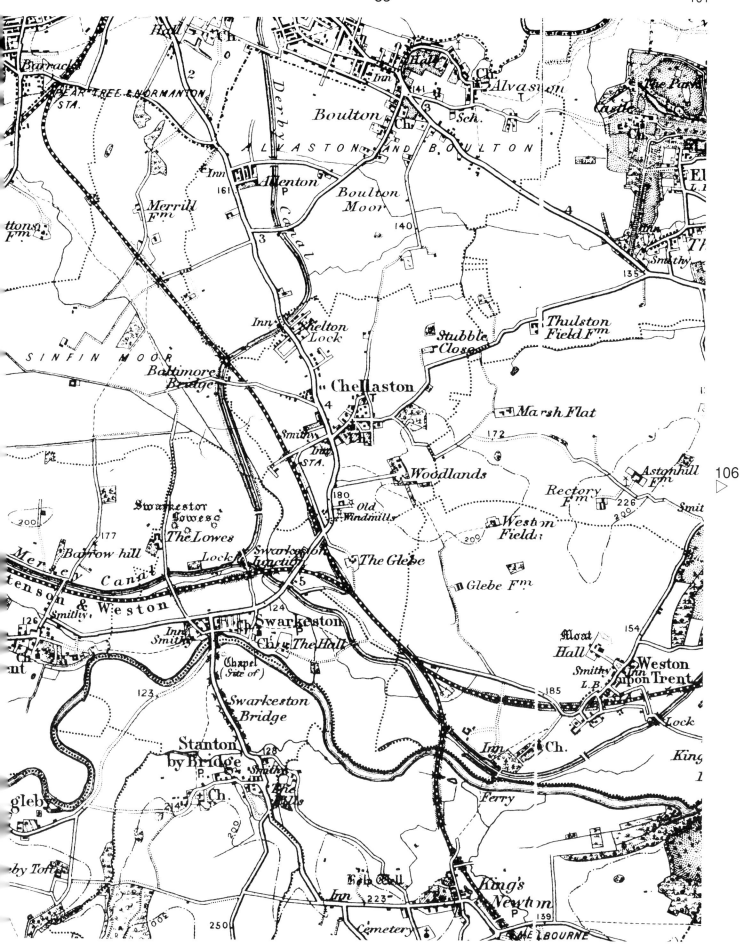

Surveyed 1879 - 83. Revised 1905 - 06. Published 1908.

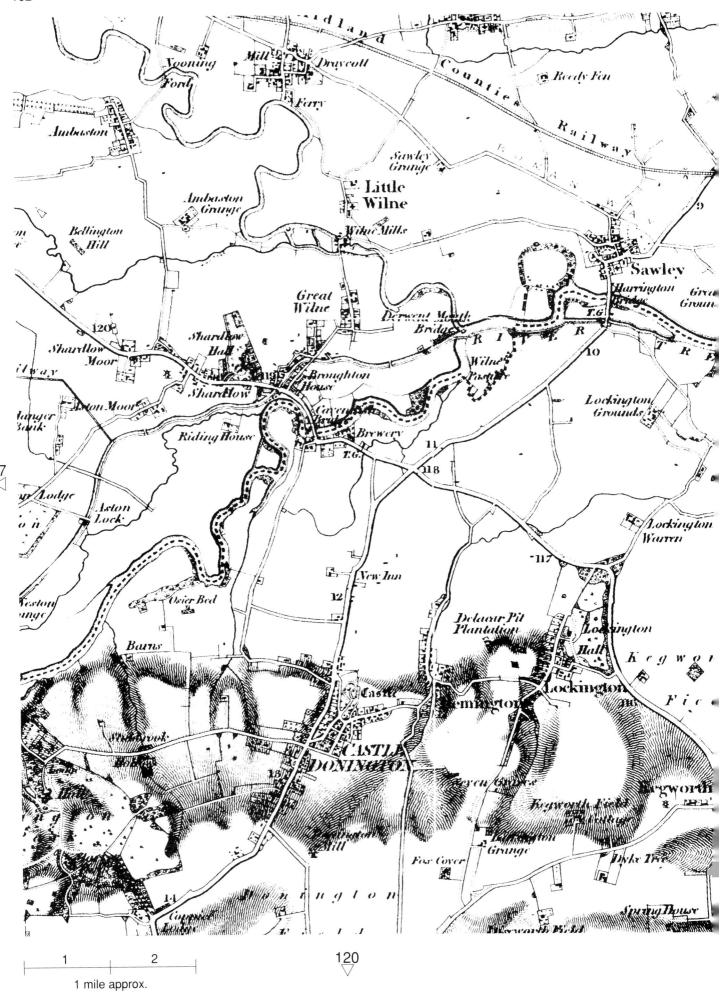

1   2

1 mile approx.

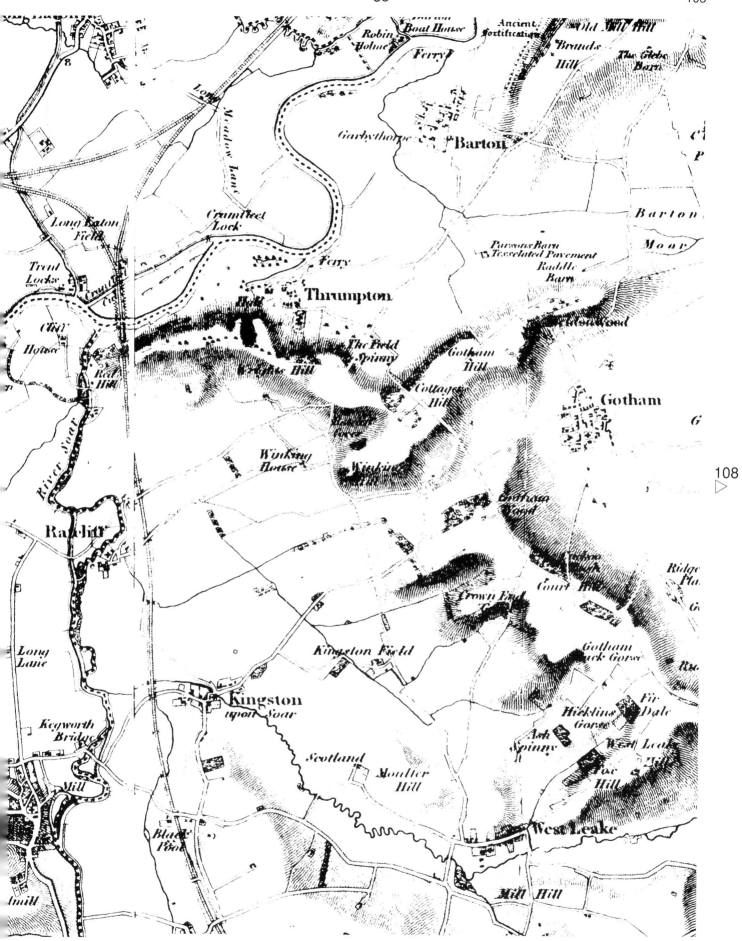

Published 1836.

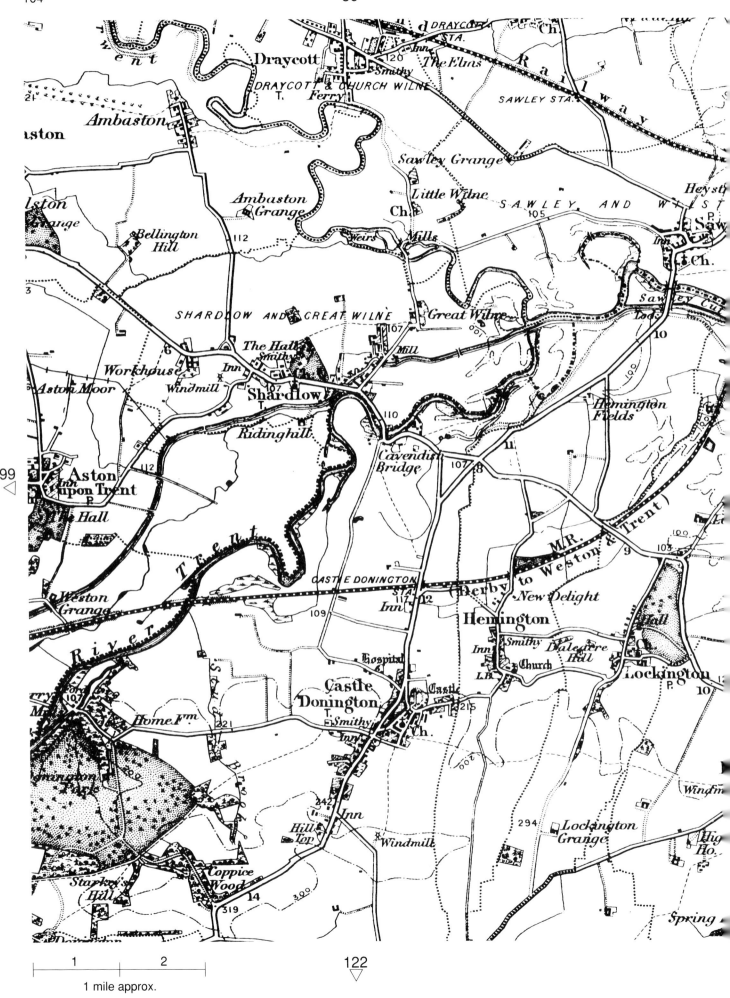

1   2

1 mile approx.

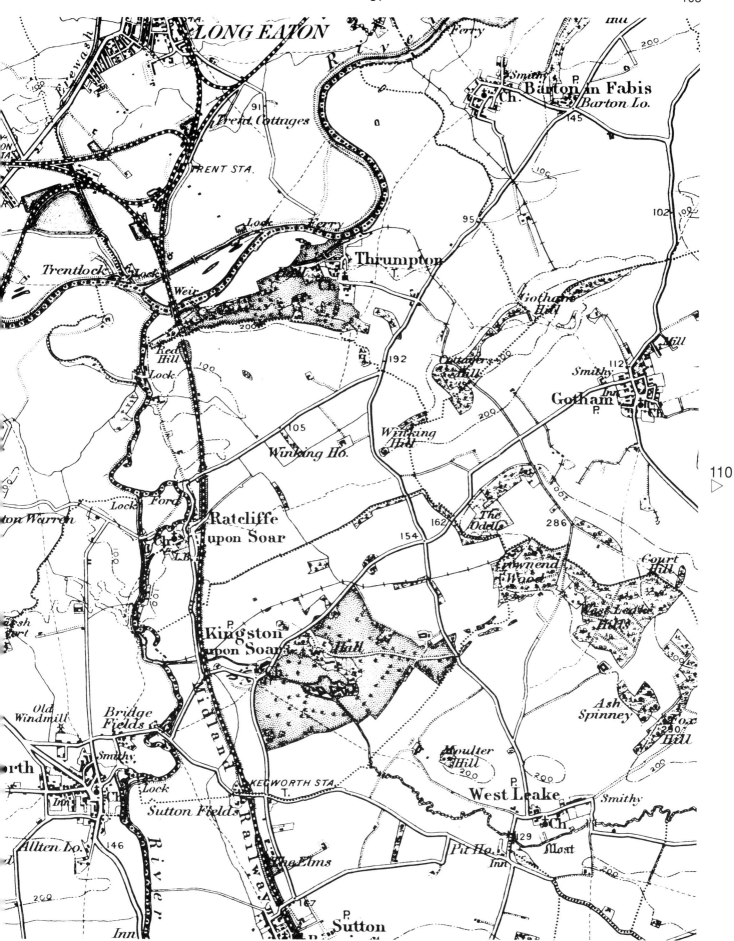

Surveyed 1879 - 83. Revised 1895 - 96. Published 1896.

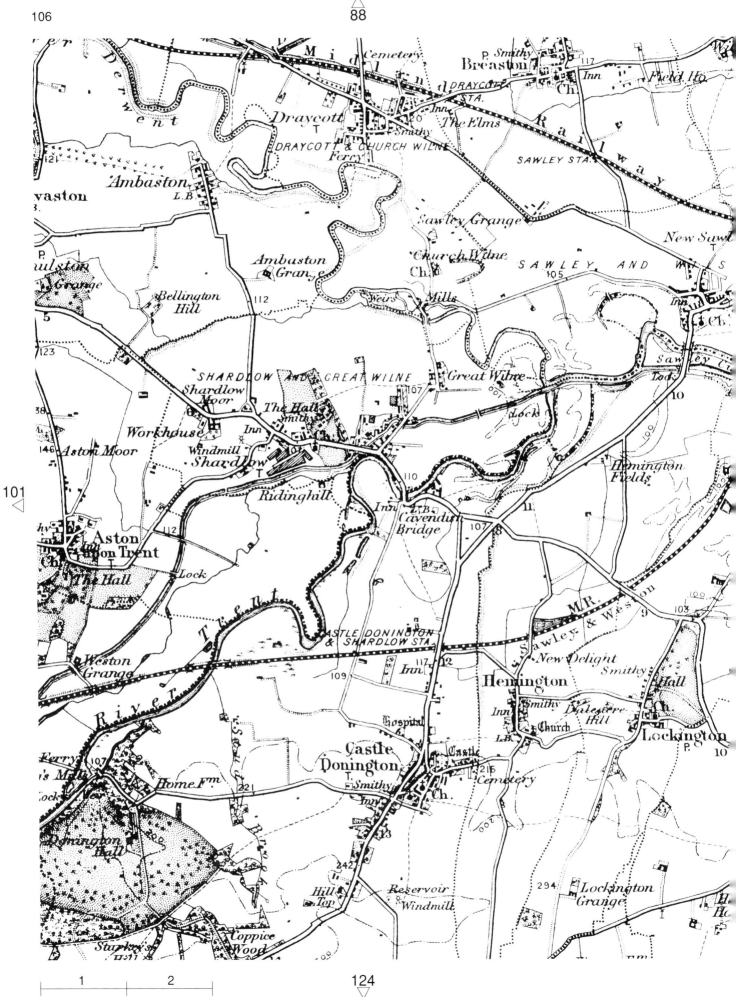

1 mile approx.

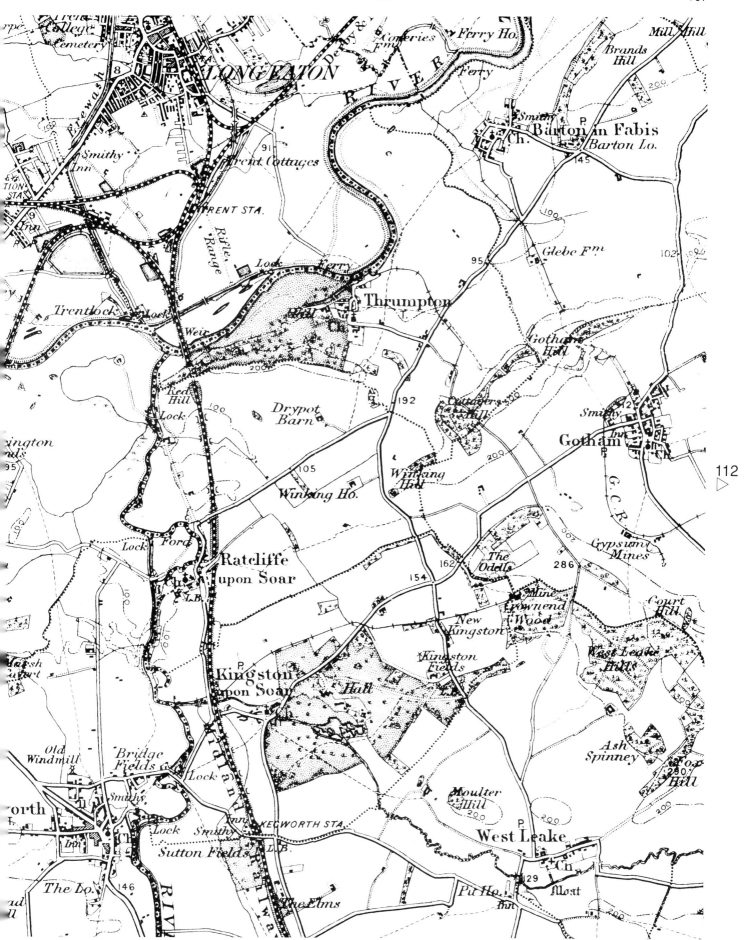

Surveyed 1879 - 83. Revised 1905 - 06. Published 1908.

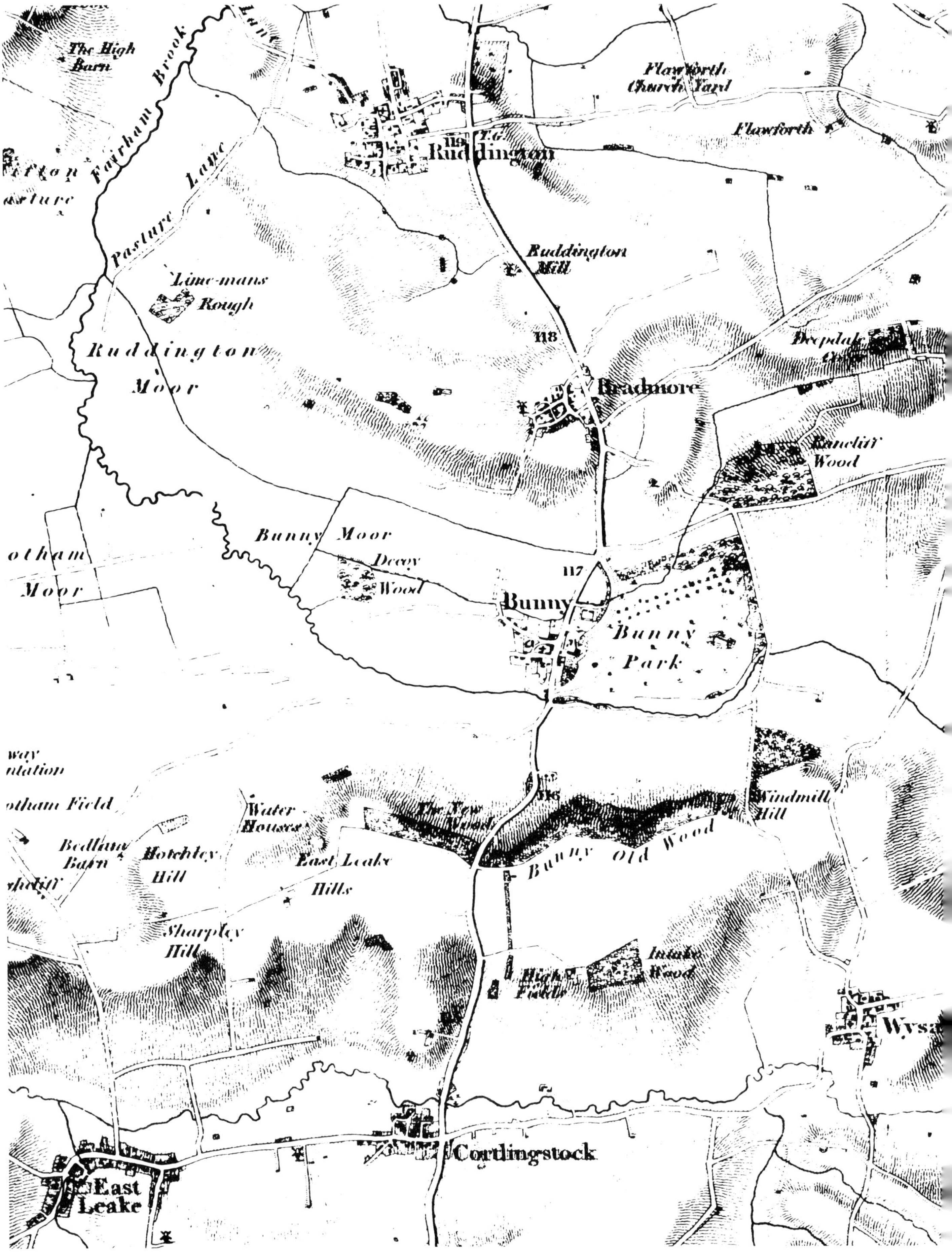

The High Barn

Fairham Brook

Pasture Lane

Lane

Ruddington

Flawforth Church Yard

Flawforth

ton asture

Ruddington Mill

Line-mans Rough

Ruddington Moor

118

Bradmore

Drapdale

Rancliff Wood

otham Moor

Bunny Moor

Decoy Wood

117

Bunny

Bunny Park

way ntation

otham Field

Water Houses

The Yew Wood

Windmill Hill

Bedlam Barn

Hotchley Hill

East Leake Hills

Bunny Old Wood

rdcliff

Sharpley Hill

Intake Wood

High Forest

Wysa

Cortlingstock

East Leake

1   2

1 mile approx.

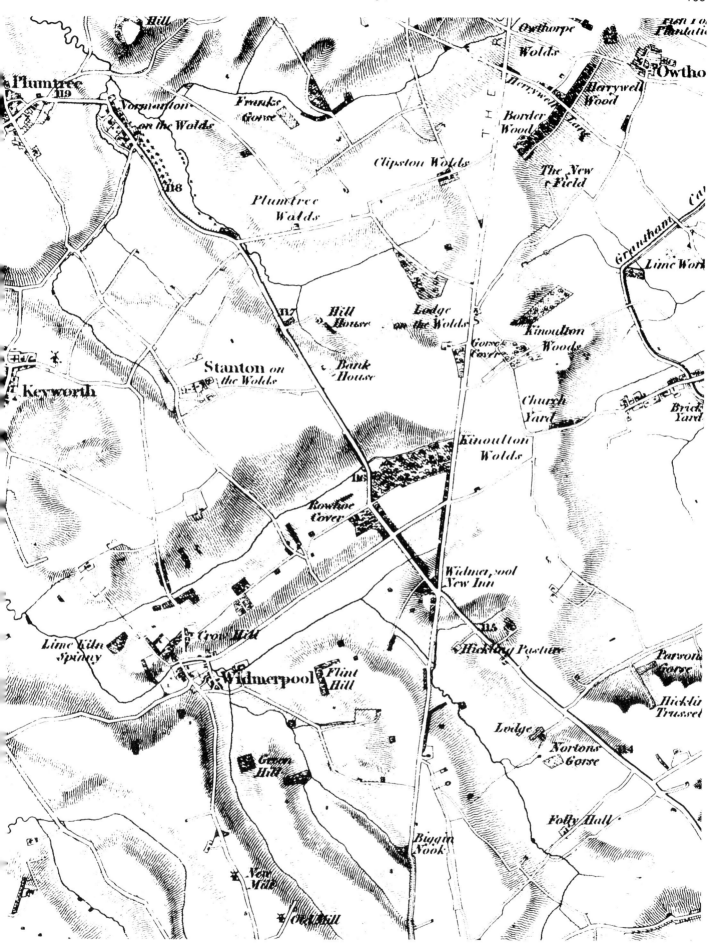

Published 1836.

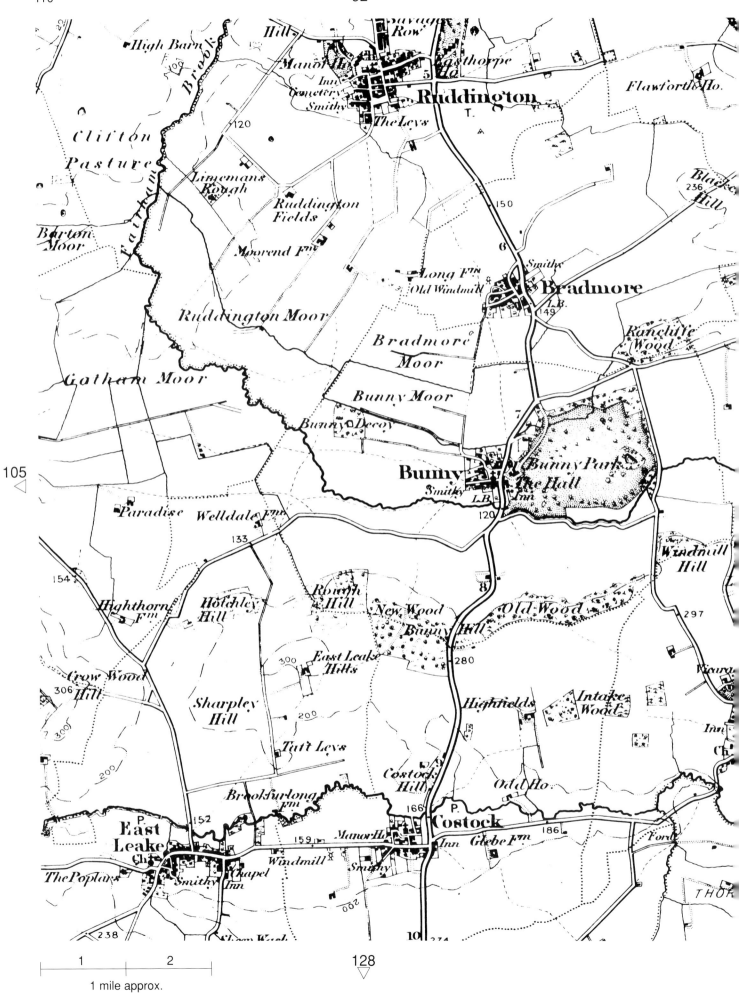

High Barn

Hill

Savage Row

Easthorpe Ho

Manor Ho

Clifton

Inn

Cemetery

Smithy

Ruddington

The Levs

Flawforth Ho.

Brook

Pasture

Barton Moor

Limemans Rough

120

Ruddington Fields

150

Black Hill

236

6

Moorend Fm

Long Fm

Old Windmill

Smithy

Bradmore

L.B.

149

Ruddington Moor

Rancliffe Wood

Bradmore Moor

Gotham Moor

Bunny Moor

Bunny Decoy

7

Bunny Bunny Park

Smithy The Hall

L.B. Inn

120

Paradise

Welldale Fm

133

Windmill Hill

154

Crow Wood

306 Hill

Highthorn Fm

Hotchley Hill

Rough Hill

New Wood

Old Wood

297

8

Bunny Hill

280

East Leake Hills

300

Sharpley Hill

200

Highfields

Intake Wood

Vicar

Inn

Ch

Tutt Levs

Brookfurlong Fm

Costock Hill

Odd Ho

166 P.

East Leake

P.

152

Ch

159

Manor Ho

Costock

Inn

Grebe Fm

186

Ford

The Poplars

Smithy Inn

Chapel

Windmill

Smithy

THOR

200

238

10

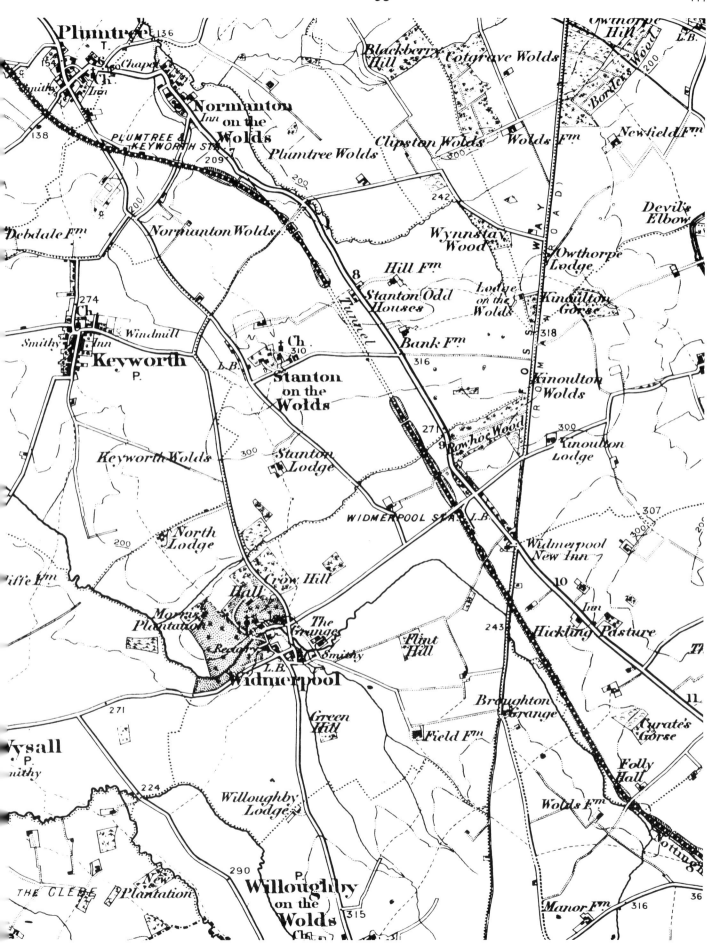

Surveyed 1882 - 86. Revised 1898. Published 1899.

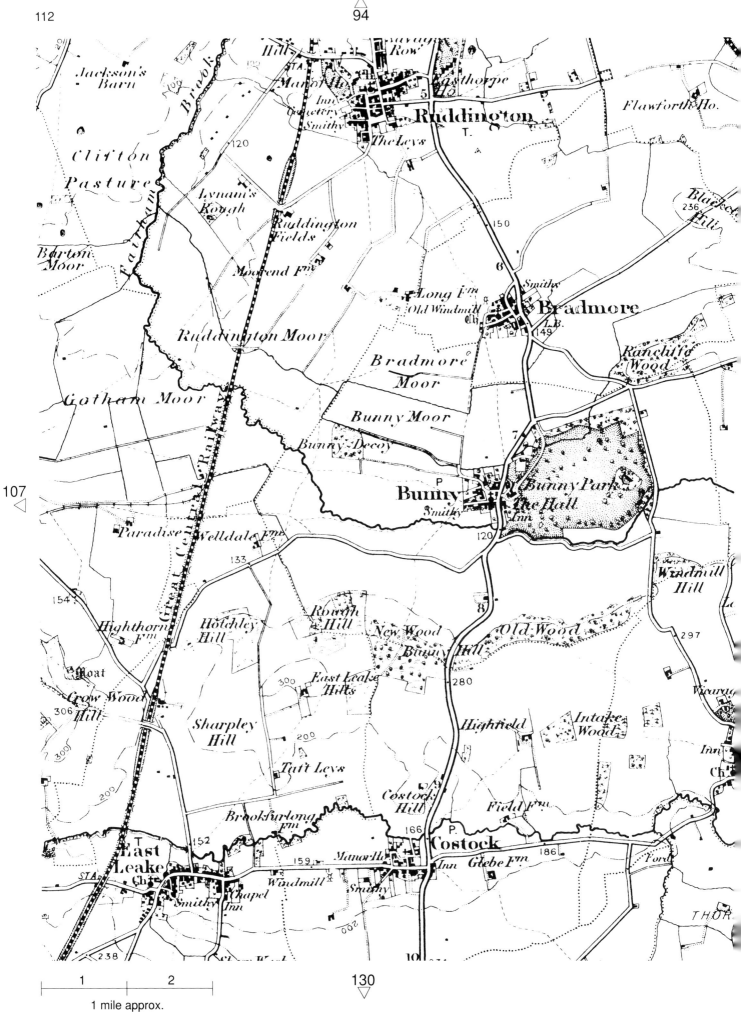

94

Jackson's
Barn

Brook

Manor Ho

Hill

Savage
Row

Eastthorpe

5

Ruddington
T.

Flawforth Ho.

Inn
Cemetery
Smithy

The Leys

Clifton

Pasture

Lynam's
Rough

Ruddington
Fields

120

Moorend Fm

150

Long Fm
Old Windmill

Ch

Smithy

Bradmore
L.B.
149

Black
Hill
236

Barton
Moor

Ruddington Moor

Bradmore
Moor

Ranchffe
Wood

Gotham Moor

Bunny Moor

Bunny Decoy

7

107

Paradise

Welldale Fm

133

Bunny
P
Smithy

Bunny Park
The Hall
Inn

120

Windmill
Hill

154

Highthorn
Fm

Hotchley
Hill

Rowth
Hill

New Wood

Old Wood

8

297

280

Moat

Crow Wood
Hill
306

300

Sharpley
Hill

300

East Leake
Hills

Bunny Hill

200

Highfield

Intake
Wood

Vicarage

Inn
Ch

Tutt Leys

200

Costock
Hill

Field Fm

Brookfurlong
Fm

166
P

Costock

186

Ford

East
Leake
Ch

152

T

159

Manor Ho
Windmill

Inn
Smithy

Glebe Fm

STA

Smithy Inn

Chapel

200

THOR

238

10

130

1   2

1 mile approx.

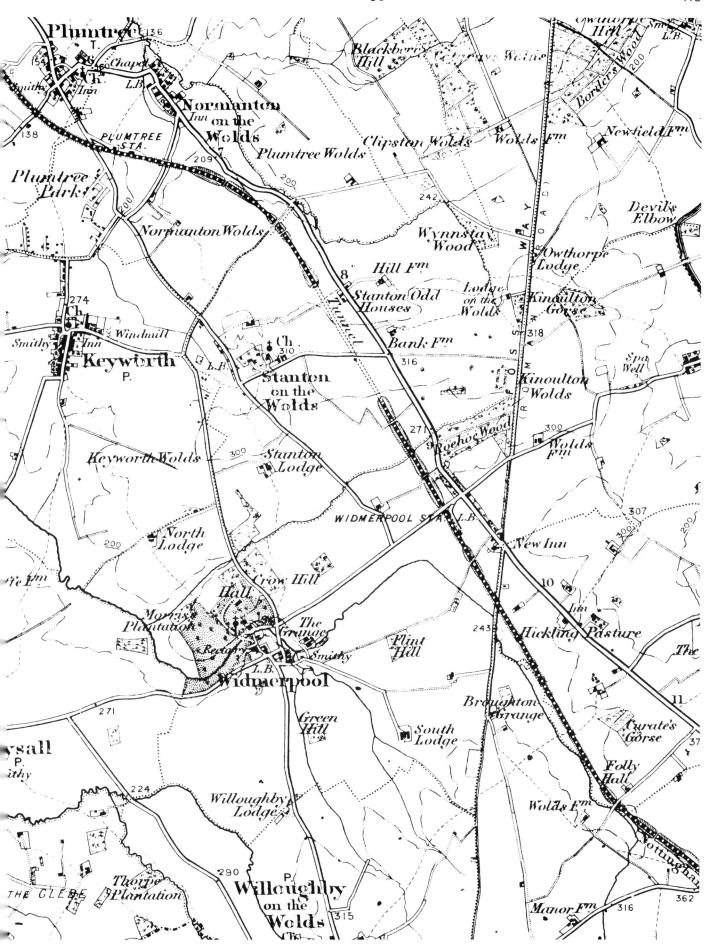

Surveyed 1882 - 86. Revised 1906. Published 1908.

1   2

1 mile approx.

97

Melbourne
Wilson Mill
Brick Yard
Wood Houses
Broadstone
New England
Prior Fields
Breedon
on the Hill
Park Spinny
Staunton Harold
Staunton
Worthington Field
Worthington
Lount Colliery
Lount
Newbold
Breedon
Cloud
Wood
Coleorton
Railway
The Common
Old Parks
Ashby
Old Parks
Stone
Quarries
The Dale
The Paddock
Railway

120

Published 1836.

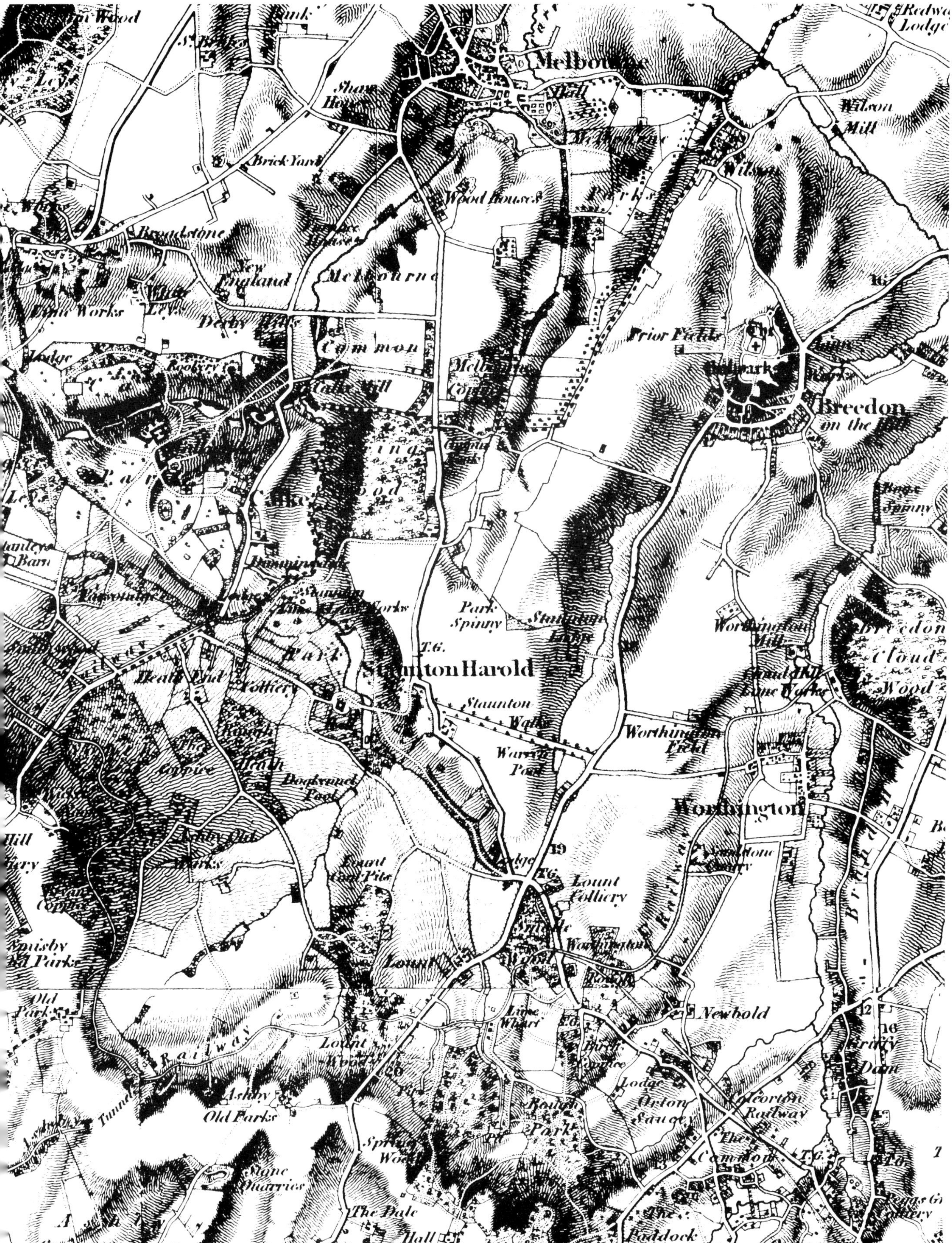

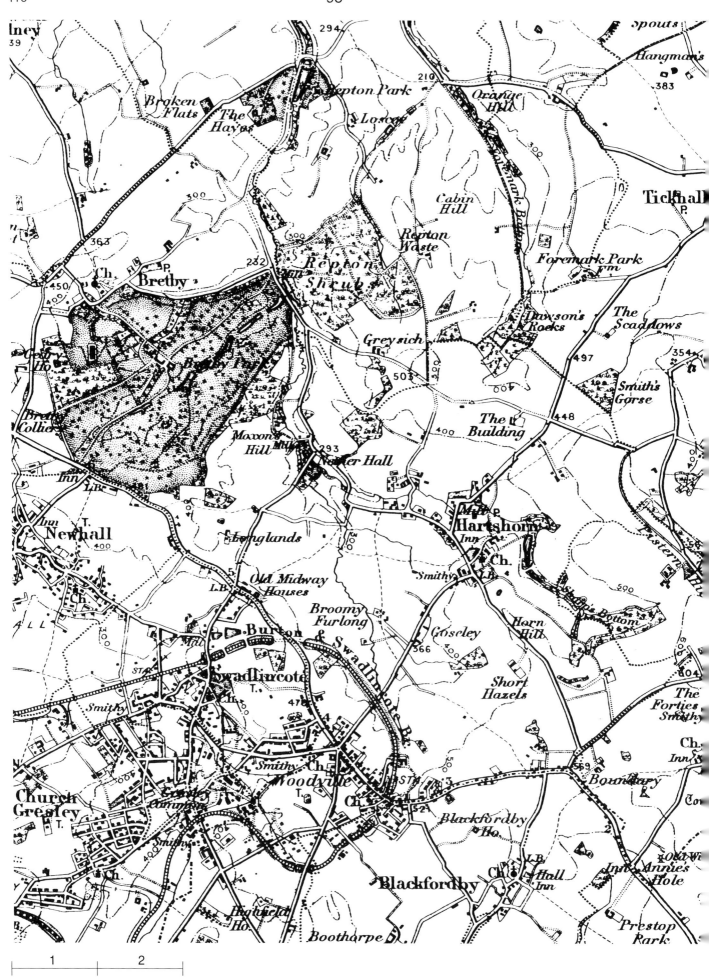

1 mile approx.

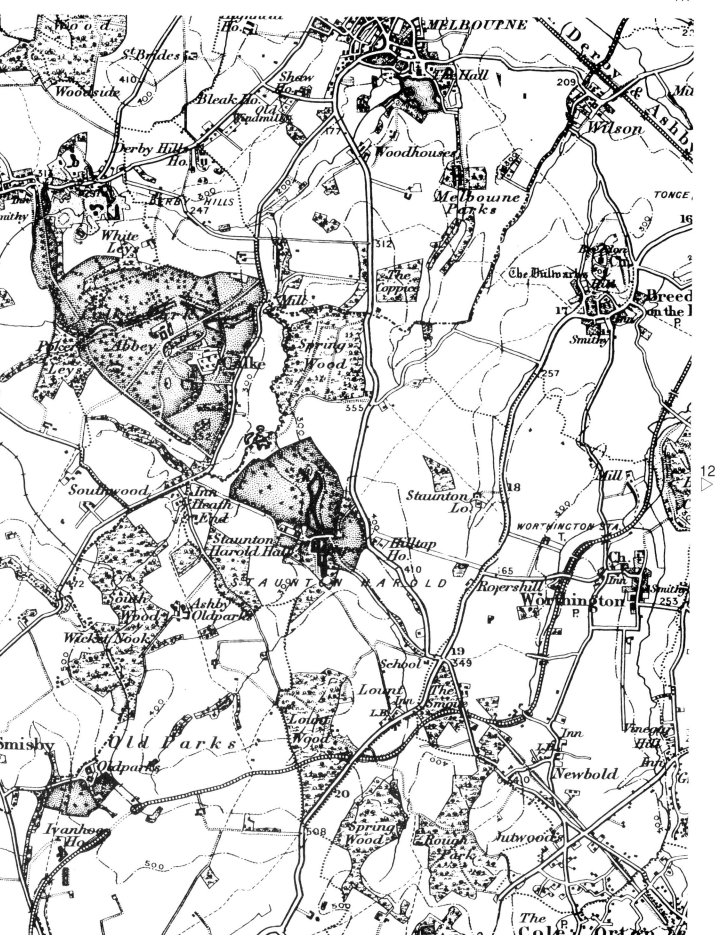

Surveyed 1879 - 83. Revised 1895 - 96. Published 1896.

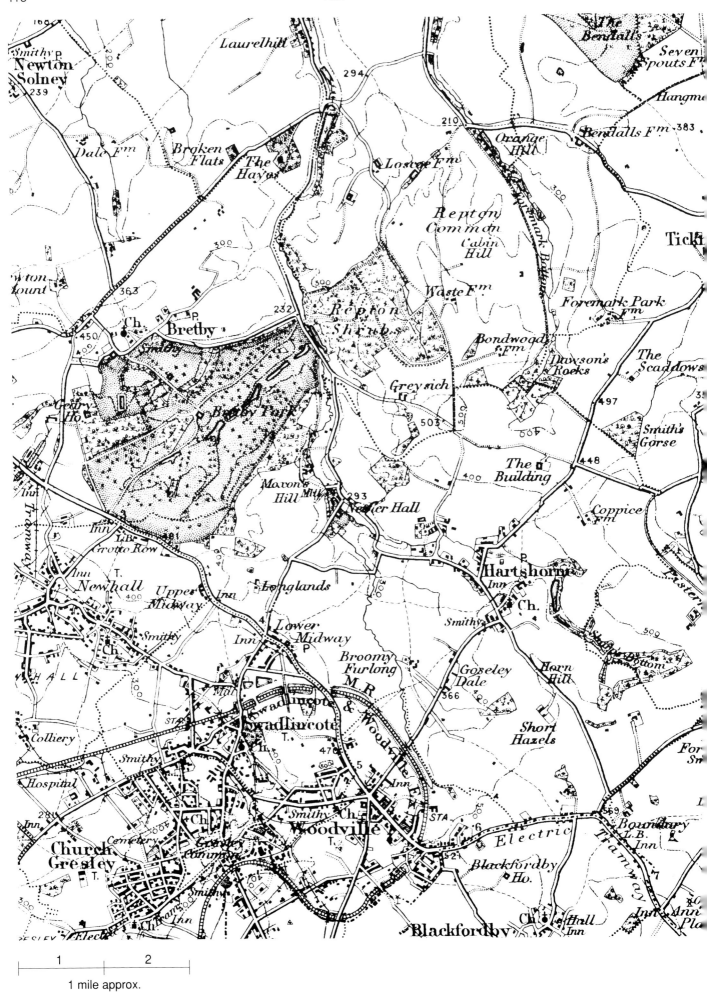

1   2

1 mile approx.

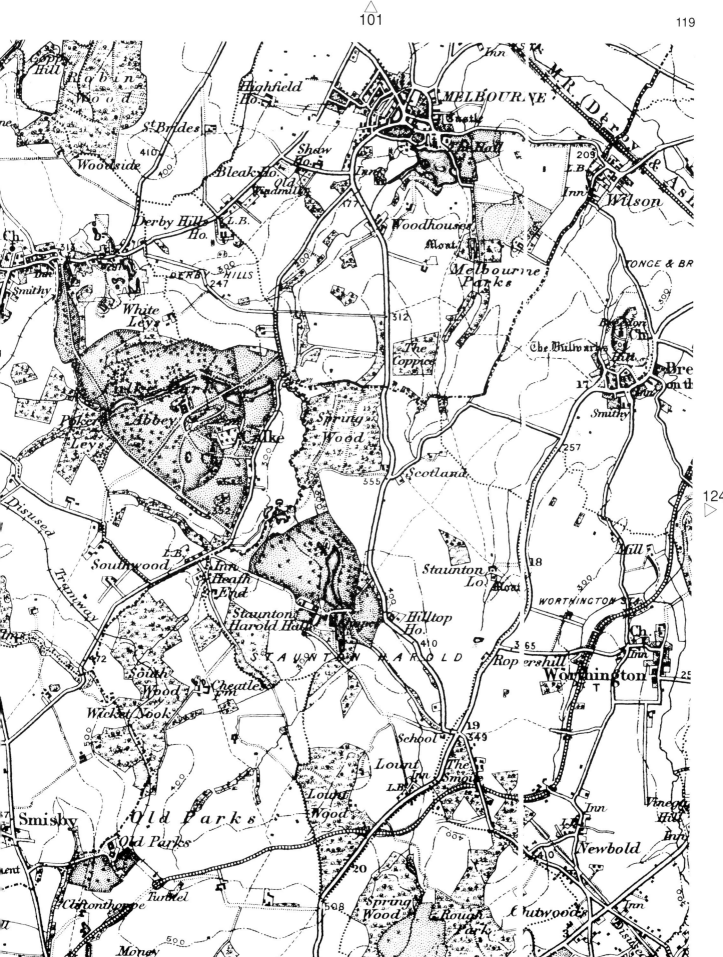

Surveyed 1882 - 86. Revised 1906. Published 1908.

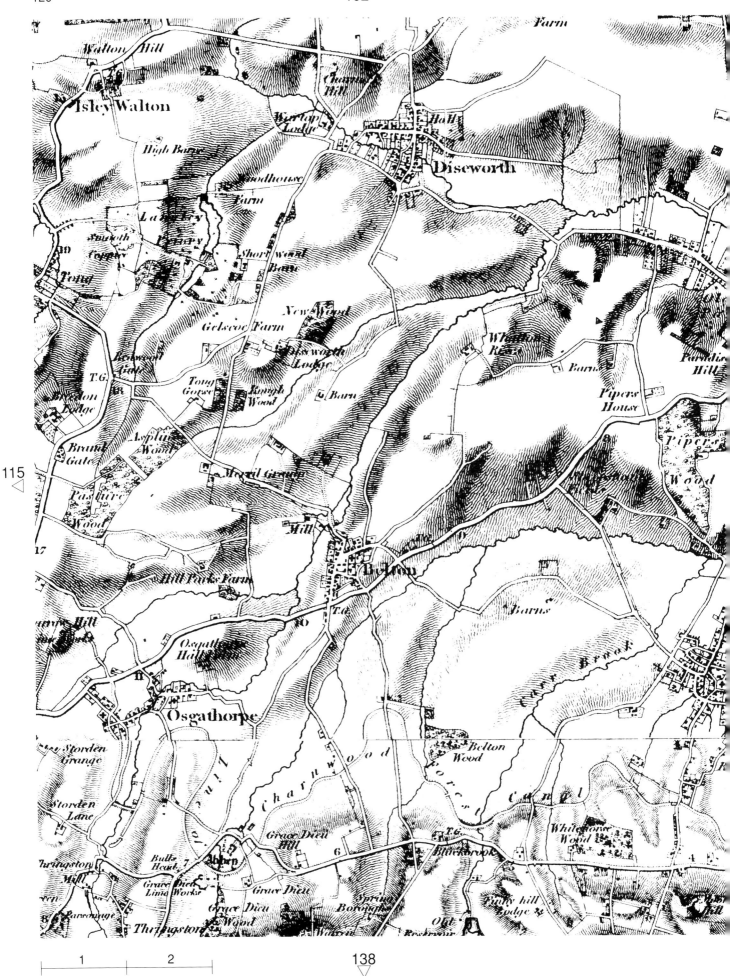

1   2

1 mile approx.

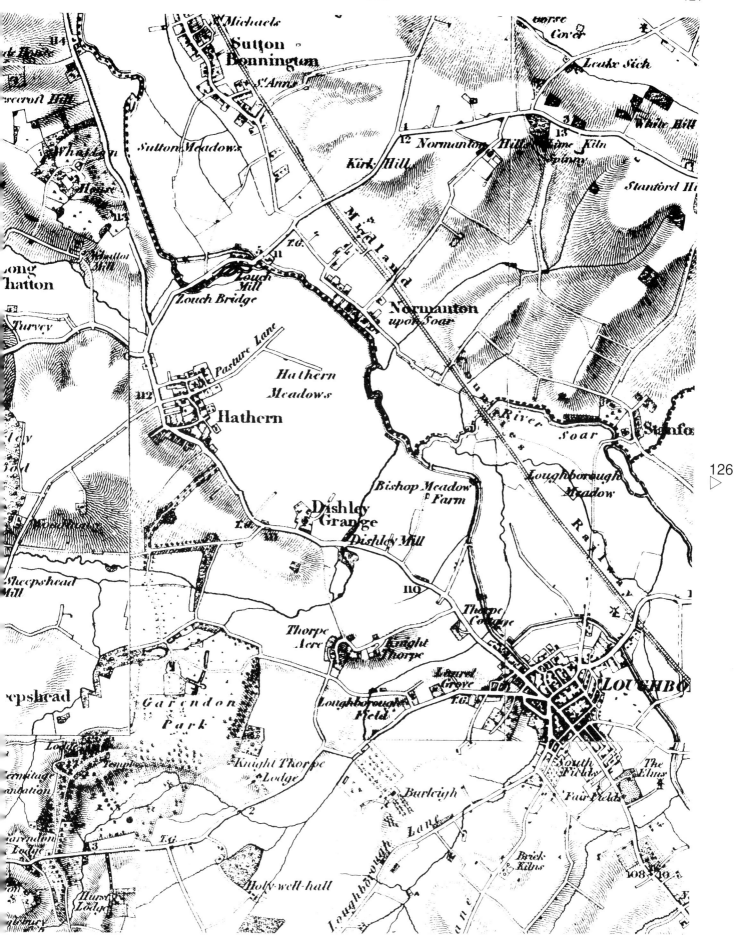

Park Fm.

Amber
Hill

Ch. Isley
Walton

Charnock
Hill

Bleak Ho.

15

200

300

Smithy Inn Diseworth

Ch.

P.

183

Long Wha

STA.

183

Wooden Nook

LANGLEY PRIORY

172

Langley Priory

L.

Tonge

268

200

Westmeadow Brook

Lo
Wha

P.

on
Hill

Whatton Rise

Moat

271

Breedon
Lo.

Asplin
Wood

320

Merril Grange

Highfield Ho.

8

338

Pasture
Wood

Merril
Grange

Windmill
Hill

210

Woodlands

reedon
oud Wood

300

210

Mill

Ch. Belton

7

Grace Dieu Brook

263

Breedon
Brand

Hillparks

Smithy
Inn

P.

Barrow
Hill

Inn

230

6

19

Shepshed

T.

300

5

283

Osgathorpe

West
End

P.

Fishpool Grange

Smithy

Ch.

Oxley Grange

Stordon
Grange

Inn

Low Wood

L. & N. W. R.

rffydam

373

278

259

Dieu Priory

6

Blackbrook

Mill

348

Inn

Spring Barrow
Lo.

Windmill

Fenny
Hill

Fenny Spring

Grace Dieu
Manor

Thringstone

P.

Inn

Smithy

The Hermitage

1   2

1 mile approx.

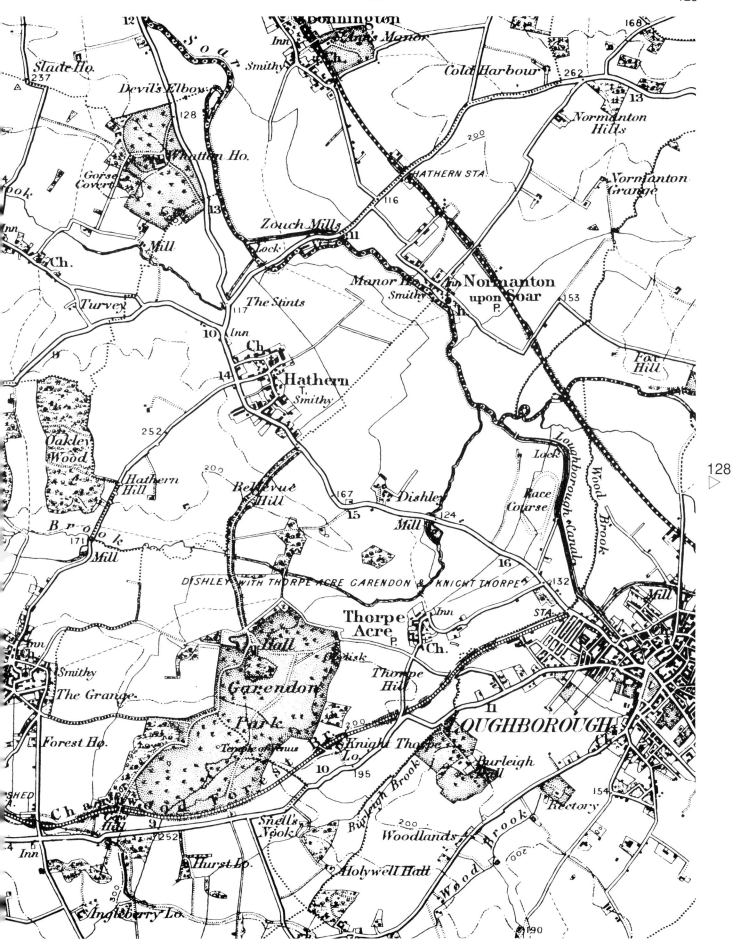

Surveyed 1879 - 83. Revised 1895 - 96. Published 1896.

Gimbro Fm

Finger

Spring

Dorrington
Park Fm

225

Bleak Ho.

Ambro
Hill

Ch.

Isley
Walton

L.B.
15

Charnwood
Hill

Smithy Inn

Diseworth

Ch.

P
183

Mill

High Barn

200

Woodhouse
Fm

Long Wha

EEDON
STA

16

183

Wooden Nook

172

L.
Wh

LANGLEY PRIORY

Langley Priory

268

200

200

Tonge

Scatherne
Fm

Whatton Rise

Piper Fm

edon
e Hill

L.B.

Moat

Breedon
Lo.

Asplin
Wood

Merril
Grange

Merril Grange

Highfield Ho.

27

8

320

338

Pasture
Wood

300

210

Windmill
Hill

210

Woodlands

Breedon
Cloud Wood

Mill

Ch.

Belton

P

7

200

Hillparks
Fm

Smithy
Inn

263

Breedon
Brand

230

Grace

Dieu

Brook

195

Barrow
Hill

Inn

300

6

SHEPSHE

West
End

5

283

Osgathorpe

P

Fishpool Grange

Smithy

Inn

Ch.

Low Woods

Old

Oxley Grang

Stordon
Grange

Moat

4

Old Canal

Canal

L. & N. W. R.

Griffydam

P
373

259

HALT

Dieu Priory 6

Blackbrook

78

7

eggs Green

Inn

348

Inn

Spring Barrow
Lo.

Fenny Spring

L.B.

Windmill

Fenney
Hill

1   2

1 mile approx.

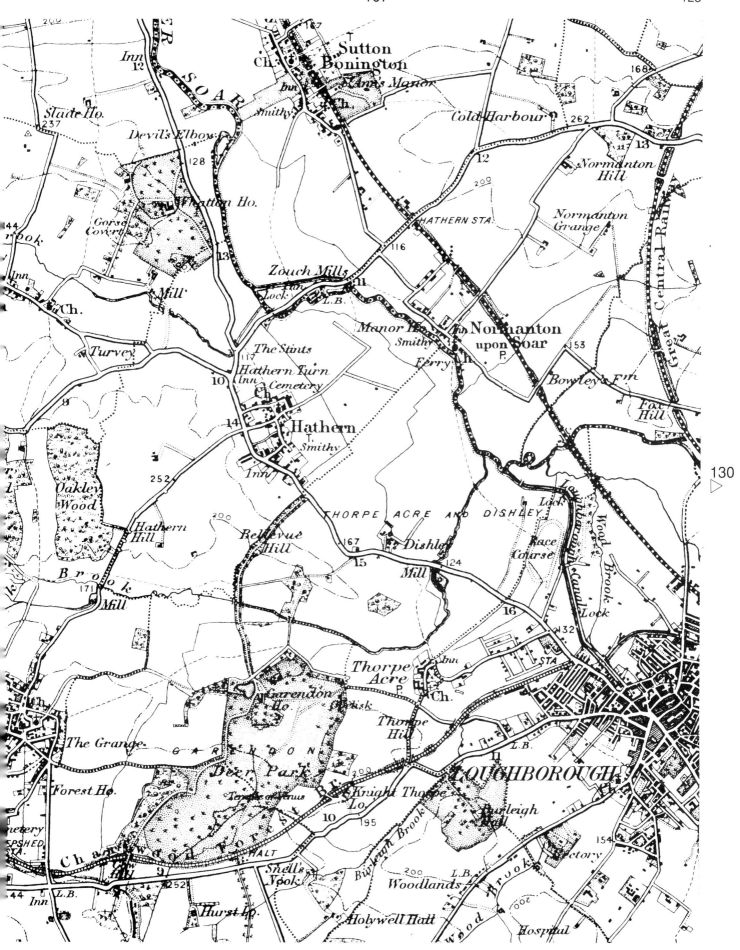

Surveyed 1882 - 86. Revised 1906. Published 1908.

114

The Lings

Rempstone
Old Church yard

Rempstone Hall

2

Stanford
Hall

Rempstone
Hill

Thor
in Gle

115

Rempstone

Wimesw

ls 14

T.G.

Blackmoor Spinny

Riggels
Spinny

Hoton
Hills

Hoton

112

Hoton
Spinny

The Dale
Plantation

Ice house
Plantation

Wimeswold
Mill

Moat hill
Spinny

Fox
Crofts

The Lings

111

Prestwold

Meadow
Plantation

Meer hill
Spinny

Burton
on the Wolds

Cotes

10

Lower
Mill

Burton Bandals

Cuthpit Farm

Low
Farm

Deep Dale

Upper
Mill

Walton Brook

ROUGH

Walton on the

Loughborough
Moors

The Tithe
Farm

Lodge

Lime Quarries
and Kilns

Cream Lodge

less
Inn

Quorndon
Moors

Barrow Field

wdy Lane

1   2

1 mile approx.

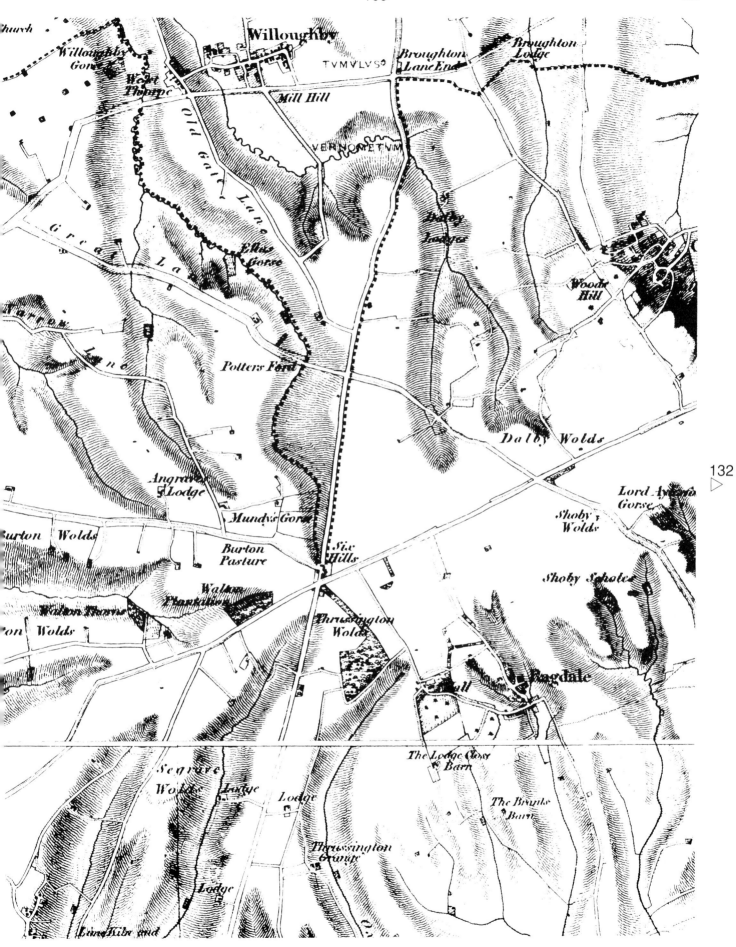

Church

Willoughby Gorse

Willoughby

West Thorpe

TVMVLVS

Broughton Lane End

Broughton Lodge

Mill Hill

VERNOMETVM

Old Gate Lane

Great Lane

Elms Gorse

Dalby Lodge

Narrow Lane

Woods Hill

Potters Ford

Angrave's Lodge

Mundy's Gorse

Dalby Wolds

Lord Aylesford Gorse

Shoby Wolds

Burton Wolds

Burton Pasture

Six Hills

Shoby Scholes

Walton Plantation

Walton Thorns

Thrussington Wolds

Ragdale

ton Wolds

The Lodge Close Barn

Segrave Wolds

Lodge

Lodge

The Brands Barn

Thrussington Grange

Lodge

Lime Kiln end

Published 1835.

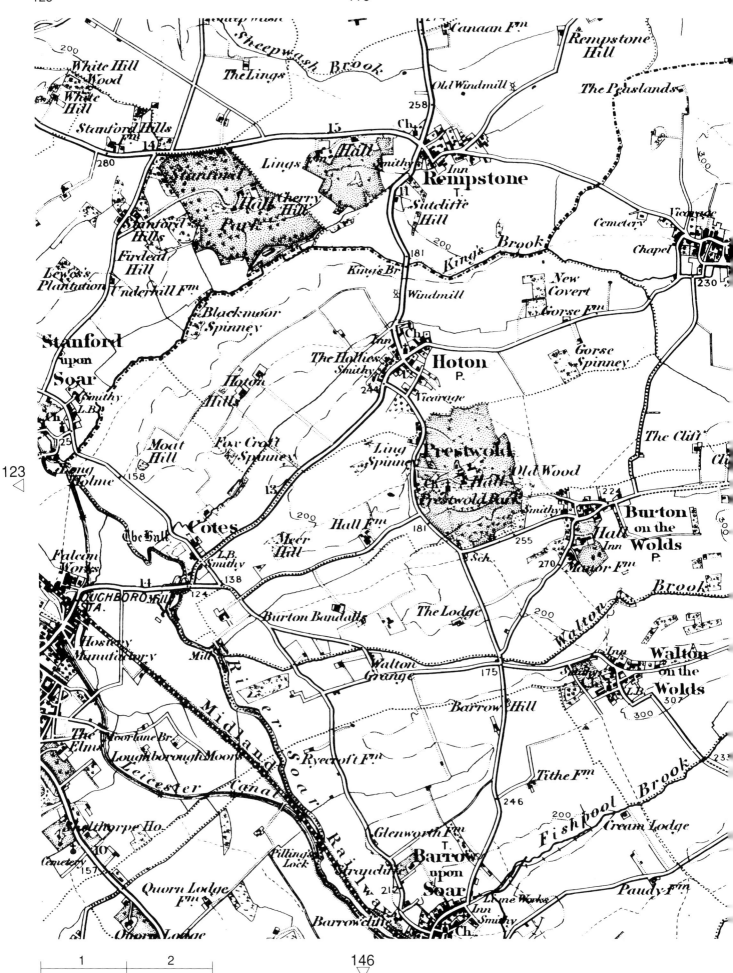

White Hill
Wood

Sheepwash

The Lings

Brook

Canaan Fm

Rempstone
Hill

The Peaslands

White
Hill

Stanford Hills
Fm

Old Windmill

258

Ch.

15

Stanford

Lings

Hall

Smithy

Inn

Rempstone
T.

Stanford
Hall
Park

Cherry
Hill

Sutcliffe
Hill

Vicarage

Cemetery

Chapel

230

Firdeat
Hill

Lewes's
Plantation

Underhall Fm

181

King's Br

Windmill

King's
Brook

New
Covert

Gorse Fm

Blackmoor
Spinney

The Hollies

Inn

Ch.

Hoton
P.

Gorse
Spinney

Stanford
upon
Soar

Hoton
Hill

Smithy

244

Vicarage

Old Wood

The Cliff
Ch.

Smithy

125

Moat
Hill

Fox Croft
Spinney

Ling
Spinney

Prestwold
Hall

224

Ch.

Long
Holme

158

13

Prestwold Park

Smithy

Burton
on the
Wolds
P.

Cotes

200

Meer
Hill

Hall Fm

181

Hall

Inn

The Hall

L.B.

255

Falcon
Works

Smithy

270

Manor Fm

138

Brook

LOUGHBOROUGH
STA.

124

The Lodge

200

Walton
on the
Wolds

Hosiery
Manufactory

Mill

Burton Bandalls

Walton

Inn

307

The
Elms

Moorlane Br.

Walton
Grange

175

Barrow Hill

300

Leicester

Canal

Loughborough Moors

Ryecroft Fm

Tithe Fm

246

Fishpool

Brook

232

Shelthorpe Ho.

200

Cream Lodge

Cemetery

10

157

Fillings
Lock

Glenworth Fm
T.

Brook

Quorn Lodge
Fm

212

Barrow
upon
Soar

Lime Works

Inn
Smithy

Quorn Lodge

Barrowcliffe

Ch.

Paudy Fm

River Soar

Midland

Railway

1   2

1 mile approx.

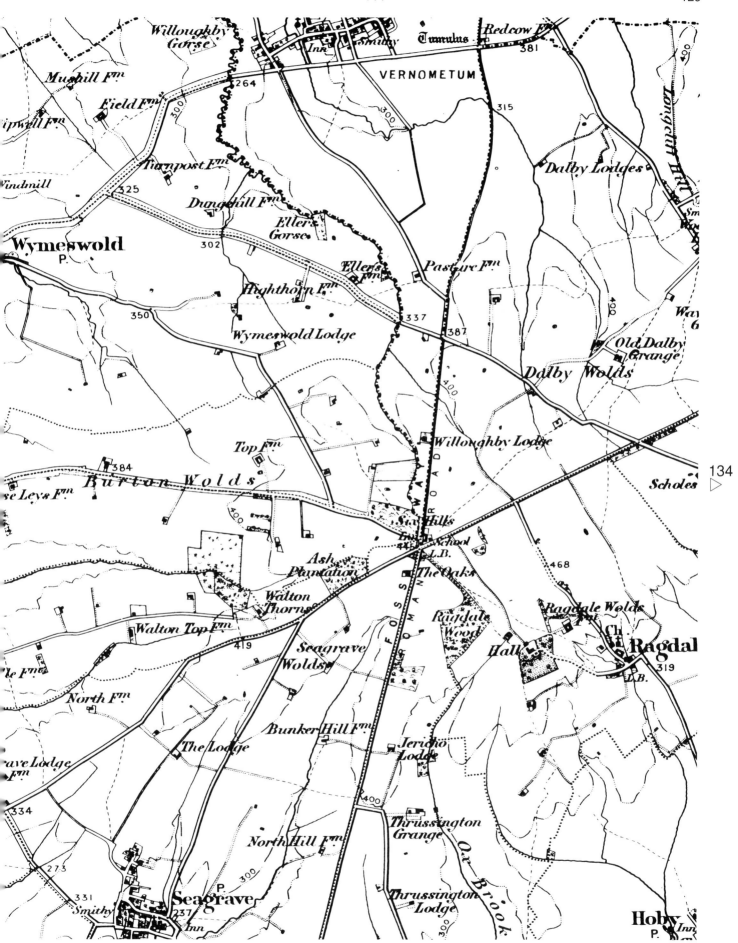

Surveyed 1882 - 86. Revised 1898. Published 1899.

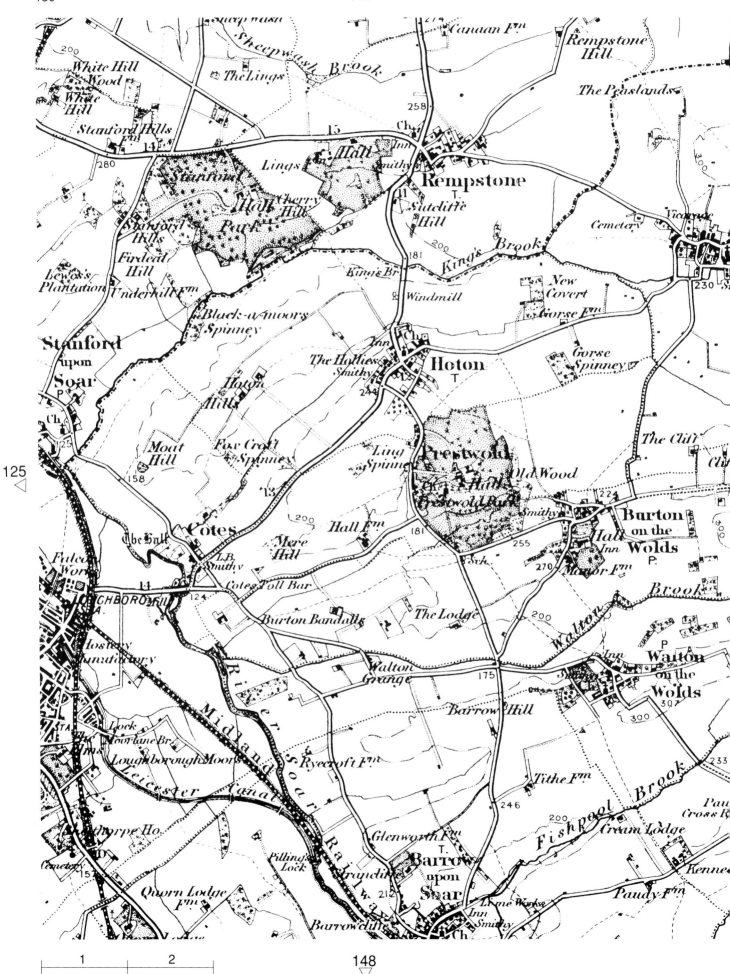

White Hill
Wood
White
Hill

Stanford Hills
Fm

280

Stanford
Hills

Firdeal
Hill

Lewis's
Plantation

Underhill Fm

Stanford
upon
Soar

Ch

125

Sheepwash
Sheepwash Brook

The Lings

Lings Hall

Lings

Stanford
Hall Park
Cherry
Hill

258

Ch

15

14

200

Black-a-moors
Spinney

King's Br

Hoton
Hill

Moat
Hill

Fox Croft
Spinney

158

13

Cotes

The Salt

Falcon
Works

LOUGHBOROUGH

Hosiery
Manufactory

STA

Lock

Moorlane Br.

Loughborough Moors

Leicester Canal

Thorpe Ho.

Cemetery

Quorn Lodge
Fm

The Hollies
Smithy

200

Mere
Hill

124

Cotes Toll Bar

Burton Bandalls

River Soar

Ryecroft Fm

Pilling's
Lock

Braunstone

212

Barrowcliffe

Canaan Fm

Rempstone
Hill

The Peaslands

274

300

REMPSTONE
T.
Inn
Smithy

Sutcliffe
Hill

181

King's Brook
200

Windmill

Inn
Ch

Smithy

HOTON
T.

244

Ling
Spinney

Hall Fm

181

Sch

Walton
Grange

Cemetery

New
Covert

Gorse Fm

Gorse
Spinney

PRESTWOLD
Hall
Prestwold Park

Old Wood

Smithy

255

175

The Lodge

Barrow Hill

200

Glenworth Fm
T.

BARROW
upon
Soar

Lime Works
Inn
Smithy
Ch

The Cliff

Cl

BURTON
on the
Wolds
P.
Hall
Inn

Manor Fm

270

222

Brook

Tithe Fm

246

Fishpool Brook

Cream Lodge

Paudy Fm

Walton
Brook

Inn

WALTON
on the
Wolds

300

300

Pau
Cross R

Kenne

233

Vicarage

230

1   2

1 mile approx.

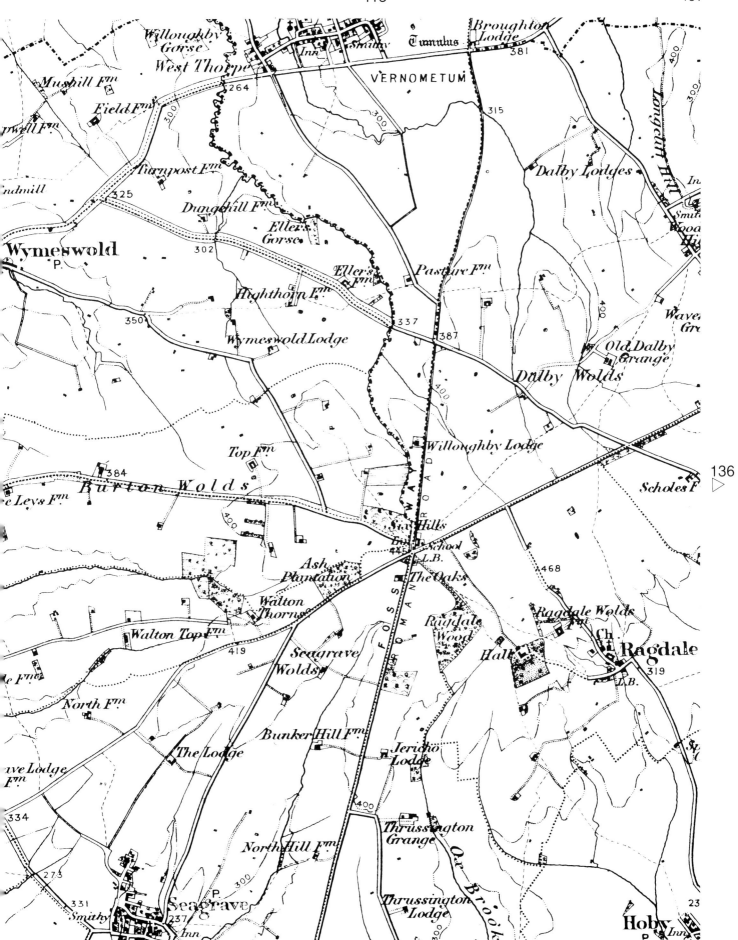

Surveyed 1882 - 86. Revised 1906. Published 1908.

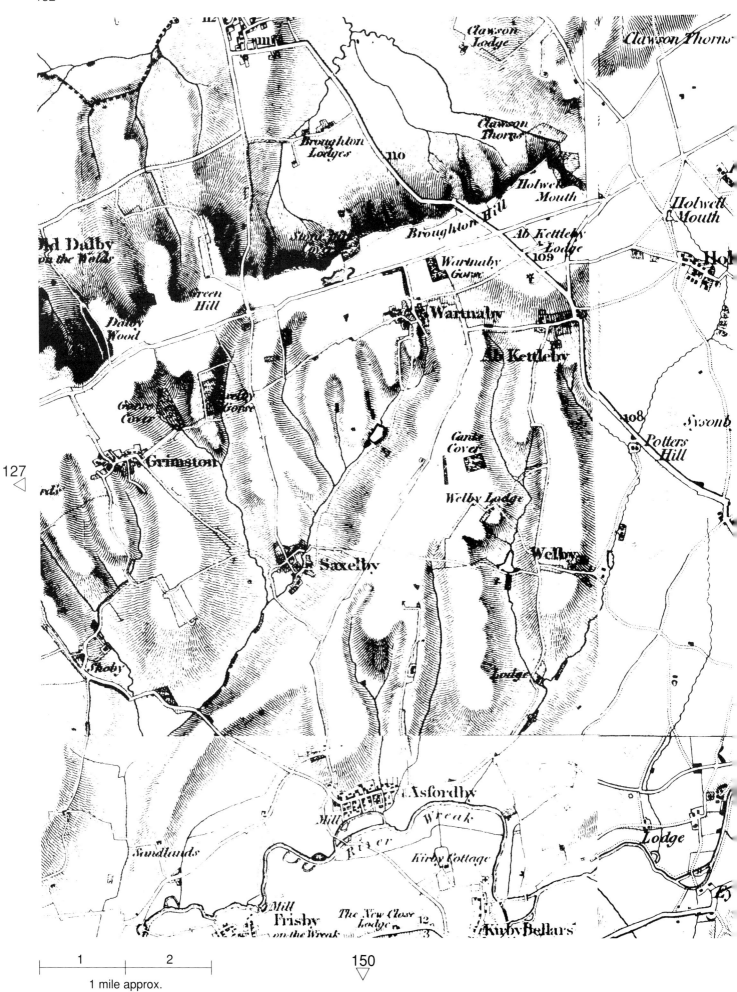

127 ◁

1 mile approx.

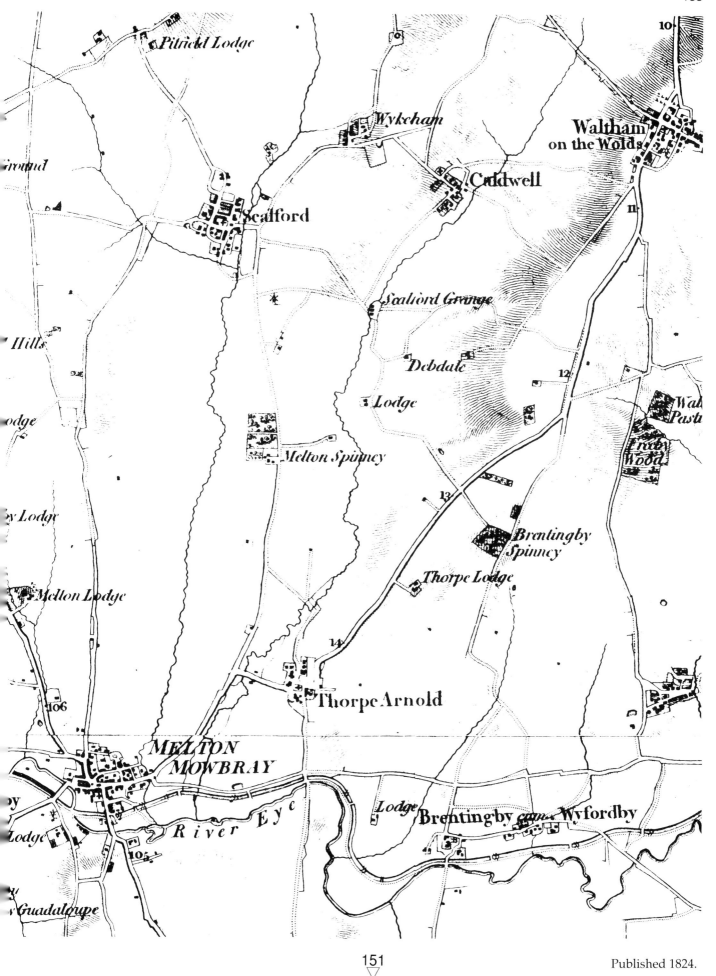

Published 1824.

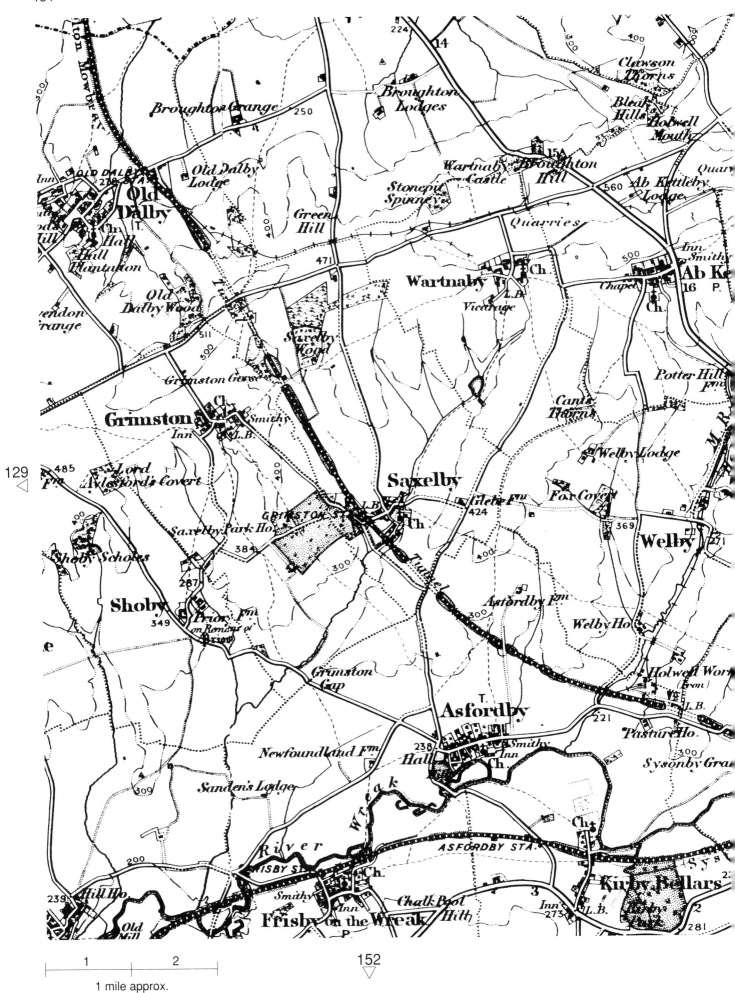

134

1 mile approx.

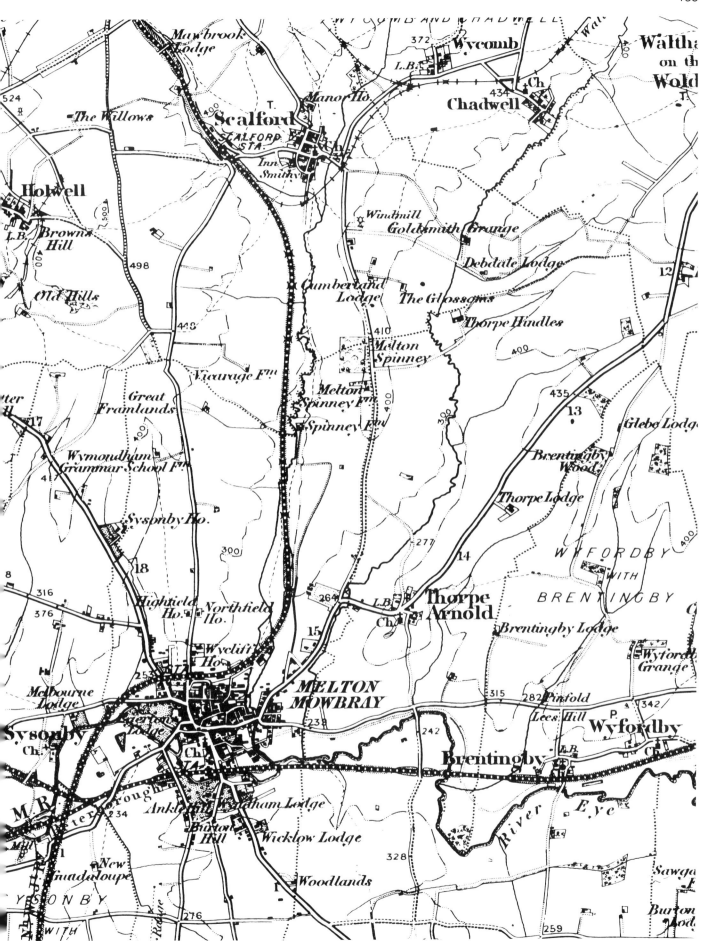

Surveyed 1882 - 86. Revised 1898. Published 1899.

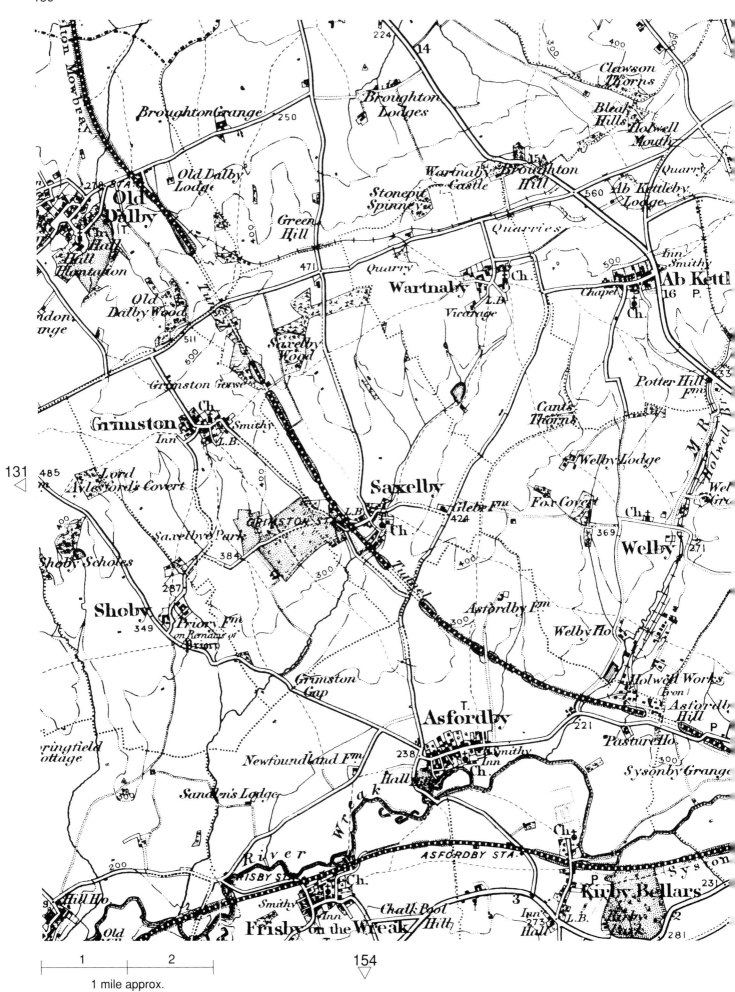

1

2

1 mile approx.

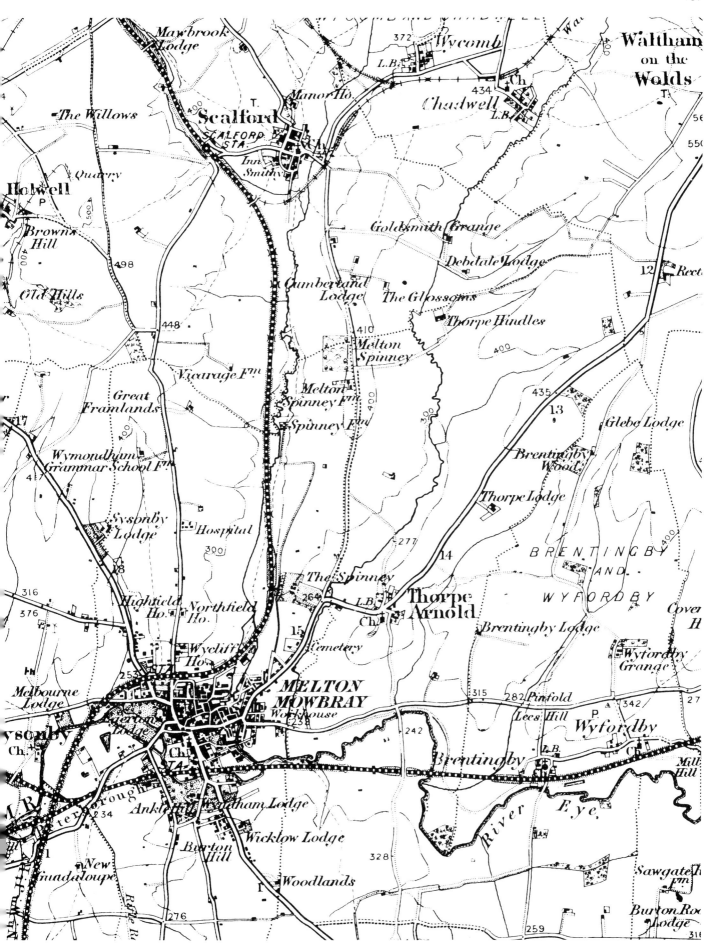

155

Surveyed 1882 - 86. Revised 1906. Published 1908.

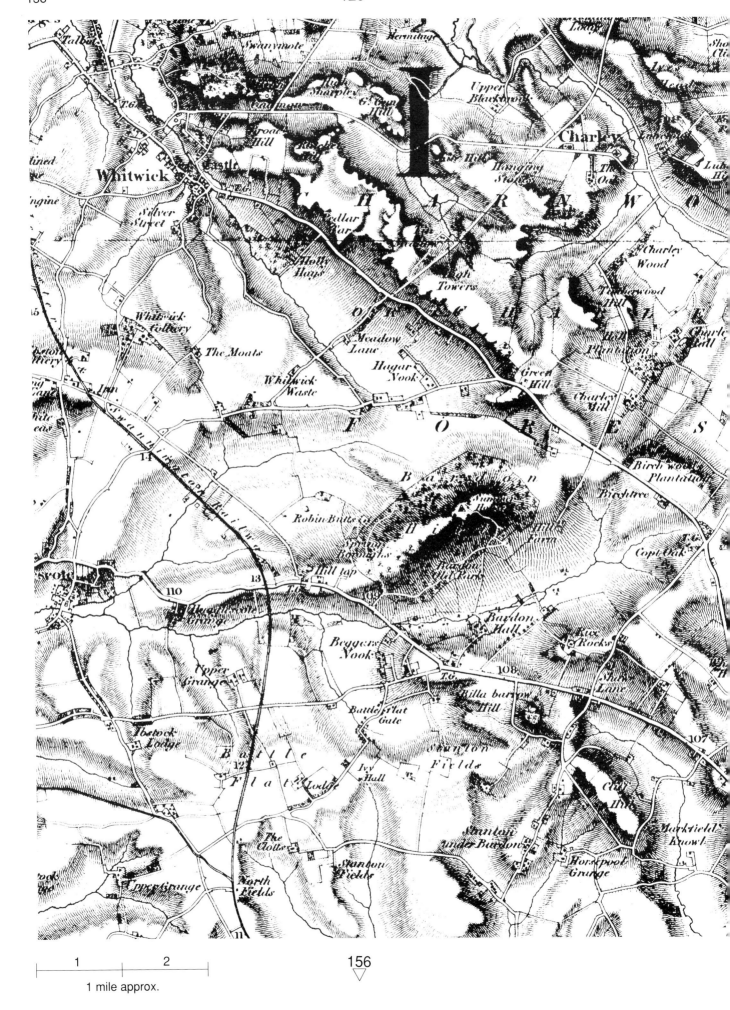

1   2

1 mile approx.

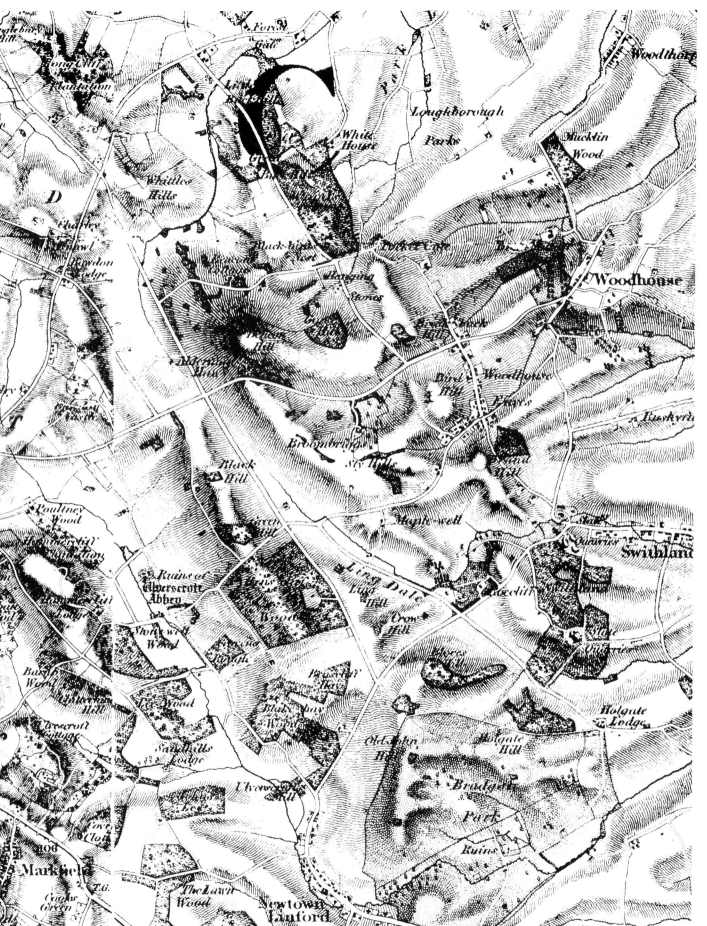

Published 1835.

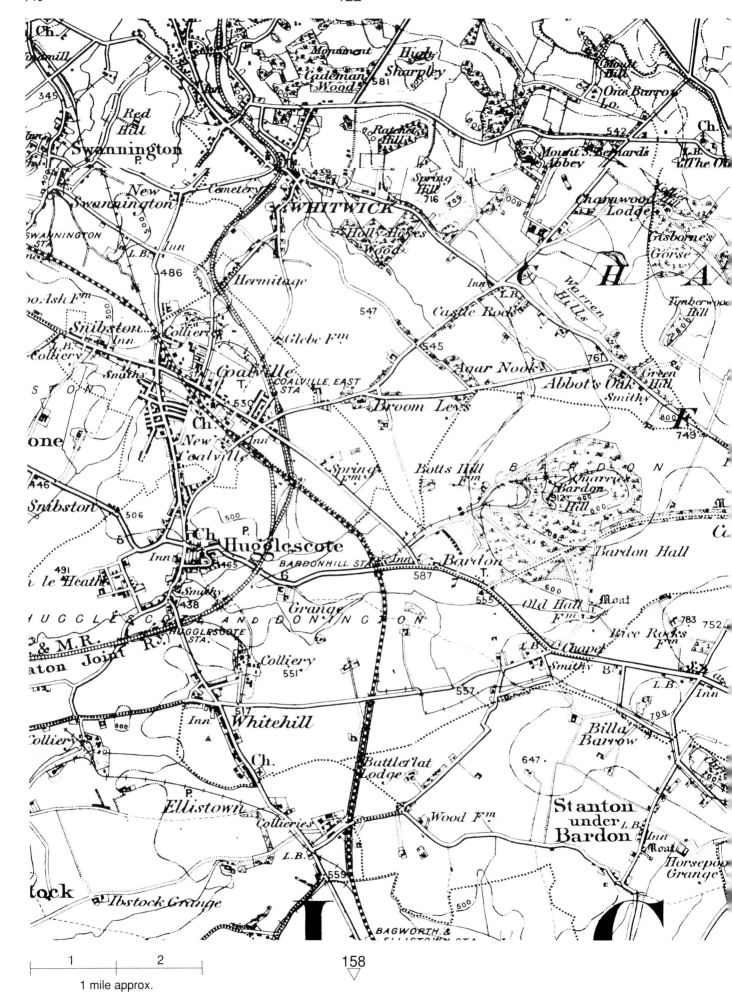

1   2

1 mile approx.

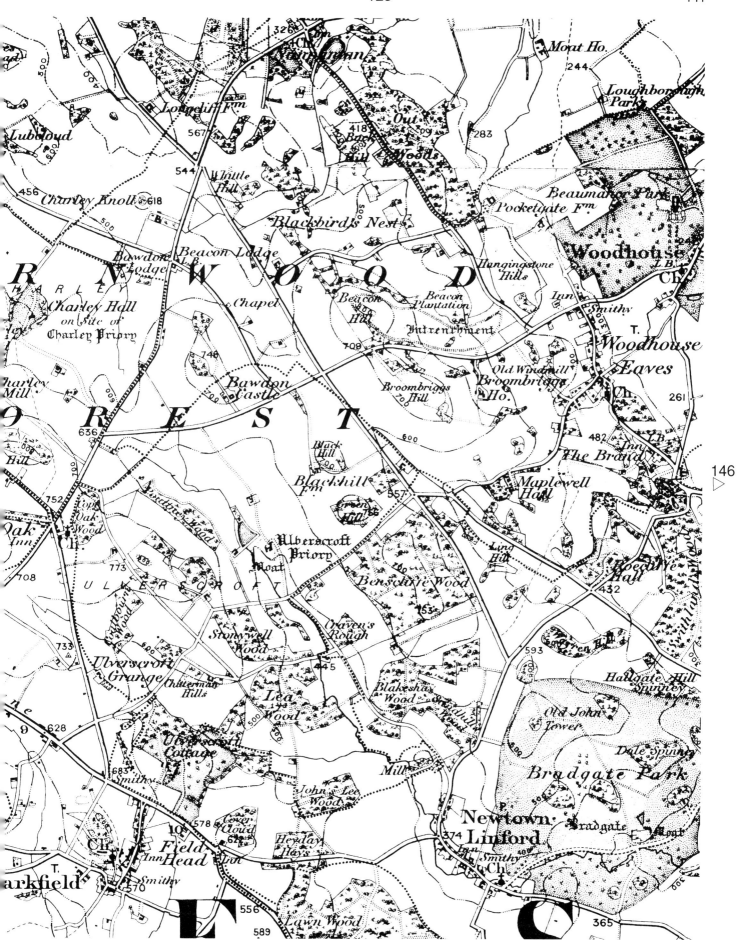

Surveyed 1881 - 86. Revised 1898. Published 1899.

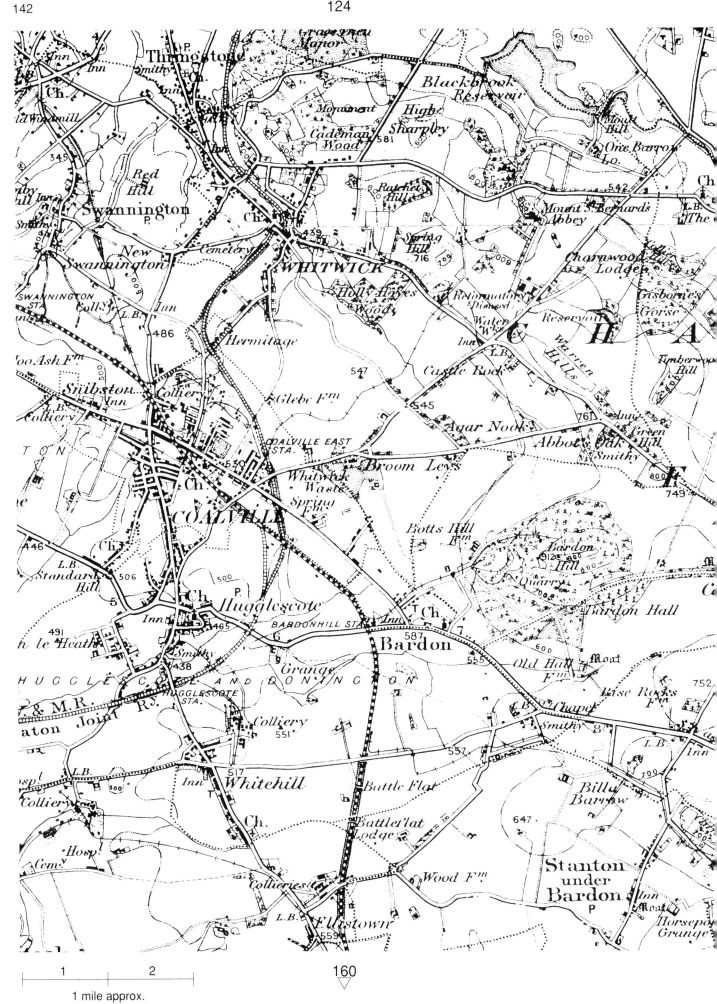

1 mile approx.

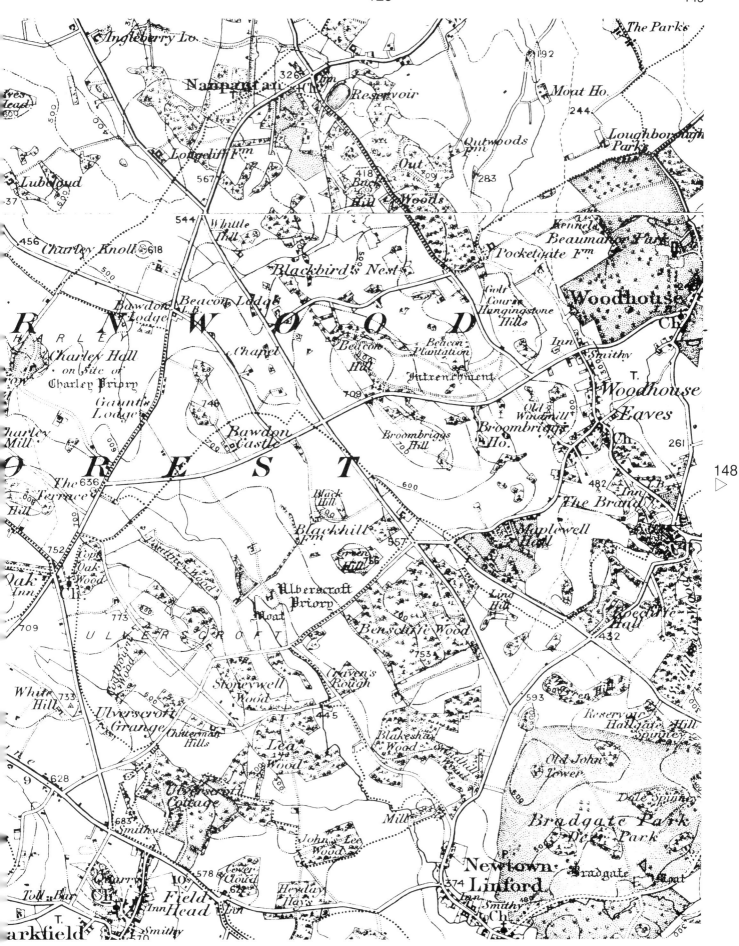

Surveyed 1879 - 86. Revised 1905 - 06. Published 1908.

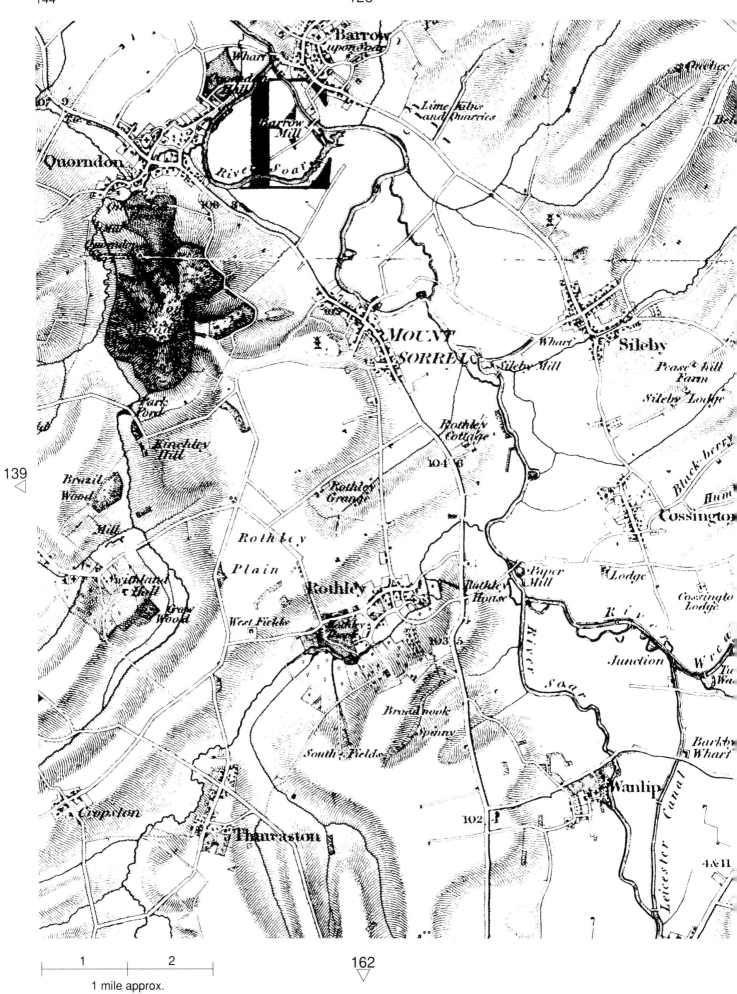

144

Barrow
upon Soar

Wharf

Barrow
Hill

Lime Kilns
and Quarries

Barrow
Mill

Quorndon

River Soar

Quorndon

MOUNT
SORREL

Wharf

Sileby

Sileby Mill

Pease hill
Farm

Sileby Lodge

Harts
Ford

Rothley
Cottage

Finchley
Hill

104 6

Black berry

Brazil
Wood

Rothley
Grange

Hum

Cossington

Mill

River

Rothley
Plain

Wreak

Southland
Hall

Rothley

Rothley
House

Paper
Mill

Lodge

Cossington
Lodge

Gorse
Wood

West Fields

103 5

River

Soar

Junction

Wreak

To
Wa

Broad nook
Spinny

Barkby
Wharf

South Fields

Wanlip

Cropston

102

Thurcaston

Leicester Canal

4 & 11

1	2

1 mile approx.

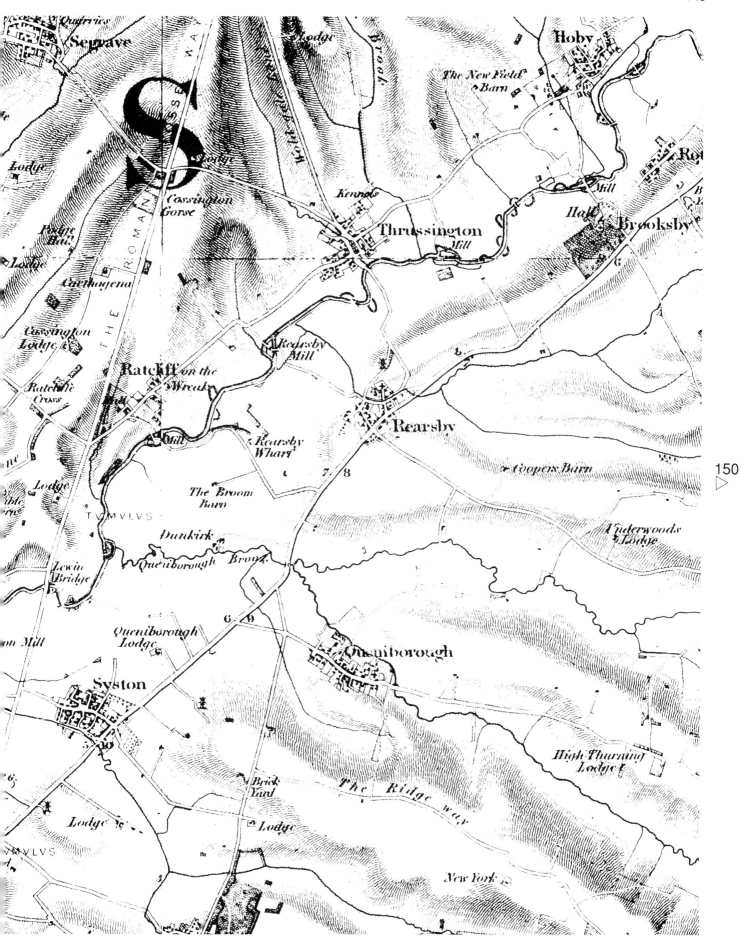

Woodthorpe

Moorfields F^m

The Hall

The Nook

152

Gypsum Mill

Inn

Lime Works

Westfield F^m

200

T.

Inn

Quorndon

Netherfield

Smithy

150

Quorndon Ha

Mill

226

Cemetery

Weir

North End

Buddon

Rawcliff
Hill

142

295

Quarry

South
End

Lock

Mill

Broad Hill

MOUNTSORREL

15

Smithy

185

Workhouse

Swithland

Rothley
Lodge

255

Reservoir

192

Rothley Lodge

Rushyfields

Kinchley
Hill

207

Rothley Plain

Cossington
P.

Rothley
Grange

230

154

141

249

190

Rothley Plain
Fm

50

Smithy Inn

220

Rothley

Mill
Lock

Swithland
P.

Ch. Hall

T.

Smithy

Lock

Crow
Wood

West Fields

The
Temple

Inn

Lodge

Sandfield Barn

236

Brook

Wanlip
Hill

280

Water Works

Mill

74

Reservoir

Inn

Wanlip

Cropston

255

Inn

Latimers Ho.

244

Thurcaston

200

Smithy
Rectory

Ch.

Smithy

257

200

226

190

Thurcaston Glebe
Lodge

281

192

1   2

1 mile approx.

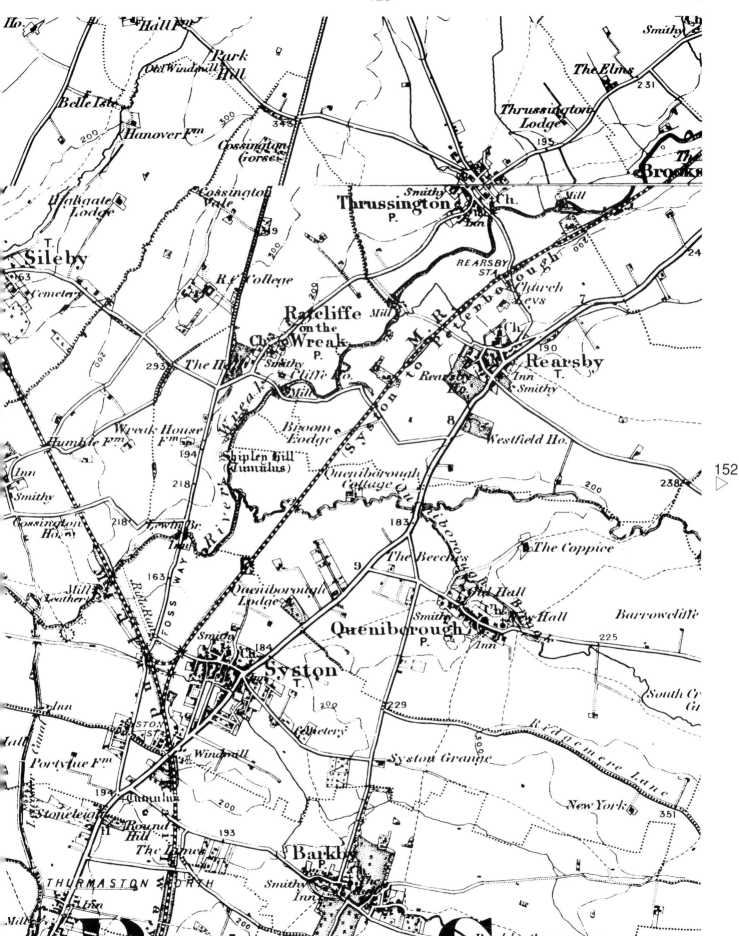

Surveyed 1883 - 86. Revised 1898. Published 1899.

Woodthorpe

Moorfields Fm

The Hall

The Nook

Westfield Fm

Gypsum Mill

Inn

Lime Works

T.

Quorndon

Smithy

Netherfield

QUORN & WOODHOUSE STA.

Inn

150

Quorndon Ho

Cemetery

North End

Weir

Inn

Lock

Buddon

Wood

Vicar's Fm

Quarry

South End

Water Works

MOUNTSORREL

Workhouse

Stockingfm

295

285

Ch

Lock

Mill

Smithy

Rushyfield

185

Swithland Reservoir

Rothley Lodge

Rothley School

192

Kinchley Hill

Rothley Plain

Cossington
P.

Rothley Plain Fm

Rothley Grange

Cemy

249

230

154

150

Smithy

Inn

Rothley

Swithland
P.

Ch

Hall

Smithy

Crow Wood

West Fields

Inn

The Temple

Sandfield Barn

L.B. STA.

Brook

Bybrook Lodge

236

Broadnook Spinney

Wanlip Hill

280

Water Works

Mill

Inn

L.B.

Reservoir

Inn

255

Cropston

Latimer's Ho

Ch

Thurcaston

Wanlip

Smithy

Rectory

244

257

226

190

200

Thurcaston Glebe Lodge

192

1   2

1 mile approx.

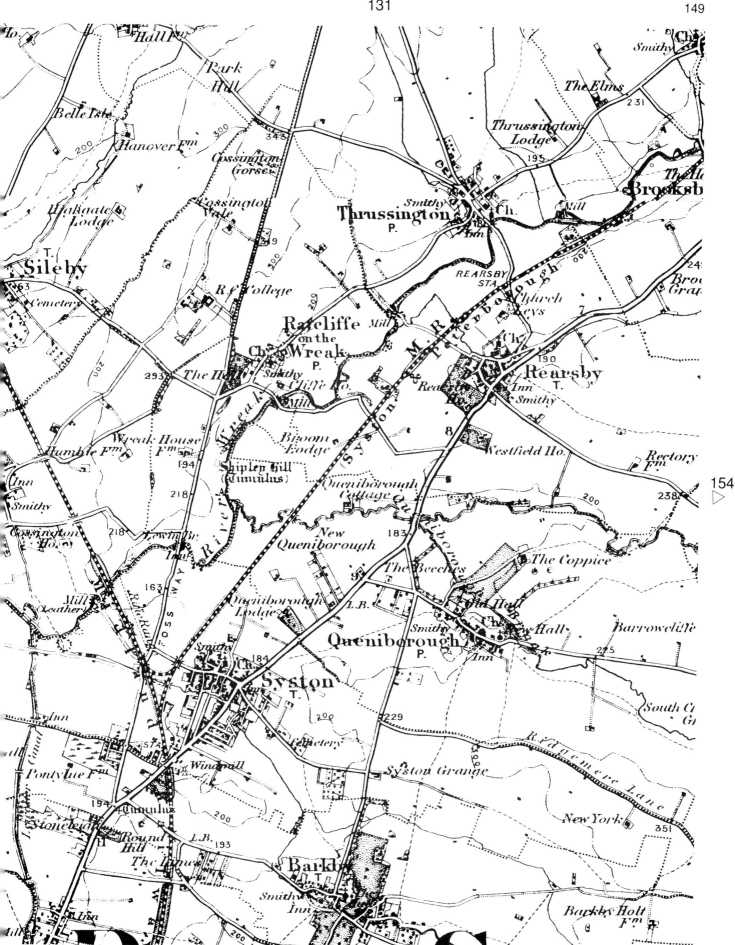

Surveyed 1883 - 86. Revised 1906. Published 1907.

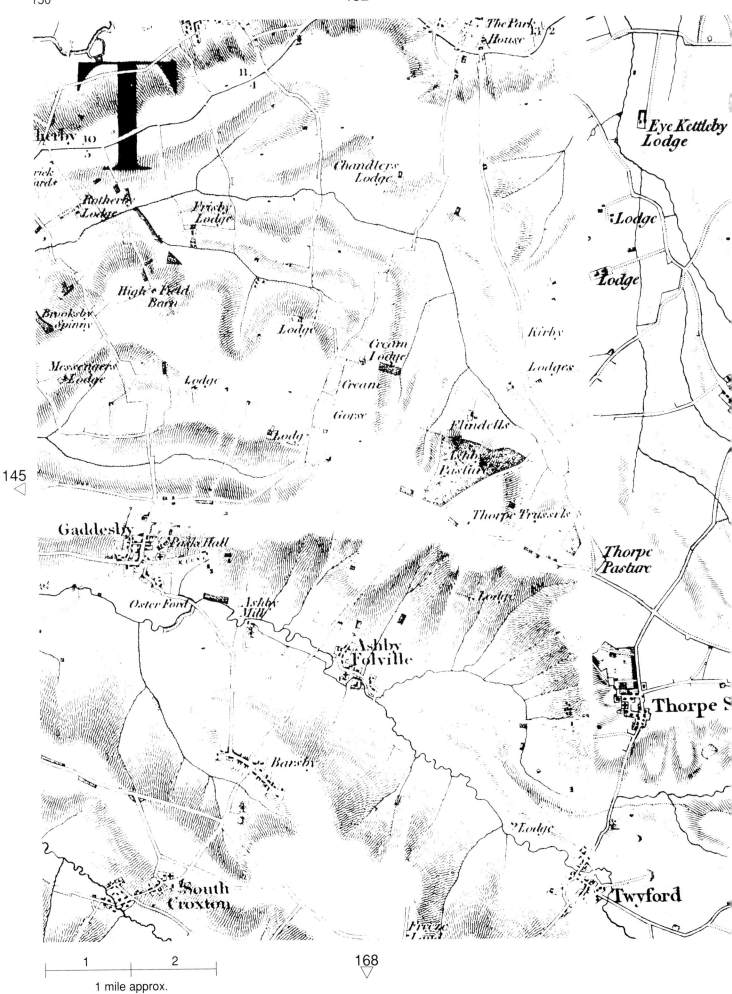

Eye Kettleby Lodge

The Park House

T̲herby 10

rick ards

Rotherby Lodge

Frisby Lodge

Chandlers Lodge

Lodge

Lodge

High Field Barn

Brooksby Spinny

Lodge

Kirby

Messengers Lodge

Lodge

Cream Lodge

Lodges

Creane

Lodge

Gorse

Lodg

Flindells

Ashby Pastur

Thorpe Trussels

Gaddesby

Park Hall

Thorpe Pasture

Oster Ford

Ashby Mill

Chorlep

Ashby Folville

Barsby

Lodge

Thorpe S

South Croxton

Twyford

1	2

1 mile approx.

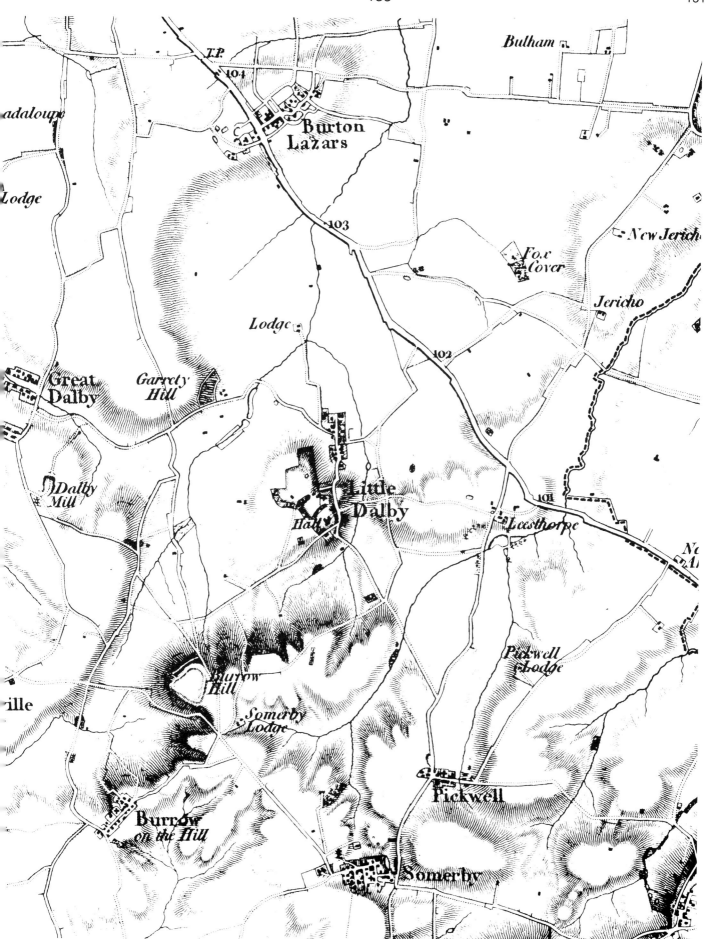

Published 1824.

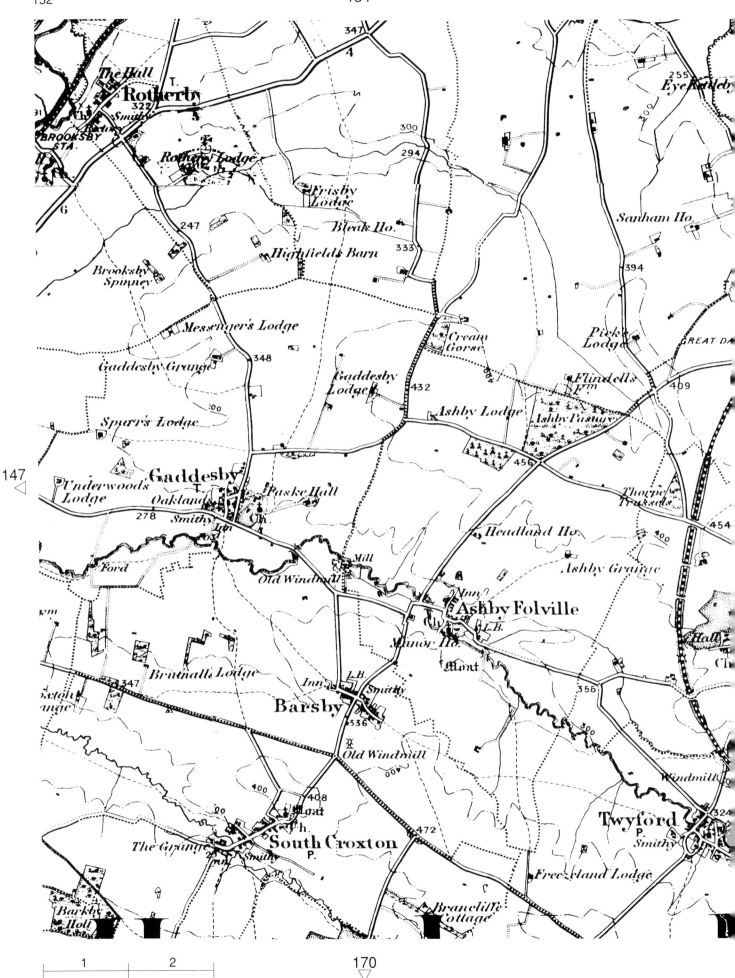

The Hall

Rotherby

Brooksby
Sta.

Rotherby Lodge

Frisby
Lodge

Bleak Ho.

Highfields Barn

Brooksby
Spinney

Messenger's Lodge

Gaddesby Grange

Gaddesby
Lodge

Spurr's Lodge

Underwood's
Lodge

Gaddesby

Oaklands

Paske Hall

Smithy Inn

Ch.

Ford

Old Windmill

Mill

Cream
Gorse

Ashby Lodge

Ashby Pasture

Flindell's
Frm

Pick
Lodge

Sanham Ho.

Eye Kettleby

GREAT DA

Thorpe
Trussels

Headland Ho.

Ashby Grange

Inn

Ashby Folville

L.B.

Manor Ho.

Mont

Hall

Ch.

Brutnalls Lodge

Inn

L.B.

Smithy

Barsby

Old Windmill

The Grange

Inn Smithy

South Croxton
P.

Ch.

Freezeland Lodge

Windmill

Twyford
P.

Smithy

Barkby
Holt

Brancliffe
Cottage

1   2

1 mile approx.

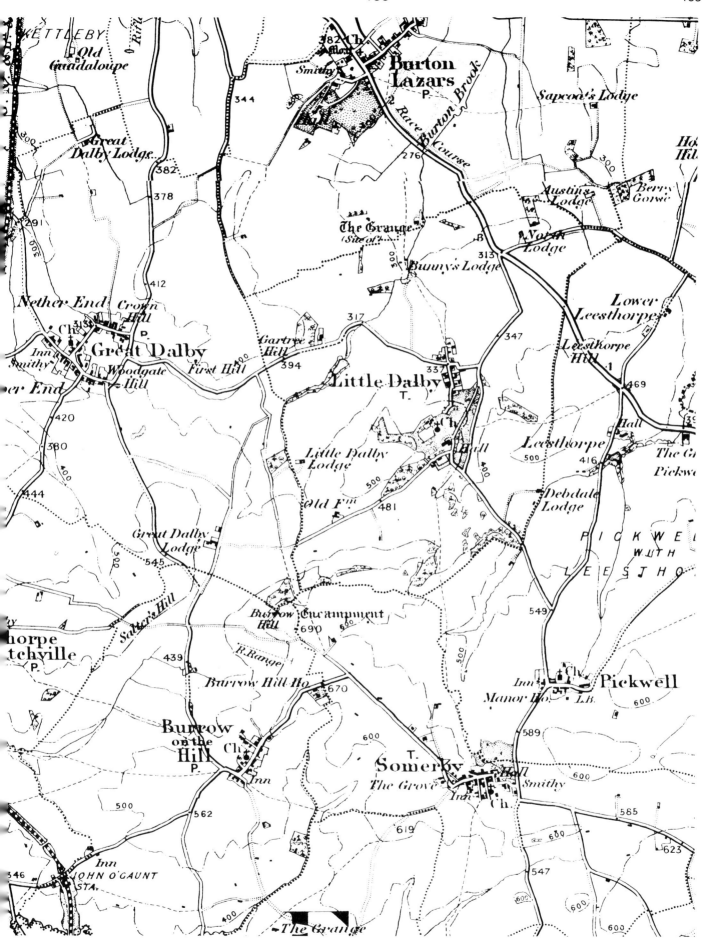

Surveyed 1883 - 86. Revised 1898. Published 1899.

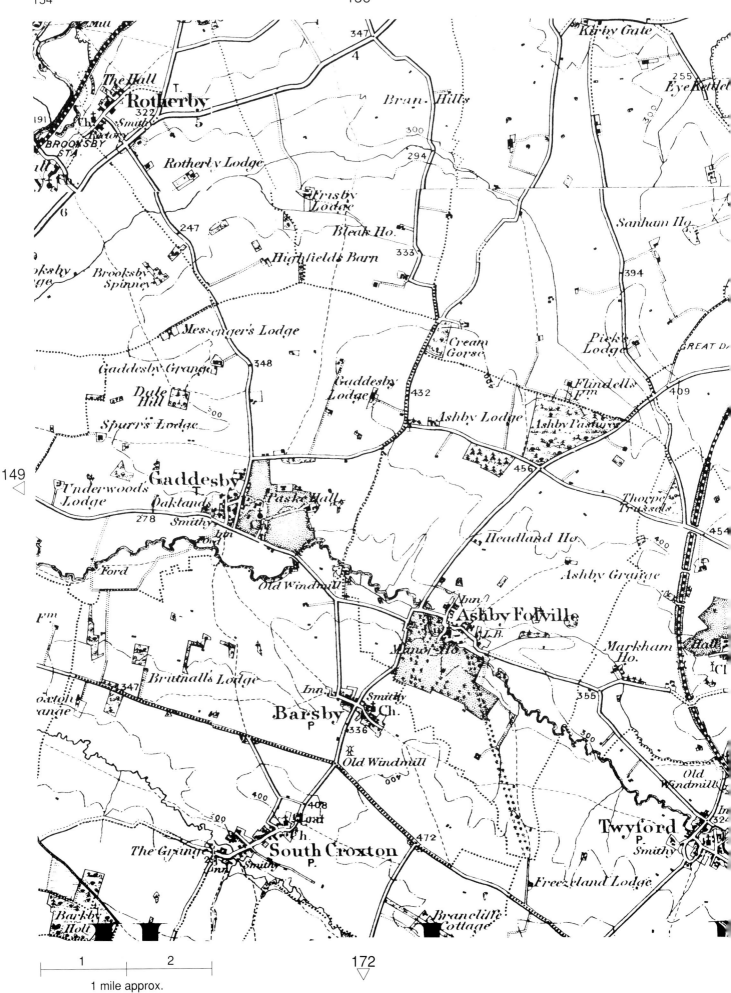

347
4

Kirby Gate

Eye Kettle

255

The Hall

Rotherby

322

Smithy

5

191

BROOKSBY
STA.

6

Rotherby Lodge

Bran Hills

300

294

Frisby Lodge

Sanham Ho

247

Bleak Ho

333

394

*Brooksby
Spinney*

*Brooksby
ge*

Highfields Barn

Messenger's Lodge

*Cream
Gorse*

*Picks
Lodge*

GREAT D

348

Gaddesby Grange

*Gaddesby
Lodge*

432

*Flindells
Fm*

409

*Dale
Hill*

300

Spurr's Lodge

Ashby Lodge

Ashby Pasture

456

Gaddesby

*Underwoods
Lodge*

Oaktands

Paske Hall

*Thorpe
Trussels*

278

Smithy

Headland Ho

400

454

Ford

Inn

Ford

Old Windmill

Ashby Grange

Inn

Ashby Folville

L.B.

*Markham
Ho.*

Hall

Ct

Brutnall's Lodge

Manor Ho

'm

347

*oxton
ange*

Inn

Smithy

Barsby

Ch.

355

P

336

Old Windmill

400

300

400

408

*Old
Windmill*

Inn

Ch.

472

Twyford

324

The Grange

South Croxton

P

Inn

Smithy

Smithy

P

Freezeland Lodge

*Barkby
Holt*

*Brancliffe
Cottage*

1   2

1 mile approx.

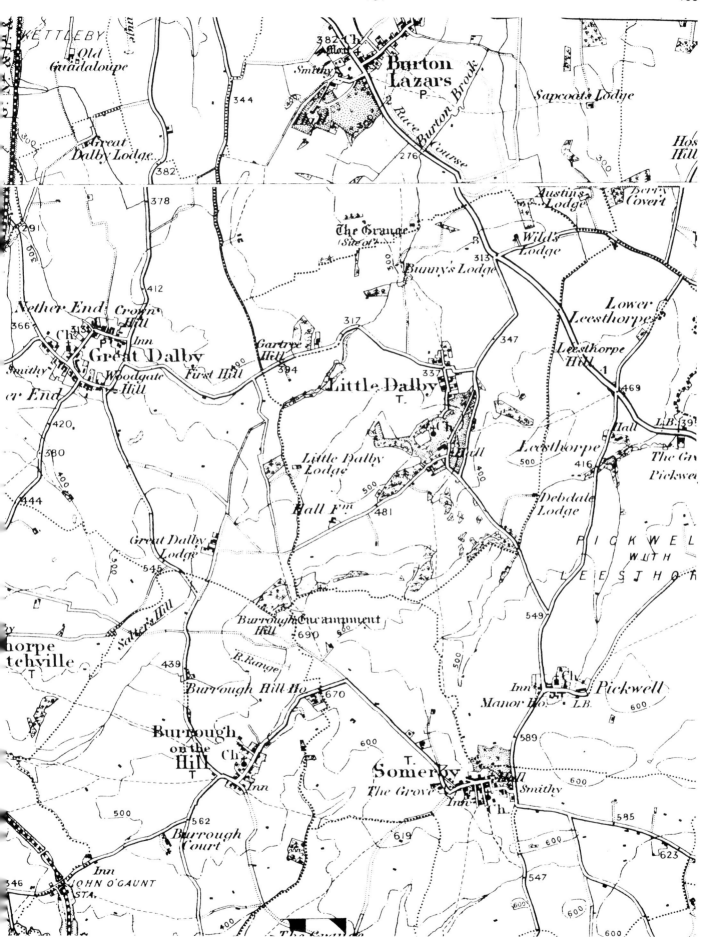

Surveyed 1883 - 86. Revised 1906. Published 1907.

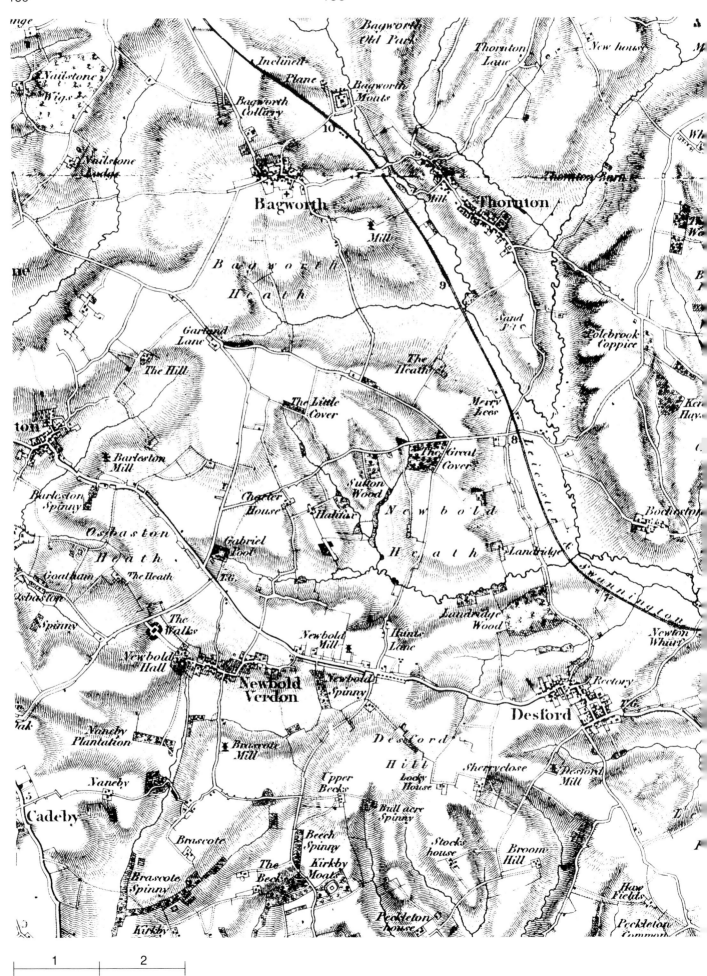

1 mile approx.

Published 1835.

△
140

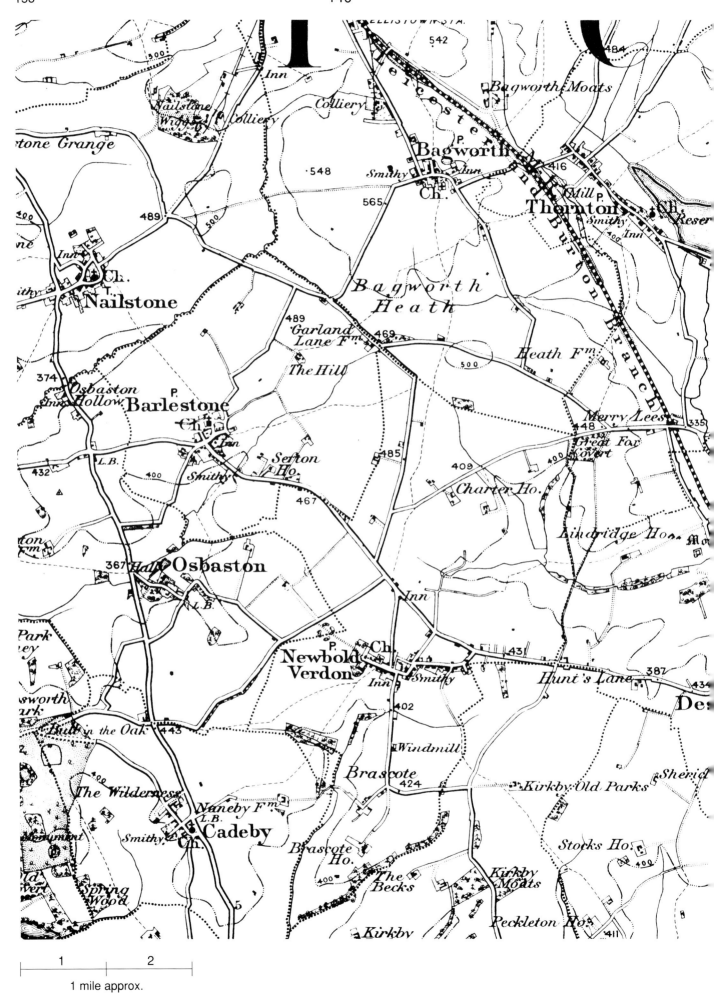

ELLISTOWN STA.

542

484

Bagworth Moats

Colliery

Colliery

Nailstone Wigston

tone Grange

500

·548

Smithy   Inn   Bagworth
Ch.

Mill   P

489   565   Thornton   Ch.   Reser

500   Smithy   Inn

Inn   100

ne   Bagworth   Heath

Ch.   489   469

Nailstone   Garland
Lane Fm.   Heath Fm.

The Hill   500

374   Osbaston   P
Inn   Hollow   Barlestone   Merry Lees
Ch.   148   335

Great For
Covert

432   L.B.   Inn   485   400

400   Smithy   467   409   Charter Ho.

ton   Lindridge Ho   Mo
Fm.

367   Hall   Osbaston

L.B.   Inn

Park   ey   Ch.   43

P   Newbold   Inn   Smithy   Hunt's Lane   387
Verdon   434

sworth   Des
ark   402

Bull in the Oak   443   Windmill

Brascote   Kirkby Old Parks   Sheric
424

The Wilderness   Naneby Fm.   Kirkby Old Parks
L.B.

Monument   Smithy   Cadeby   Stocks Ho.   400
Ch.   Brascote
Ho.   400

Spring   The   Kirkby
Wood   5   400   Becks   Moats   Peckleton Ho
411

Kirkby

1   2

1 mile approx.

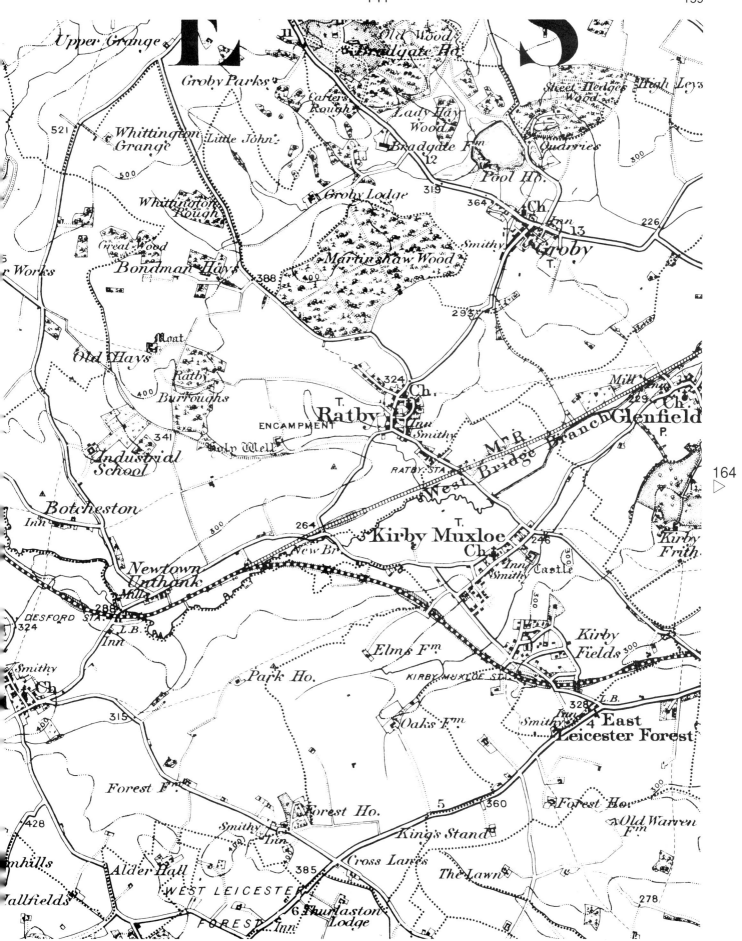

Surveyed 1881 - 86. Revised 1898. Published 1899.

Ibstock Grange

Hosp.

I

BAGWORTH & ELLISTOWN STA.

C

L.B.

Inn

542

500

484

Bagworth Moats

Nailstone Wigg

Colliery

Colliery

Colliery

stone Grange

Bagworth

548

P.

Mill

416

Smithy

Man

Thornton

Ch.

Smithy

Inn

Ch.

565

400

489

500

400

Inn

Bagworth

Ch.

Heath

Colly

Nailstone

489

469

Garland

Heath Fm

Smithy

Lane Fm

The Hill

500

374

485

Merry Lees

Osbaston

P.

448

335

Inn Hollow

Barlestone

Great Fox

Ch.

Covert

L.B.

409

Lindridge Ho

432

Osbaston

400

Mo

Gate

Smithy

Newholm

Charter Ho.

467

ton

Fm

Osbaston

367

Hall

Osbaston

Field

Park

Goatham

Inn

ney

L.B.

431

worth

Ch.

Hunt's Lane

387

P.

Newbold

434

Verdon

Inn

Smithy

Des

402

Old

443

Windmill

Ol

in the Oak

Windm

The Wilderness

Brascote

Sherid

424

Kirkby Old Parks

Naneby Fm

L.B.

Smithy

Cadeby

Brascote

Stocks Ho.

Ch.

Ho.

Kirkby

400

400

Moats

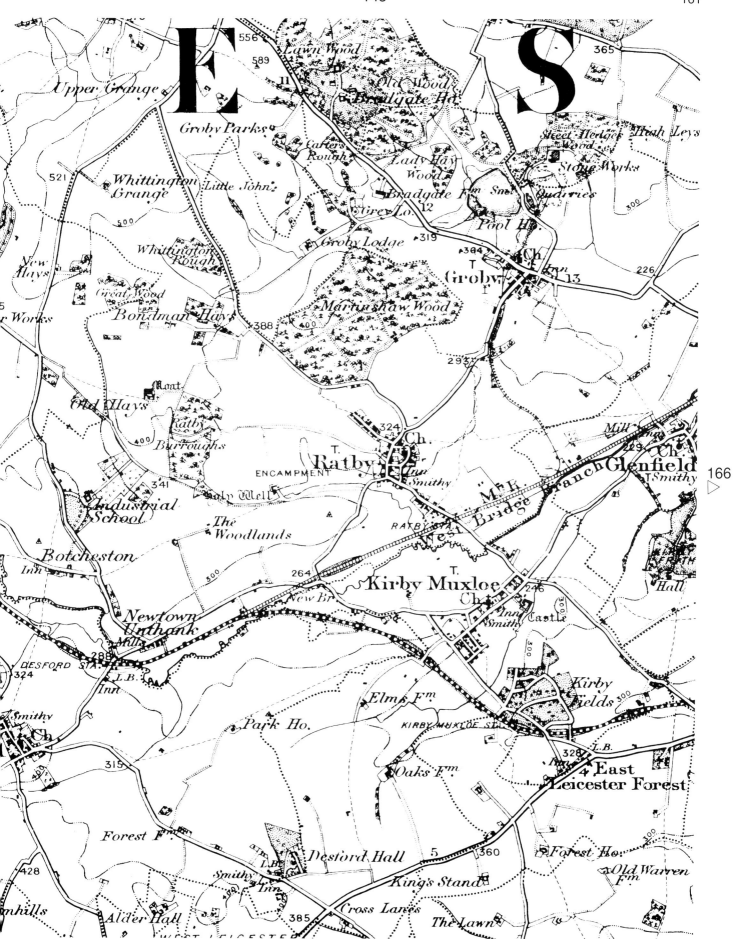

Surveyed 1881 - 86. Revised 1905 - 06. Published 1908.

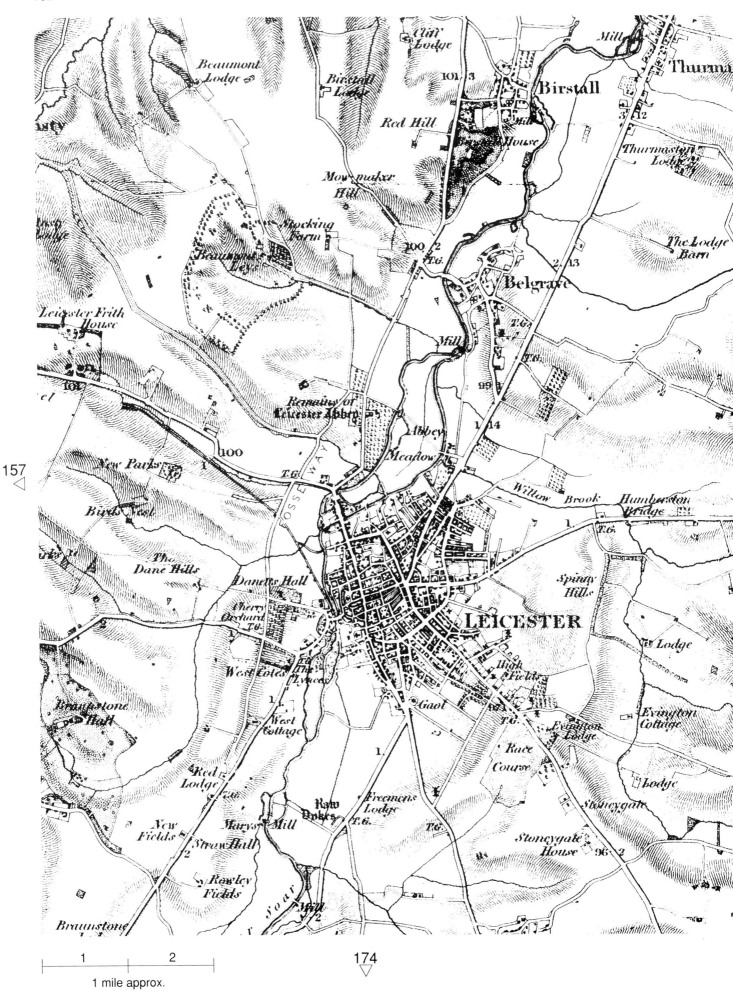

Cliff
Lodge

Mill

Thurma

Birstall
Lodge

Beaumont
Lodge

Birstall

101 3

Red Hill

Mill
House

Thurmaston
Lodge

3 12

Mow puller
Hill

200 2

The Lodge
Barn

T.G.

Stocking
Farm

Beaumont
Leys

2 13

Belgrave

T.G.

Mill

Leicester Frith
House

99

78

101

Remains of
Leicester Abbey

1 14

100

Abbey
Meadow

New Parks

1

T.G.

Willow Brook

Humberston
Bridge

Birds Nest

1

T.G.

The
Dane Hills

Spinny
Hills

Danetts Hall

LEICESTER

Cherry
Orchard
T.G.

West Cotes

Lodge

The
Lymes

High
Fields

Evington
Cottage

Braunstone
Hall

West
Cottage

Gaol

T.G.

Evington
Lodge

Red
Lodge

1.

Race
Course

Lodge

New
Fields

Marys Mill

Raw
Dykes

Freemens
Lodge

T.G.

Stoneygate

Straw Hall

2

T.G.

Stoneygate
House

96 2

Rowley
Fields

Soar

Mill

Braunstone

1   2

1 mile approx.

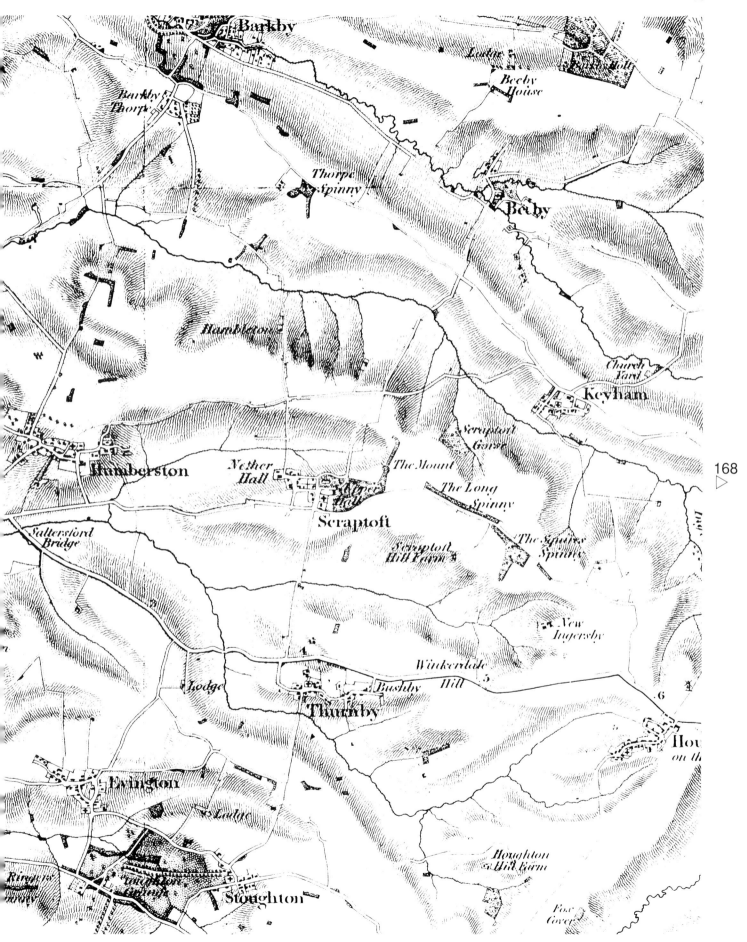

Barkby

Barkby Thorpe

Thorpe Spinny

Beeby House

Beeby

Humbleton

Church Yard

Keyham

Scraptoft Gorse

Humberston

Nether Hall

The Mount

The Long Spinny

Scraptoft Hall

Scraptoft

Saltersford Bridge

Scraptoft Hill Farm

The Squires Spinny

New Ingersby

Lodge

Winkendale Hill

Bushby

Thurnby

Hou

Evington

Lodge

Houghton Hill Farm

Stoughton

Fox Cover

Published 1835.

Cliff Lodge

The Lawn

Rectory

Burstall

P.

Inn

Braumont Lodge

Burstall Hill Park

Smithy

Smithy

Austey

Mill

Sewage Farm

Mowmacre Hill Fm

Mowmacre Hill

BEAUMONT LEYS

.311

Cemetery

257

Stocking Fm

173

Anstey Pastures

Beaumont Leys

300

200

246

Reservoir

Mill

The Gynsills

218

Leicester Frith

Bels

St John's Stone

GLENFIELD STA.

188

Glenfield Frith

Glenfield Tunnel

Gilroes

Leicester Abbey

Abbey Meadow

Moat Birds Nest

M. R.

.220

16

New Parks

NEW PARKS

New Found Pool

185

Braunstone Frith

300

Ashleigh Ho

200

2

Leicester & Bur

210

Highway Spinney

313

Braunstone Ho.

195

300

Victoria Park

Ch

Lunatic Asylum

L. R.

Smithy

Braunstone

St Mary's Mills

India Rubber Wks

Freemen's Common

Clarendon Park

New Fields

239

Rowley Fields

Hat Lodge

Ch

266

200

FOSS WAY

LUBBESTHORPE

Braunstone Lodge

189

Aylestone Park

Vicarage

1   2

1 mile approx.

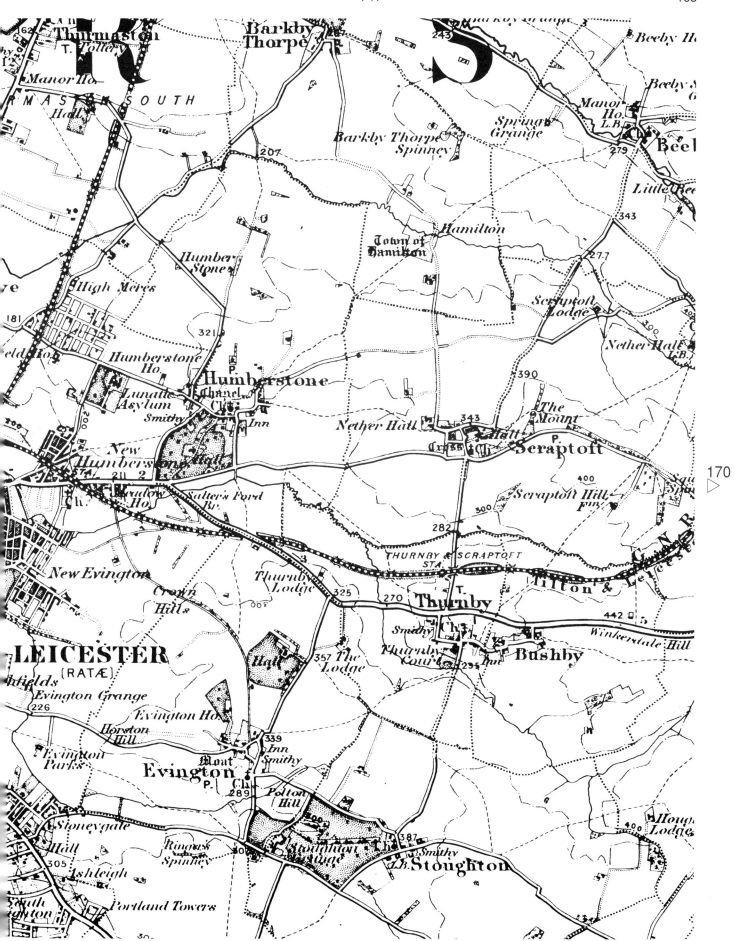

Surveyed 1883 - 86. Revised 1898. Published 1899.

1 mile approx.

Surveyed 1883 - 86. Revised 1906. Published 1907.

Bagsby Lodge

Street Hill

The Porters Lodge

Hinks Gorse

Car Bridge

The

South

Austin's Lodge

Loseby Lodge

Oaks

Loseby

Hungerton

Quenby Lodge

Manor House

Halstead Field

Foxhole Spinny

Quenby Hall

Cold Newton

Hanners Lodge

The Hill House

Old Ingersby

Botes Lodge

Lodges

Botany bay Cover

Cover

Hill

Fox Hill

Hulsedon Copton

Palace Hill

ighton Hill

T.G.

Billesdon Brook

8

9

10

Billesdon

S

Old Frisby

1   2

1 mile approx.

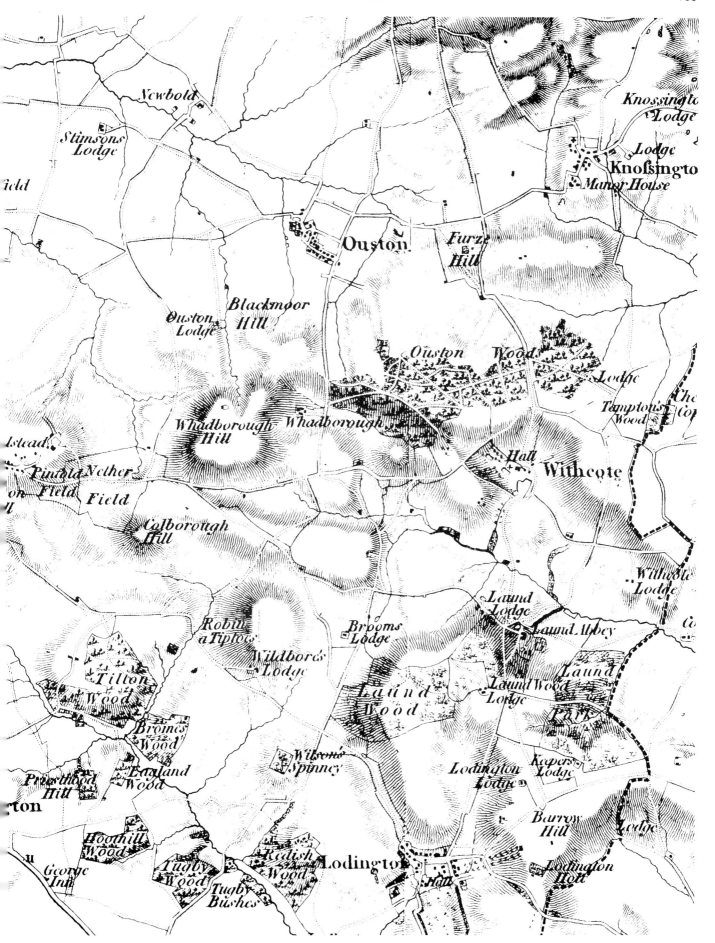

Newbold

Stinsons
Lodge

field

Knossington
Lodge

Lodge

Knossington

Manor House

Ouston

Furze
Hill

Blackmoor
Hill

Ouston
Lodge

Ouston Wood

Lodge

Tampton's
Wood

Che
Co

Whadborough
Hill

Whadborough

Hall

Withcote

lstead

Pinfold Nether
Field Field

Colborough
Hill

Withcote
Lodge

Laund
Lodge

Robin
a Tiptoe

Brooms
Lodge

Laund Abbey

Co

Wildbore's
Lodge

Laund

Tilton
Wood

Laund
Wood

Laund Wood
Lodge

Park

Broines
Wood

Wilson's
Spinney

Keepers
Lodge

Eagland
Wood

Priesthood
Hill

Lodington
Lodge

Barrow
Hill

Lodge

ton

Hoothill
Wood

Redish
Wood

Lodington
Hall

George
Inn

Tugby
Wood

Lodington

Tugby
Bushes

Hall

Published 1824.

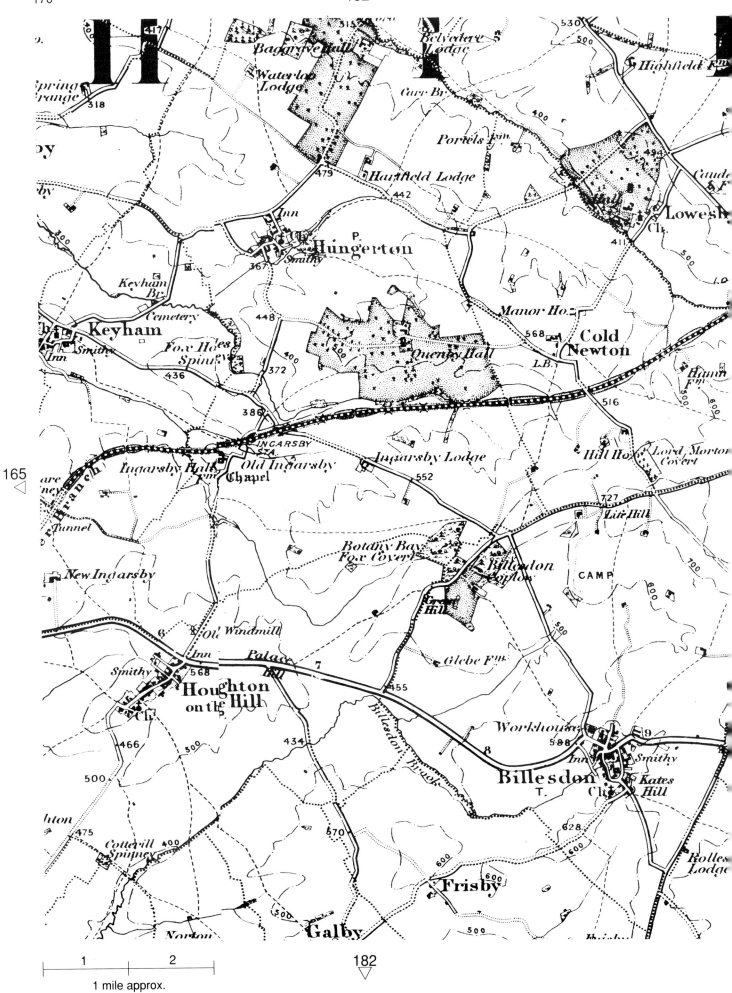

△

530

500

Highfield F

Belvedere
Lodge

Baggrave Hall

315

Waterloo
Lodge

Carr Br.

400

491

Lowesb

318

Spring
Grange

417

Portels F

Hartfield Lodge

479

442

411

Ck.

500

Inn

P.

Hungerton

367

Smithy

Manor Ho.

568

L.B.

Cold
Newton

Keyham
Br.

Cemetery

448

Hann
F

Keyham

Inn
Smithy

Fox Holes
Spinney

372

400

Quenby Hall

516

600

436

386

165
△

INGARSBY
STA.

Ingarsby Hall

Old Ingarsby

Inn

Chapel

Ingarsby Lodge

552

Hill Ho

Lord Morton
Covert

Branch

Tunnel

727

Lit Hill

New Ingarsby

Botany Bay
Fox Covert

Billesdon
Coplow

CAMP

700

Great
Hill

600

Old Windmill

6

Palace

7

Glebe F

500

Inn

Smithy

568

Bp

455

Houghton
on the Hill

Workhouse

588

9

Ch.

466

500

434

8

Inn

Smithy

628

Billesdon

T.

Ch.

Kates
Hill

500

475

570

600

500

Cotterill
Spinney

400

600

Frisby

Rolles
Lodge

500

Norton

Galby

500

△
▽

1   2

1 mile approx.

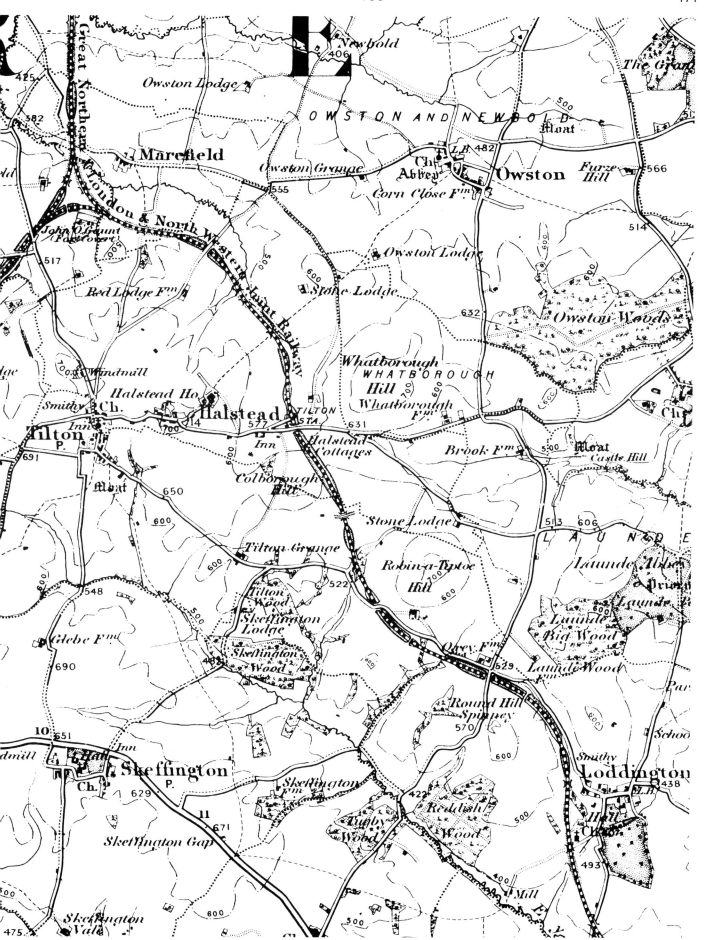

Surveyed 1883 - 86. Revised 1898. Published 1899.

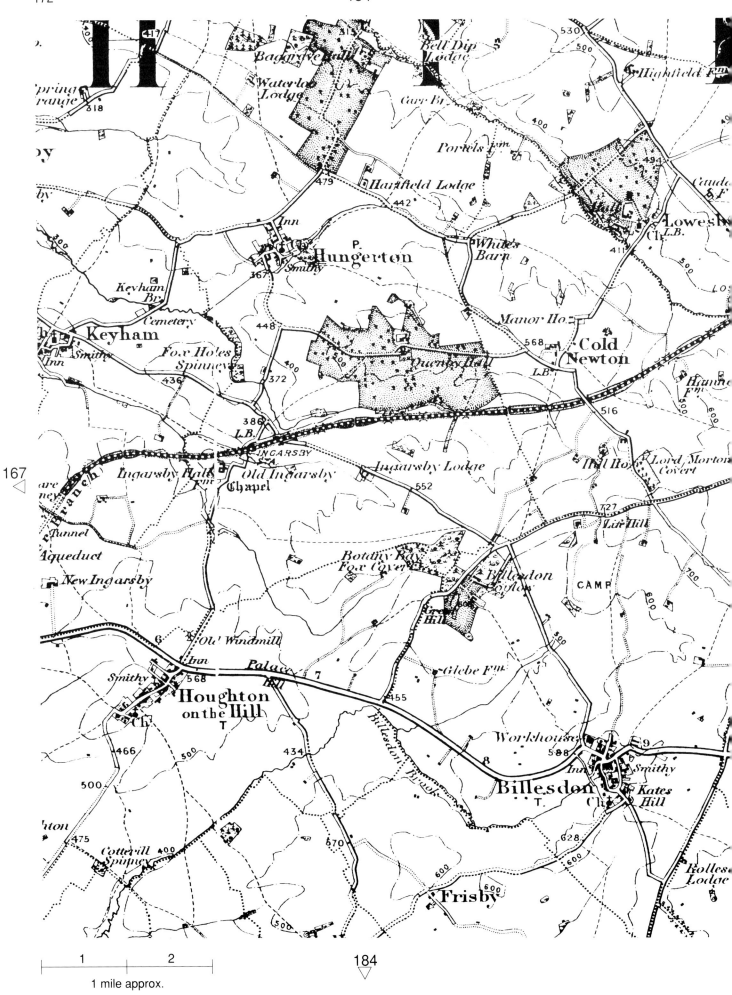

1 mile approx.

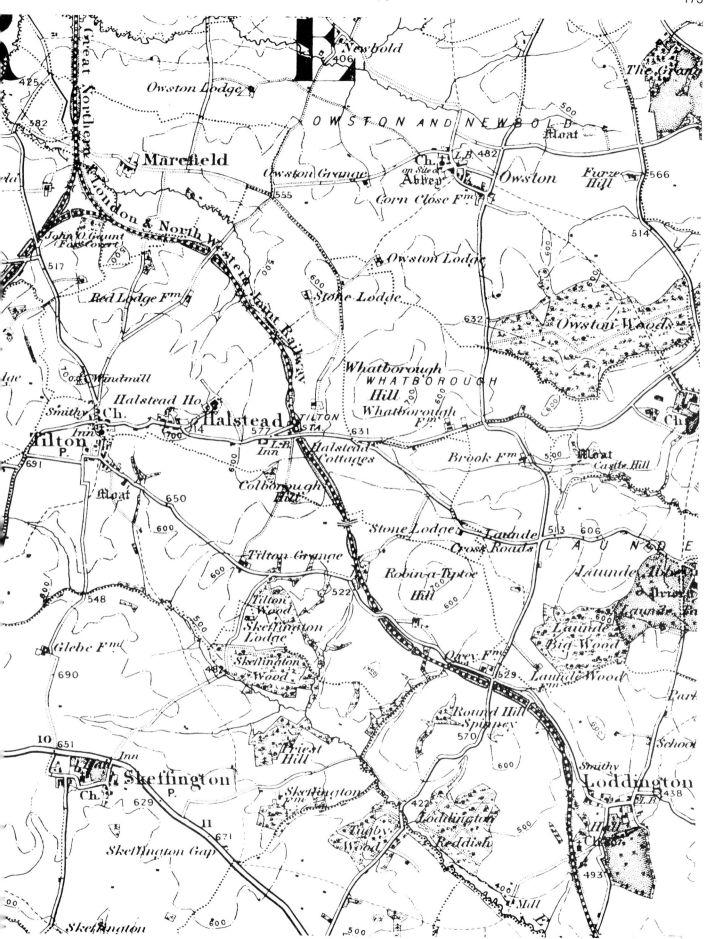

Surveyed 1883 - 86. Revised 1906. Published 1907.

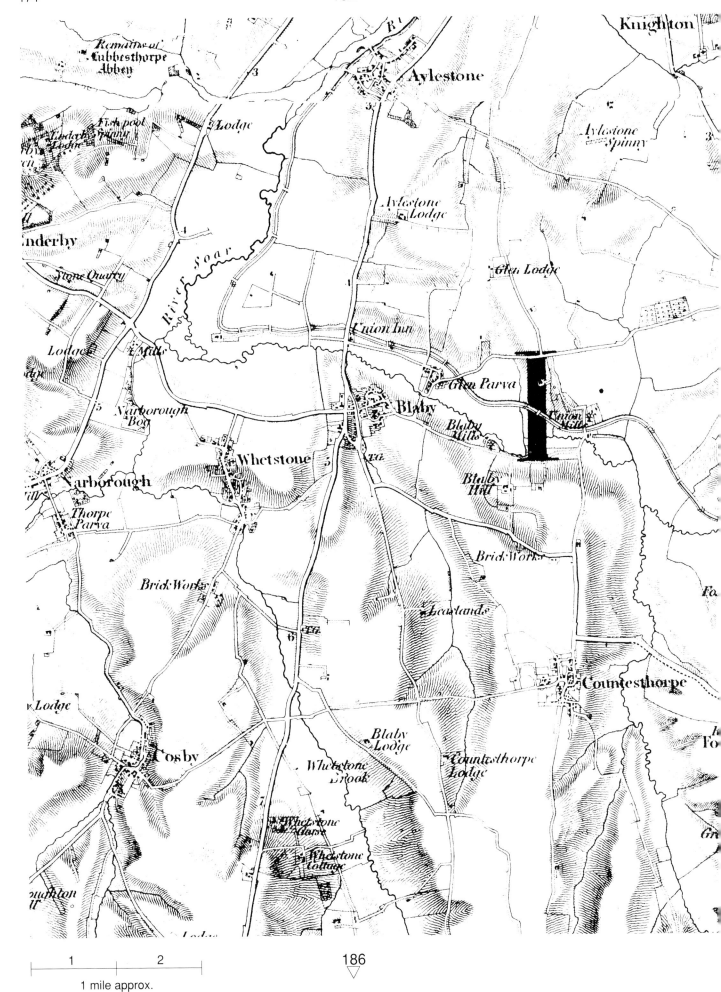

1   2

1 mile approx.

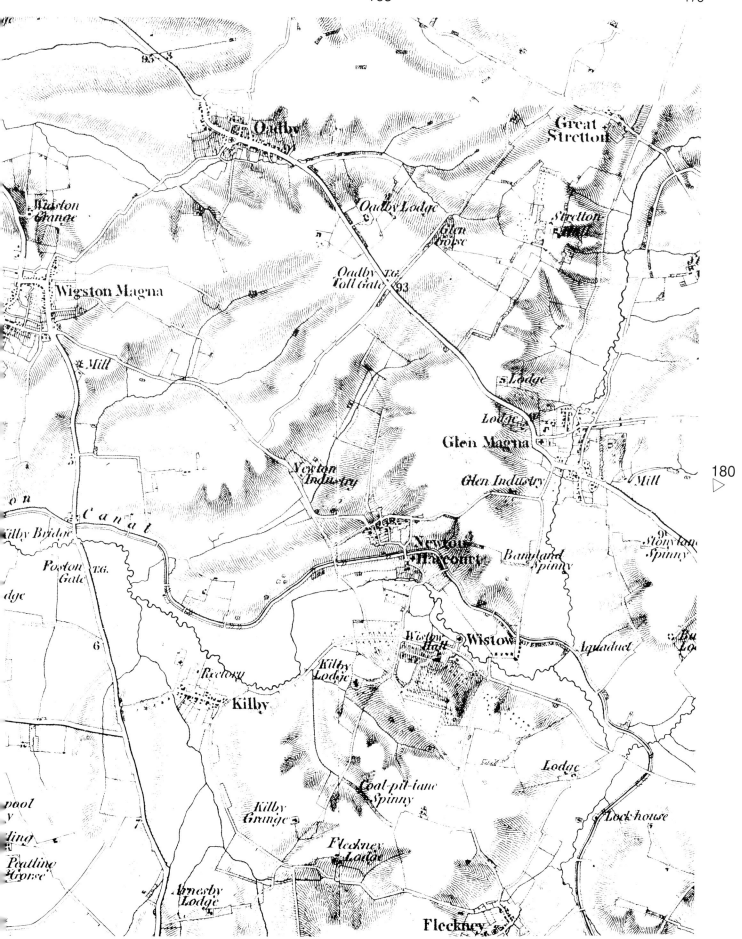

Published 1835.

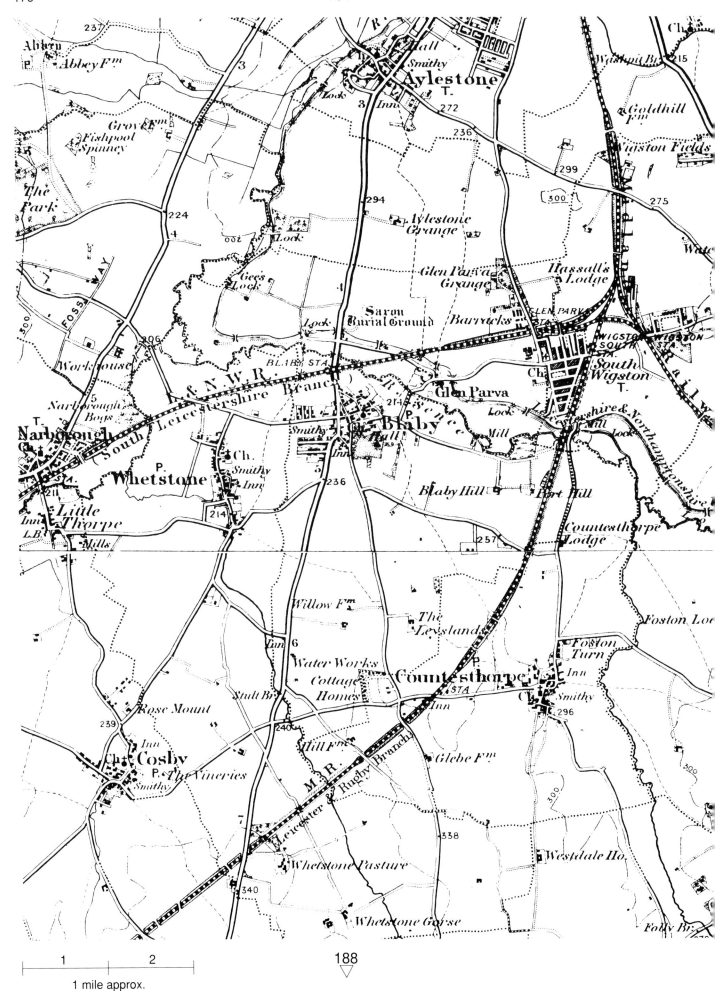

1   2

1 mile approx.

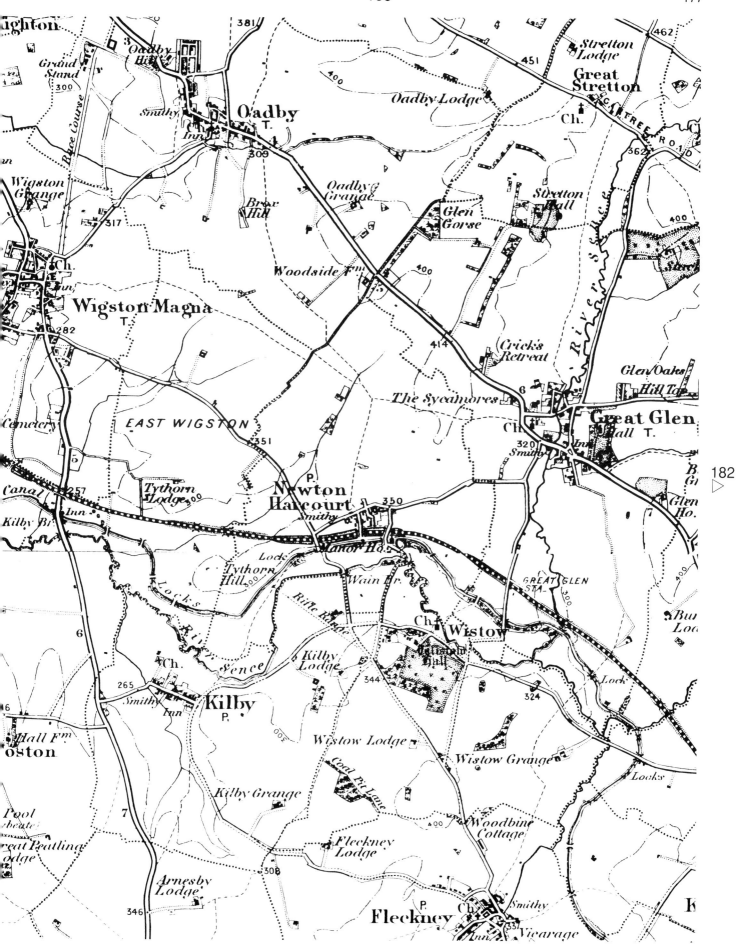

Surveyed 1883 - 86. Revised 1897. Published 1898.

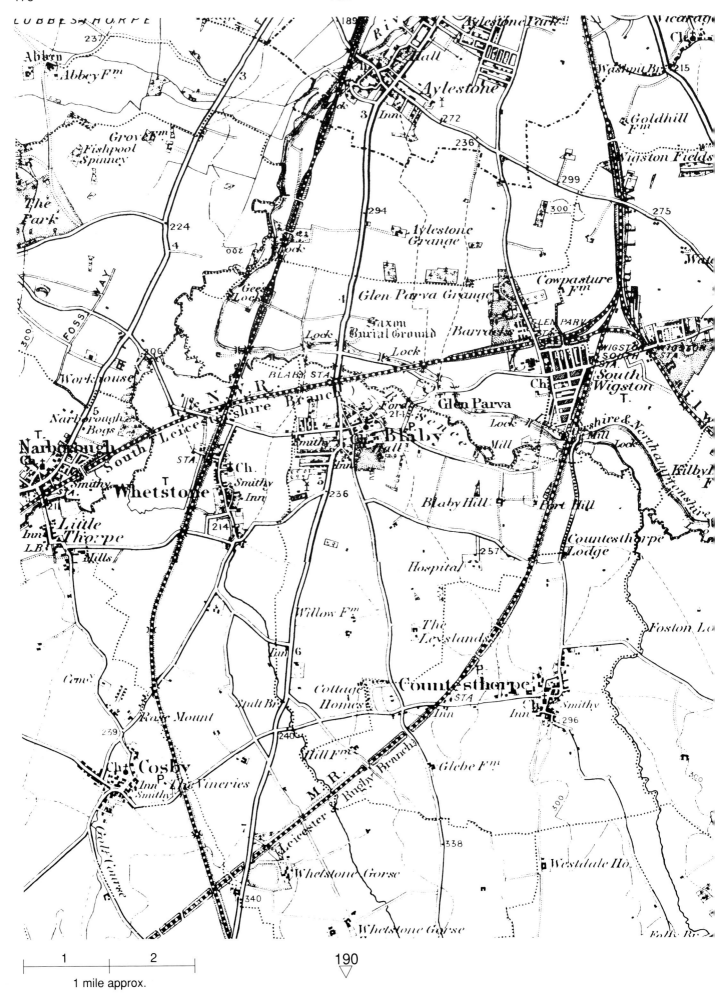

1 mile approx.

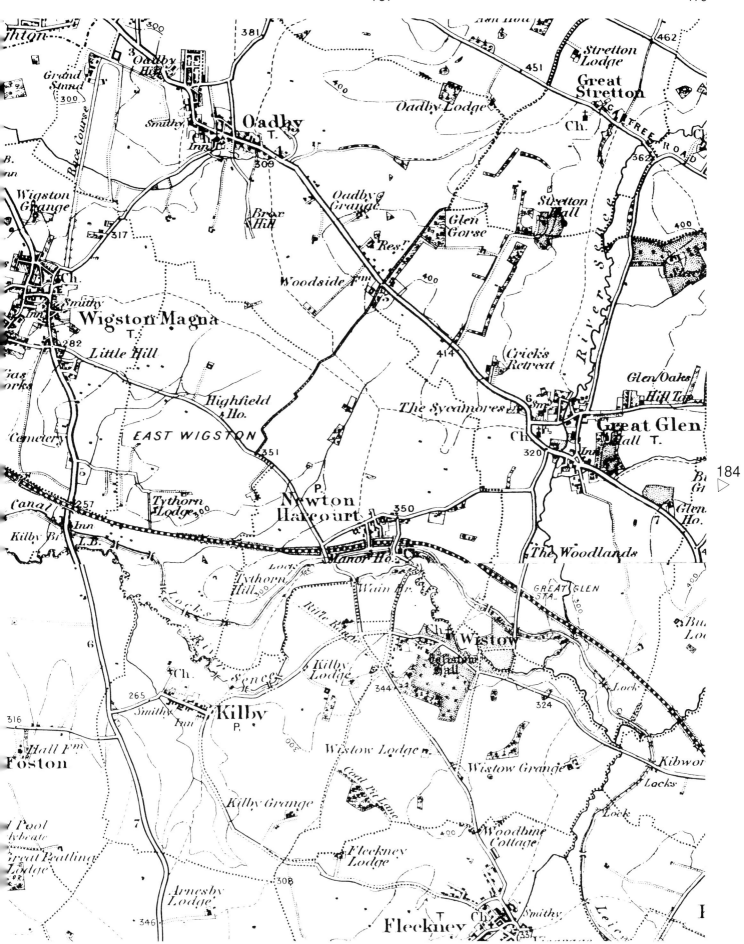

Surveyed 1883 - 86. Revised 1906. Published 1907.

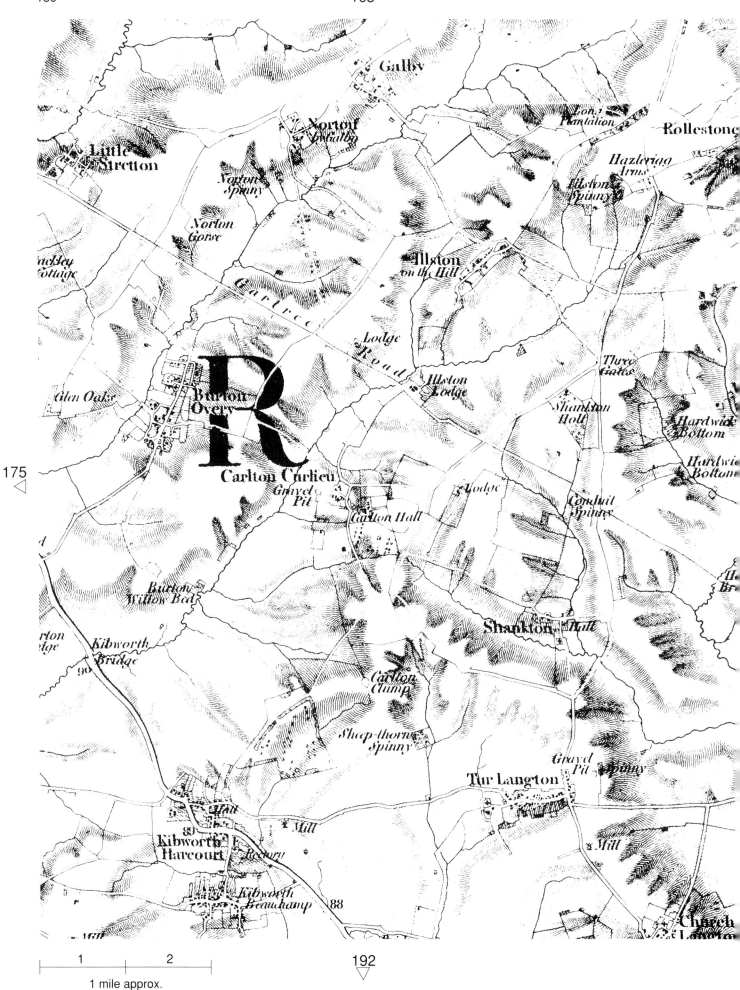

Galby

Norton
Gedalby

Long
Plantation

Rollestone

Little
Stretton

Hazlerigg
Arms

Norton
Spinny

Illston
Spinny

Norton
Gorse

Illston
on the Hill

Hinckley
Cottage

Gartree

Lodge

Road

Three
Gates

Glen Oake

Burton
Overy

Illston
Lodge

Shankton
Holt

Hardwick
Bottom

R

Carlton Curlieu

Gravel
Pit

Lodge

Hardwick
Bottom

Conduit
Spinny

Carlton Hall

Burton
Willow Bed

Shankton Hall

rlton
dge

Kibworth
Bridge

90

Carlton
Clump

Sheep-thorns
Spinny

Gravel
Pit Spinny

Tur Langton

Hall

Mill

Mill

Kibworth
Harcourt

80

Rectory

Kibworth
Beauchamp

88

Church
Langton

1   2

1 mile approx.

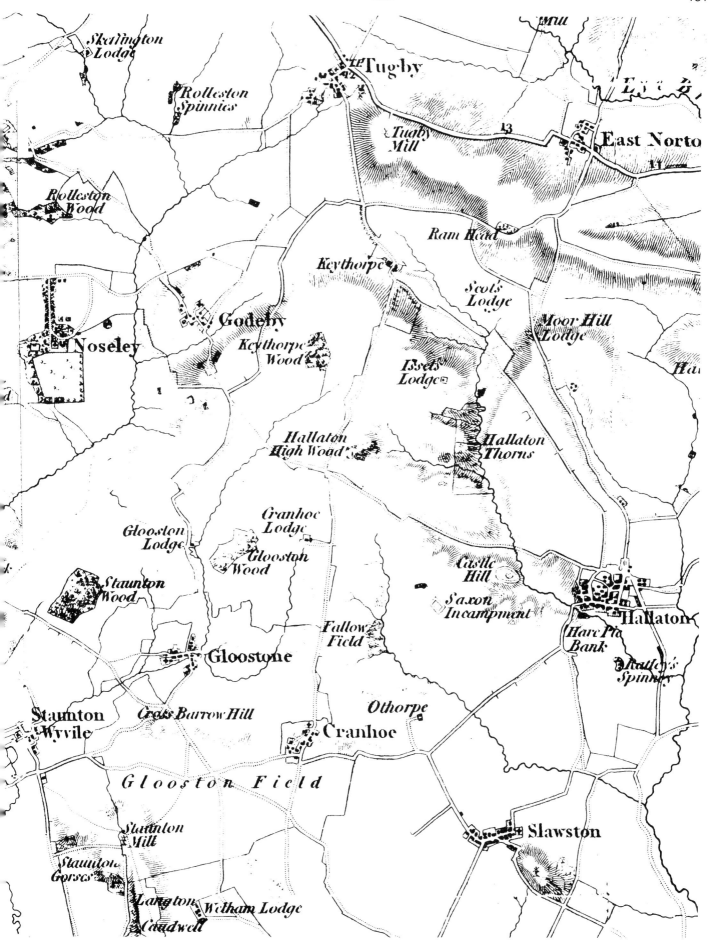

Skeffington Lodge

Rolleston Spinnies

Rolleston Wood

Tugby

Tugby Mill

East Norto

Ram Head

Keythorpe

Scot's Lodge

Moor Hill Lodge

Godeby

Noseley

Keythorpe Wood

Issels Lodge

Ha

Hallaton High Wood

Hallaton Thorns

Glooston Lodge

Cranhoe Lodge

Glooston Wood

Castle Hill

Hallaton

Staunton Wood

Saxon Incampment

Hare Pie Bank

Hatlo's Spinney

Glooston

Fallow Field

Staunton Wyvile

Cross Barrow Hill

Othorpe

Cranhoe

Glooston Field

Slawston

Staunton Mill

Staunton Gorses

Langton

Welham Lodge

Caudwell

Published 1824.

Gorse
Ch.
Lodge

Manor Ho.
574
152
635

Smithy
Ashlands
Long Plant.
Rolleston
575

Little
Stretton
King's
Norton Ch.
Manor Ho.
L.B.
600

Smithy
Galby
Lodge
Illston
on the
Hill Ch.
576
Millfield
Clump

471
Inn
L.B.
Smithy
Manor Ho.
500
600

313
Bleak
Ho.
491
589

Hall
N O S

425
Three Gates
555
Cotton
Ho.

Scotland
Illston Grange
Shangton
Holt

P.
527
400

Ch.
Burton Overy
394
Shangton
Grange

Inn
Smithy
Ch.
Carlton
Curlieu
Carlton
Grange
478
Conduit
Spinney

177
Burton
Grange
L.B.
Hall
400

358
468

421

Shangton
Ch.

ton
lge
500
The Hall

333
348

483
Tur Langton Lodge

Kibworth Hall
400

Sheepkorns
Spinney
King Charles's

Kibworth
Harcourt
Tur Langton
P.
Croxfield
Spinney

447
327
Manor Ho.
Inn
420

TUMULUS
Inn
350
Windmill
Smithy Ch.
288

9
Ch.

KIBWORTH
Smithy
10

Kibworth Beauchamp
WEST LANGTON
Ch.
410
Chu
Lang

292
M

1   2
194

1 mile approx.

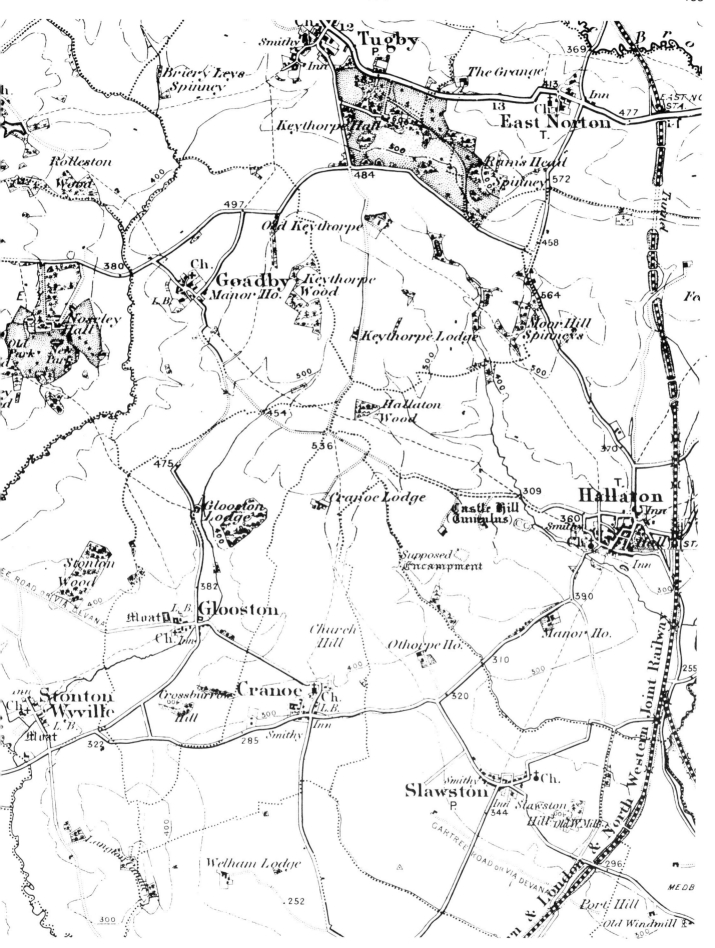

Surveyed 1883 - 86. Revised 1897. Published 1898.

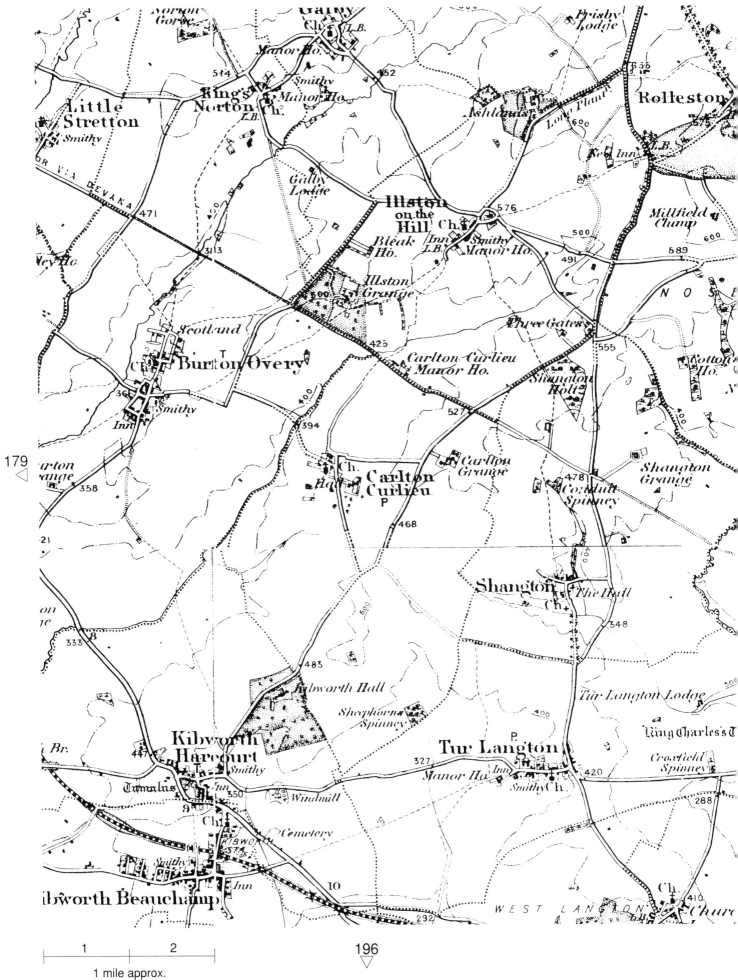

Norton
Gorse

Frisby
Lodge

Galby
Ch.

L.B.

Rolleston

Manor Ho.

514

452

Ashlands

Long Plant.

600

Little
Stretton

King's
Norton Ch.

Smithy

Manor Ho.

635

L.B.

New Inn

L.B.

Smithy

Millfield
Clump

VIA

DEVANA

471

Galby
Lodge

Illston
on the
Hill

576

500

600

589

313

Bleak
Ho.

Ch.

Inn
L.B.

Smithy

Manor Ho.

491

N O S

ey Ho.

500

Illston
Grange

N

Scotland

425

Three Gates

555

Cotton
Ho.

Burton Overy

T

Carlton Curlieu
Manor Ho.

Shangton
Holt

367

Smithy

527

400

478

Shangton
Grange

Inn

394

Hall

Ch.

Carlton
Curlieu

Carlton
Grange

Conduit
Spinney

arton
Grange

358

P

468

400

321

Shangton
Ch.

The Hall

on
ie

333

8

500

348

483

Tur Langton Lodge

400

Kibworth Hall

Sheephorne
Spinney

King Charles's T

Br.

Kibworth
Harcourt

Tur Langton

Croxfield
Spinney

447

Smithy

327

Manor Ho.

Inn

420

Tumulus

Inn

350

Windmill

Smithy Ch.

288

9

Ch.

Cemetery

KIBWORTH

Smithy

Inn

10

ibworth Beauchamp

W E S T   L A N G T O N

Ch.

410

292

Church

1

2

1 mile approx.

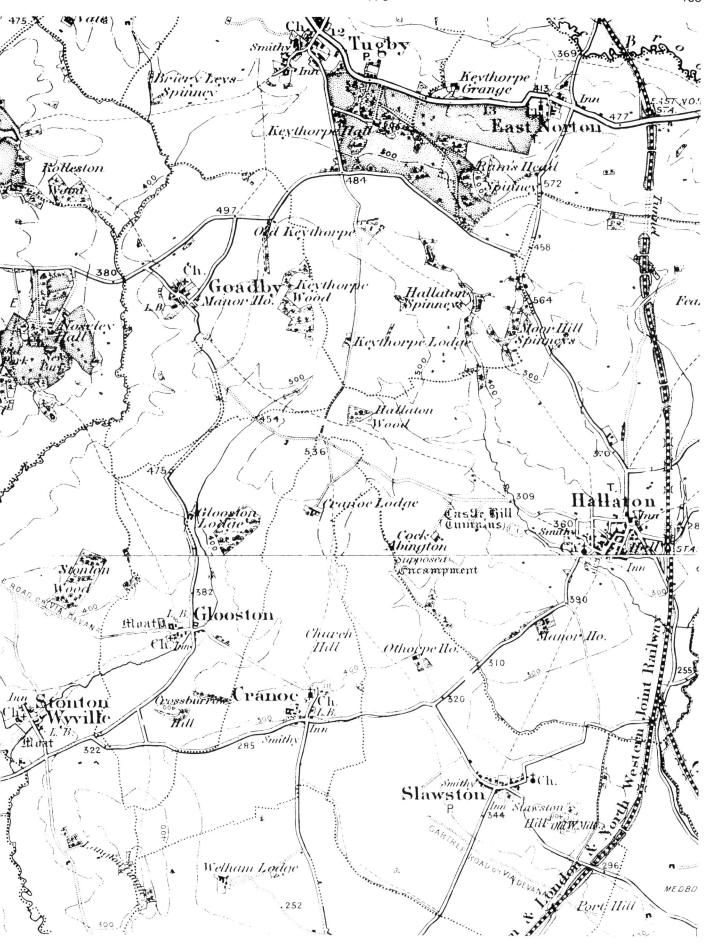

Surveyed 1883 - 86. Revised 1906. Published 1907.

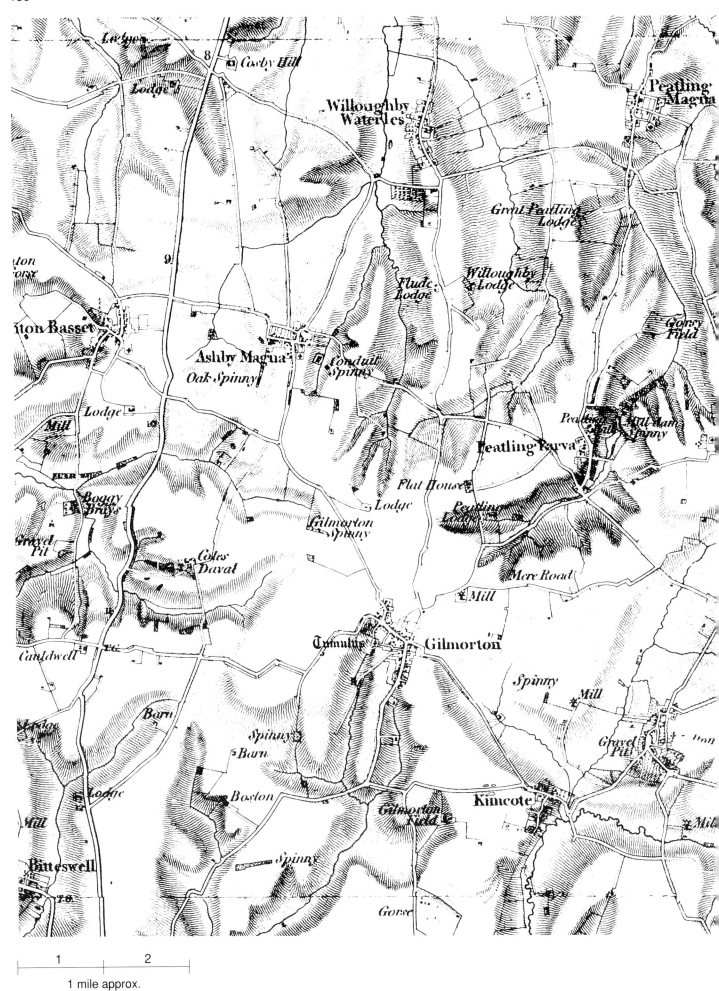

1 mile approx.

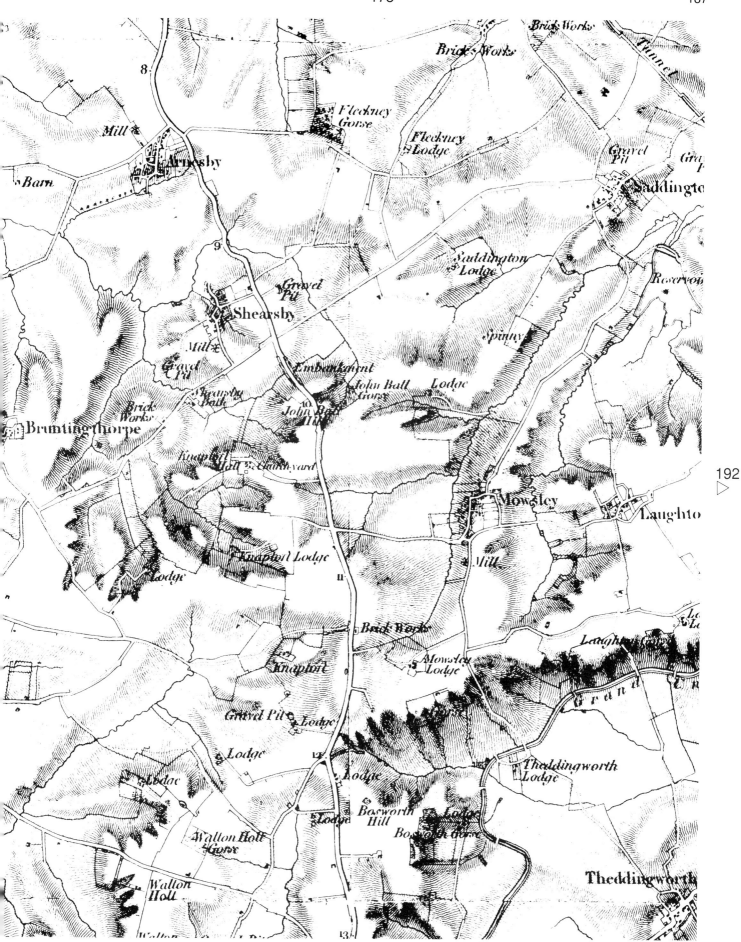

8

Mill

Barn

Arnesby

Fleckney
Gorse

Fleckney
Lodge

Brick Works

Brick Works

Gravel
Pit

Gra
P

Saddington

9

Gravel
Pit

Shearsby

Saddington
Lodge

Reservoir

Mill

Spinny

Brunting thorpe

Brick
Works

Gravel
Pit

Shearsby
Bath

Embankment

John Ball
Gorse

John Ball
Hill

Lodge

Knaptoft
Hall & Church yard

Mowsley

Laughto

Lodge

Knaptoft Lodge

Mill

Brick Works

Knaptoft

Mowsley
Lodge

Laught

Gravel Pit
Lodge

Lodge

Lodge

Lodge

Thaddingworth
Lodge

Lodge

Bosworth
Hill

Lodge

Walton Holt
Gorse

Lodge

Bosworth Gorse

Theddingworth

Walton
Holt

13

Published 1835.

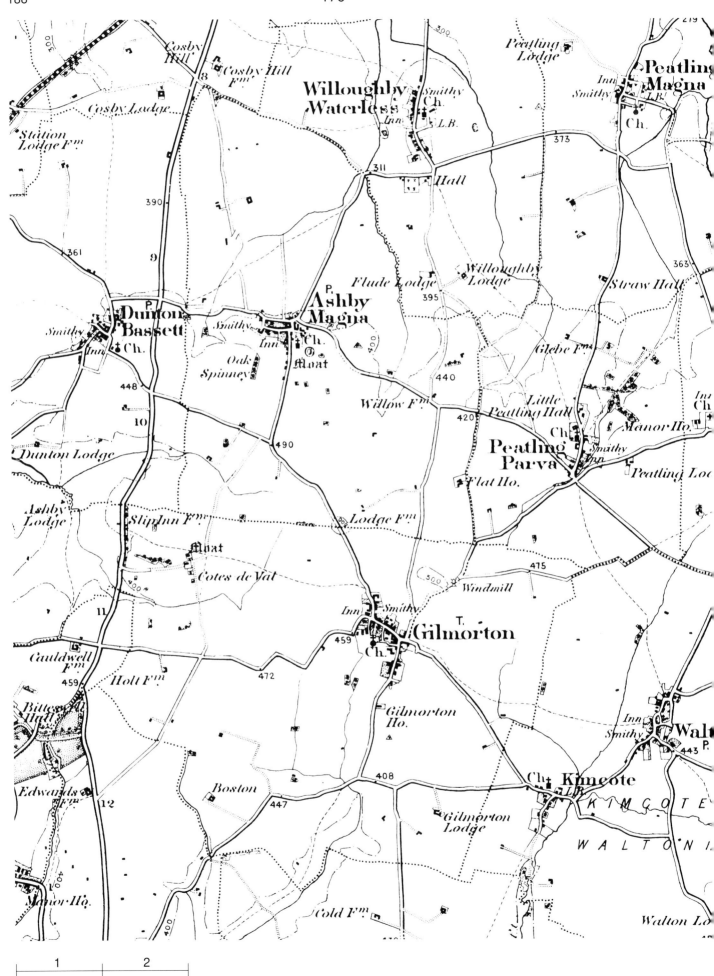

1 mile approx.

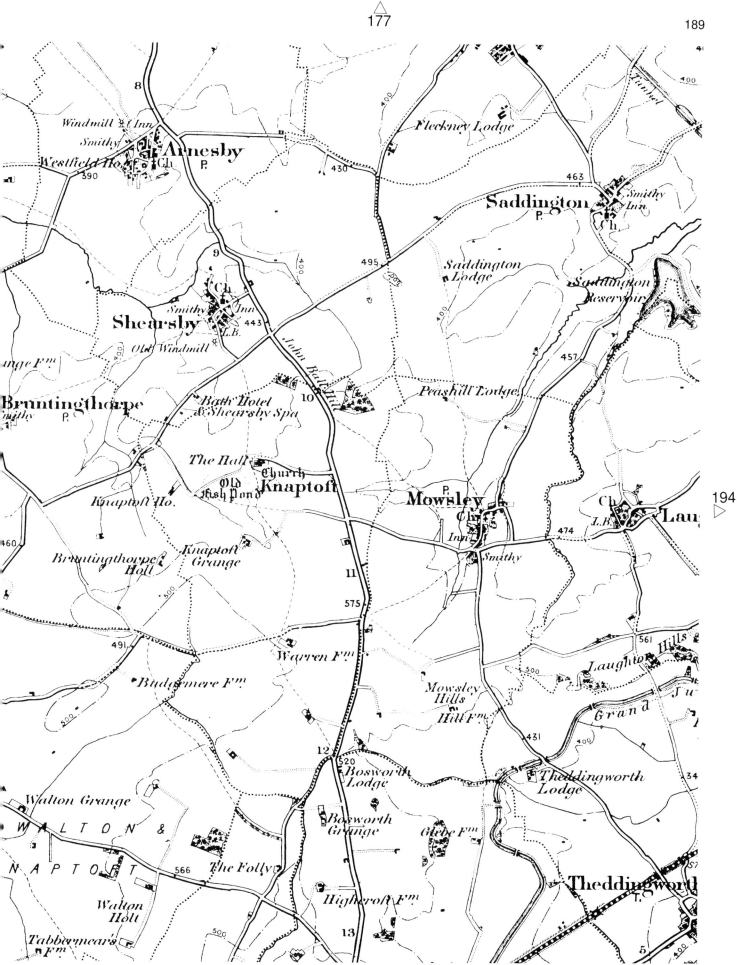

Windmill & Inn

Smithy

Westfield Ho.

St. Arnesby

Ch.

P.

390

Fleckney Lodge

430

463

Saddington

P.

Smithy Inn

Ch.

495

Saddington Lodge

Saddington Reservoir

457

Ch.

Smithy Inn

Shearsby

L.B.

443

Old Windmill

John Ball Hill

Bath Hotel & Shearsby Spa

Peashill Lodge

ange Fm

Bruntingthorpe

mithy

P.

The Hall

Old Fish Pond

Church Knaptoft

Mowsley

P.

Ch.

Inn

Ch.

L.B.

Lau

474

Knaptoft Ho.

Smithy

460

Bruntingthorpe Holt

Knaptoft Grange

561

Laughton Hills

491

Warren Fm

Mowsley Hills

Hill Fm

Grand

Ju

Budgemere Fm

500

431

400

Theddingworth Lodge

-34

Walton Grange

520

Bosworth Lodge

Bosworth Grange

Glebe Fm

Theddingworth

W A L T O N &

N A P T O F T

566

The Folly

Highcroft Fm

T.

Walton Holt

Tabbermears Fm

500

5

400

Surveyed 1883 - 86. Revised 1897. Published 1898.

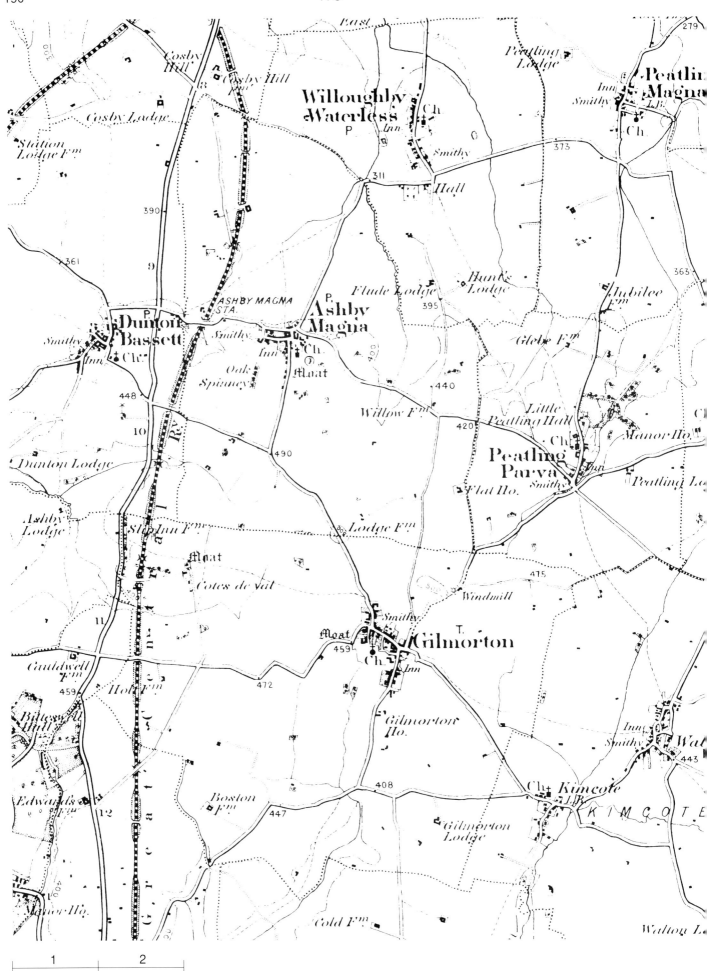

178

Cosby
Hill

Cosby Hill

Cosby Hill

Willoughby
Waterless
P

Peatling
Lodge

Peatling
Magna

Inn

Smithy

L.B.

Ch.

Cosby Lodge

Inn

Station
Lodge F.m

311

Hall

Smithy

373

Hunt's
Lodge

Jubilee
F.m

Glebe F.m

279

363

390

361

9

ASHBY MAGNA
STA.

P.
Ashby
Magna

Flude Lodge

395

P.
Dunton
Bassett

Smithy

Smithy

Inn

Ch.

Inn

Ch.

Moat

Oak
Spinney

Moat

Willow F.m

440

Little
Peatling Hall

Ch.

Manor Ho.

448

Peatling
Parva

Inn

Smithy

Peatling Lo.

10

490

420

Flat Ho.

Dunton Lodge

Lodge F.m

475

Ashby
Lodge

Sta. Inn F.m

Moat

Cotes de Vat

Windmill

11

Moat
459

Smithy

T.
Gilmorton

Ch.

Inn

Cauldwell
F.m

Holt F.m

459

472

Bittes.

Gilmorton
Ho.

Inn

Smithy

Wal

443

Edwards's

12

Boston
F.m

408

Ch.

Kimcote
L.B.

447

Gilmorton
Lodge

K I M C O T E

Manor Ho.

400

Cold F.m

Walton Lo.

1

2

1 mile approx.

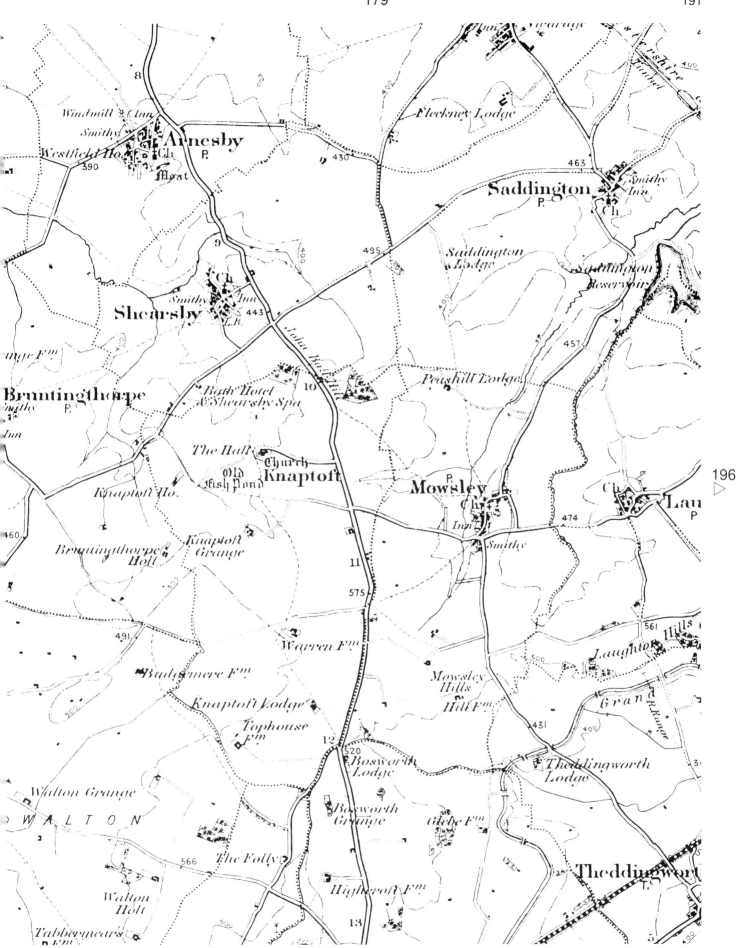

Surveyed 1883 - 86. Revised 1906. Published 1907.

Mill

Smeeton

Westerby

*Gravel
Pit*

Aqueduct

*Gravel
Pit*

Spinny

*Bull
Spiny*

Bull Barn

Works

*Langton
Hall*

Spinny

T.G.

Wide Bridge

Lodge

Debdale Wharf

*Great Bowden
Inn*

*Gunley
Wood*

Union   Can

Foxton

Gunley Hall

Gunley

Garrow Hill

*Foxton
Locks*

T.G.

*Gunley
Gorse*

*Foxton
Mill*

Great

*Brick
Works*

*Harborough
Mill*

Codad Sal

Lodge

Wharf

Canal

Mill

Spinny

MARKET

Lubenham

HARBOROUGH

Old Hall

T.G.

Papillon Hall

River   Welland

Hall

*Thorpe
Lubenham*

Pear Tree

Pear Tree Ford

*Marston
Hussell*

*Farndon
Mill*

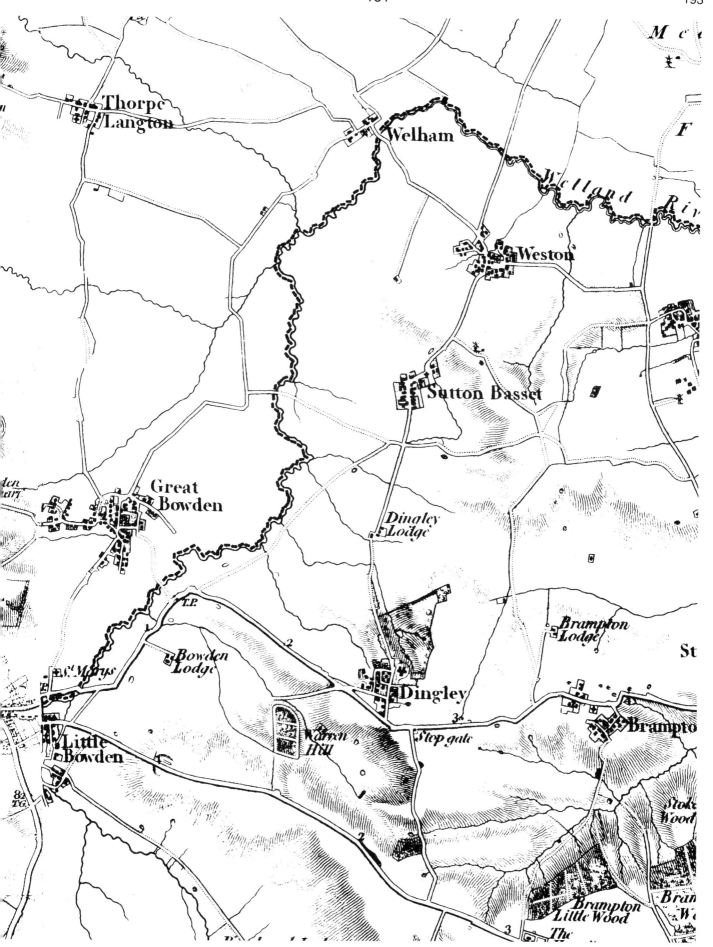

Published 1824.

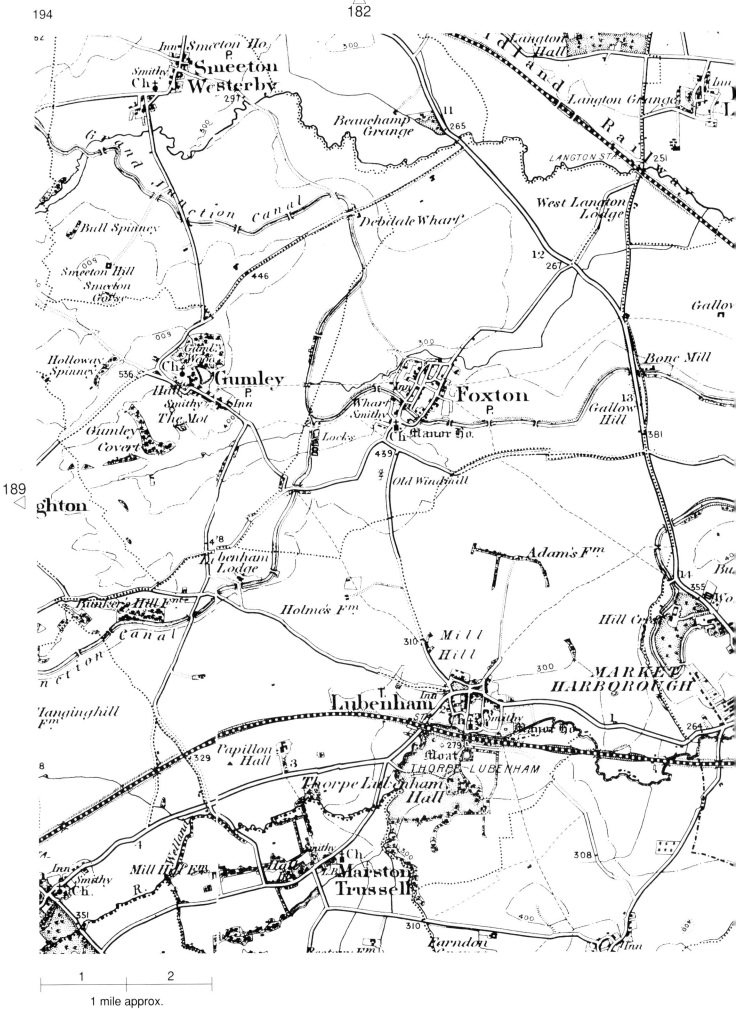

182

189

Inn Smeeton Ho.
P.
Smithy
Ch.
Smeeton
Westerby
297

d Langton
Hall

Langton Grange

Inn

Beauchamp
Grange
11
265

Langton Sta.
West Langton
Lodge
251

300

12
267

Galloy

Bone Mill

Bull Spinney

Grand Traction Canal

Debdale Wharf

446

Smeeton Hill
Smeeton
Gorse

009

Holloway
Spinney
536
Ch.
Grand
Wood

Gumley
P.

Foxton
P.

13

Gallow
Hill
381

Wharf
Smithy
Locks

Ch. Manor Ho.

439

Hall
Smithy
Inn
The Mot

Gumley
Covert

Old Windmill

ghton

Adam's Fm

14
355

478

Lubenham
Lodge

Bu
Wo

Hill Cr

Bunker's Hill Fm

Holme's Fm

Mill
Hill
310

300

MARKET
HARBOROUGH

Inn

ction Canal

Hanginghill
Fm

Lubenham

Inn
Smithy
Manor Ho.
264

Papillon
Hall
329

3

279
Moat
THORPE-LUBENHAM

8

Thorpe Lubenham
Hall

308

Welland

Mill Hill Fm

Smithy
Ch.
Marston
Trussell

300

Inn
Smithy
Ch.
R.

351

310
400

Farndon

Inn

400

1   2

1 mile approx.

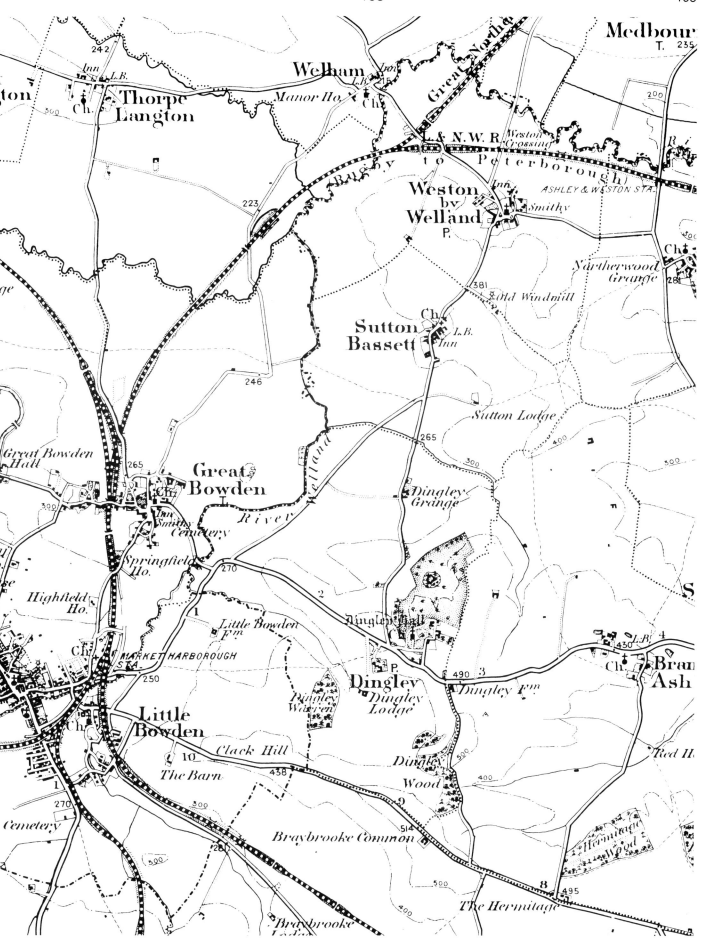

Surveyed 1883 - 86. Revised 1897. Published 1898.

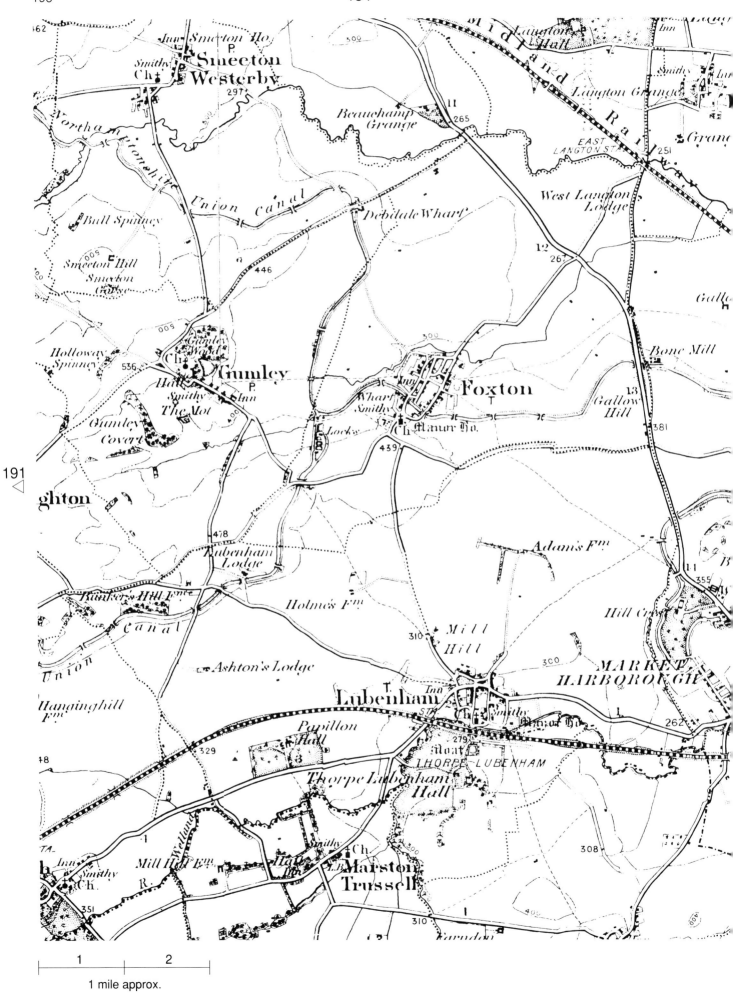

196

△
184

191
△

1

2

1 mile approx.

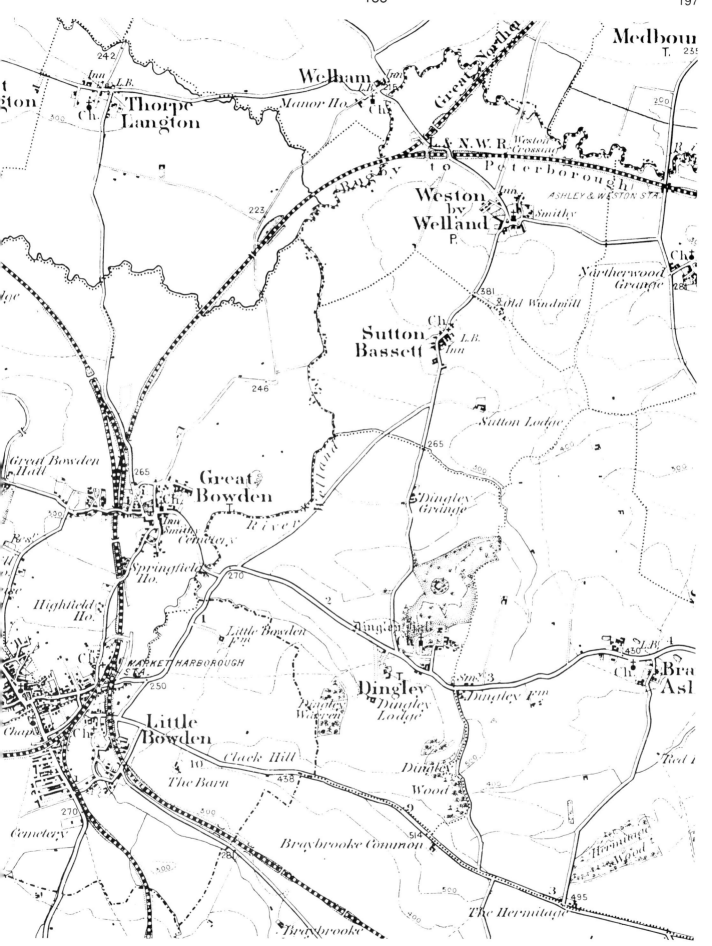

Surveyed 1883 - 86. Revised 1906. Published 1907.

BIBLIOGRAPHY

Portrait of Nottingham by Emrys Bryson. Publisher: Robert Hale 1974.

Portrait of Leicestershire by Brian Bailey. Publisher: Robert Hale 1974.

Derbyshire by Arthur Mee. Publishers: Hodder and Stoughton 1969.

Nottinghamshire by Arthur Mee. Publishers: Hodder and Stoughton 1970.

The Victoria History of the Counties of England. Editor: Christopher Elrington. Publishers: Oxford University Press.

Gazetteer

The following list of place names is not definitive; rather it is designed to stimulate the reader's interest and, used in conjunction with a modern day atlas, assists on a journey of re-discovering one's heritage.

Ab Kettleby, Leics. 132, 134, 136.
Alderwasley, Derby. 42, 44, 46.
Alfreston, Derby. 43, 45, 47.
Allestree, Derby. 79, 81, 83.
Alvaston, Derby. 97, 99, 101.
Ambaston, Derby. 102, 104, 106.
Annesley, Derby. 49, 51, 53.
Anstey, Leics. 162, 164, 166.
Arnesby, Leics. 187, 189, 191.
Arnold, Notts. 72, 74, 76.
Asfordby, Leics. 132, 134, 136.
Ashby Folville, Leics. 150, 152, 154.
Ashby Magna, Leics. 186, 188, 190.
Ashover, Derby. 24, 26, 28.
Aston on Trent, Derby. 102, 104, 106.
Ault Hucknall, Derby. 30, 32, 34.
Aylestone, Leics. 174, 176, 178.

Bagthorpe, Notts. 48, 50, 52.
Bagworth, Leics. 156, 158, 160.
Balcote, Notts. 73, 75, 77.
Bardon, Leics. 138, 140, 142.
Barkby Thorpe, Leics. 163, 165, 167.
Barkby, Derby. 145, 147, 149.
Barlestone, Leics. 156, 158, 160.
Barrow upon Soar, Leics. 126, 128, 130.
Barrow upon Trent, Derby. 97, 99, 101.
Barsby, Leics. 150, 152, 154.
Barton in Fabis, Notts. 103, 105, 107.
Beeston, Notts. 85, 87, 89.
Belper, Derby. 60, 62, 64.
Belton, Leics. 120, 122, 124.
Bilborough, Notts. 67, 69, 71.
Billesdon, Leics. 168, 170, 172.
Bilsthorpe, Notts. 37, 39, 41.
Birstall, Leics. 162, 164, 166.
Blaby, Leics. 174, 176, 178.
Blackwell, Derby. 30, 32, 34.
Blidworth, Notts. 54, 56, 58.

Bolsover, Derby. 12, 14, 16.
Bothamsall, Notts. 19, 21, 23.
Brackenfield, Derby. 25, 27, 29.
Bradmore, Notts. 108, 110, 112.
Bramcote, Notts. 85, 87, 89.
Braunstone, Leics. 162, 164, 166.
Breadsall, Derby. 79, 81, 83.
Breaston, Derby. 102, 104, 106.
Bredon on the Hill, Leics. 115, 117, 119.
Bretby, Derby. 114, 116, 118.
Brimington, Derby. 7, 9, 11.
Brinsley, Notts. 66, 68, 70.
Bulwell, Notts. 67, 69, 71.
Bunny, Notts. 108, 110, 112.
Bur on Overy, Leics. 180, 182, 184.
Burnaston, Derby. 96, 98, 100.
Burrough on the Hill, Leics. 151, 153, 155.
Burton Joyce, Notts. 73, 75, 77.
Burton Lazars, Leics. 151, 153, 155.
Burton on the Wolds, Leics. 126, 128, 130.
Bushby, Leics. 163, 165, 167.

Cadeby, Leics. 156, 158, 160.
Calverton, Notts. 73, 75, 77.
Carburton, Notts. 19, 21, 23.
Carlton Curlieu, Leics. 180, 182, 184.
Castle Donington, Leics. 102, 104, 106.
Chaddesden, Derby. 79, 81, 83.
Chellaston, Derby. 97, 99, 101.
Chesterfield, Derby. 7, 9, 11.
Chilwell, Notts. 85, 87, 89.
Church Gresley, Derby. 114, 116, 118.
Church Warsop, Notts. 18, 20, 22.
Clifton, Notts. 90, 92, 94.
Clipstone, Notts. 36, 38, 40.
Clipston, Notts. 91, 93, 95.
Coalville, Leics. 138, 140, 142.
Cold Newton, Leics. 168, 170, 172.
Colwick, Notts. 91, 93, 95.

Copt Oak, Leics. 139, 141, 143.
Cosby, Leics. 174, 176, 178.
Cossall, Notts. 67, 69, 71.
Cossington, Leics. 144, 146, 148.
Costock, Notts. 108, 110, 112.
Cotes, Leics. 126, 128, 130.
Cotgrove, Notts. 91, 93, 95.
Cotmanhay, Derby. 66, 68, 70.
Countesthorpe, Leics. 174, 176, 178.
Cranoc, Leics. 181, 183, 185.
Cropston, Leics. 144, 146, 148.
Cross Hill, Derby. 66, 68, 70.
Cuckney, Notts. 18, 20, 22.
Cutthorpe, Derby. 6, 8, 10.

Dale Abbey, Derby. 84, 86, 88.
Darley Abbey, Derby. 79, 81, 83.
Denby, Derby. 61, 63, 65.
Derby, Derby. 78, 79, 80, 81, 82, 83.
Desford, Leics. 157, 159, 161.
Dimple, Derby. 24, 26, 28.
Dingley, Northants. 193, 195, 197.
Diseworth, Leics. 120, 122, 124.
Duffield, Derby. 60, 62, 64.
Dunton Bassett, Leics. 186, 188, 190.

East Kirkby, Notts. 49, 51, 53.
East Langton, Leics. 192, 194, 196.
East Leake, Notts. 108, 110, 112.
East Leicester Forest, Leics. 157, 159, 161.
East Norton, Leics. 181, 183, 185.
Eastmoor, Derby. 6, 8, 10.
Eastwood, Notts. 66, 68, 70.
Edwalton, Notts. 90, 92, 94.
Edwinstowe, Notts. 19, 21, 23.
Elmton, Derby. 13, 15, 17.
Epperstone, Notts. 73, 75, 77.
Evington, Leics. 163, 165, 167.

Farnsfield, Notts. 55, 57, 59.
Findern, Derby. 96, 98, 100.
Fleckney, Leics. 175, 177, 179.
Forest Town, Notts. 36, 38, 40.
Foston, Leics. 175, 177, 179.
Foxton, Leics. 192, 194, 196.
Frisby on the Wreak, Leics. 132, 134, 136.

Gaddesby, Leics. 150, 152, 154.
Gamston, Notts. 90, 92, 94.
Gelding, Notts. 73, 75, 77.
Glenfield, Leics. 157, 159, 161.
Glooston, Leics. 181, 183, 185.
Goadby, Leics. 181, 183, 185.
Gorby, Leics. 157, 159, 161.
Gotham, Notts. 103, 105, 107.
Grassmoor, Derby. 7, 9, 11.
Greasley, Leics. 67, 69, 71.
Great Bowden, Leics. 193, 195, 197.

Great Dalby, Leics. 151, 153, 155.
Great Glen, Leics. 175, 177, 179.
Great Stretton, Leics. 175, 177, 179.
Gilmorton, Leics. 186, 188, 190.
Grimston, Leics. 132, 134, 136.
Gumley, Leics. 192, 194, 196.

Hallaton, Leics. 181, 183, 185.
Halstead, Leics. 169, 171, 173.
Hardstoft, Derby. 30, 32, 34.
Hartshorn, Derby. 114, 116, 118.
Hasland, Derby. 7, 9, 11.
Hayward Oaks, Notts. 54, 56, 58.
Hazlewood, Derby. 60, 62, 64.
Heanor, Derby. 66, 68, 70.
Hathern, Leics. 121, 123, 125.
Heath, Derby. 12, 14, 16.
Hemington, Leics. 102, 104, 106.
Higham, Derby. 25, 27, 29.
Highbury Vale, Notts. 72, 74, 76.
Hoby, Leics. 127, 129, 131.
Holbeck, Notts. 13, 15, 17.
Holbrook, Derby. 61, 63, 65.
Holloway, Derby. 42, 44, 46.
Holme Pierrepont, Notts. 91, 93, 95.
Holwell, Leics. 133, 135, 137.
Horsley, Derby. 61, 63, 65.
Hoton, Leics. 126, 128, 130.
Houghton on the Hill, Leics. 168, 170, 172.
Hucknall Torkard, Notts. 67, 69, 71.
Hucknall under Huthwaite, Notts. 30, 32, 34.
Humberstone, Leics. 163, 165, 167.
Hungerton, Leics. 168, 170, 172.

Ilkeston, Derby. 66, 68, 70.
Illston on the Hill, Leics. 180, 182, 184.
Ingleby, Derby. 97, 99, 101.
Inkersall, Derby. 12, 14, 16.
Isley Walton, Leics. 120, 122, 124.

Kedleston, Derby. 78, 80, 82.
Kegworth, Leics. 103, 105, 107.
Keyham, Leics. 168, 170, 172.
Keyworth, Notts. 109, 111, 113.
Kibworth Harcourt, Leics. 180, 182, 184.
Kilbourne, Derby. 61, 63, 65.
Kilby, Leics. 175, 177, 179.
Kimberley, Notts. 67, 69, 71.
Kingston upon Soar, Notts. 103, 105, 107.
King's Newton, Derby. 97, 99, 101.
Kirby Bellars, Leics. 132, 134, 136.
Kirby Muxloe, Leics. 157, 159, 161.
Kirk Hallam, Derby. 84, 86, 88.
Kirk Langley, Derby. 78, 80, 82.
Kirkby in Ashfield, Notts. 49, 51, 53.
Knaptoft, Leics. 187, 189, 191.

Lambley, Notts. 73, 75, 77.

Laughton, Leics. 187, 189, 191.
Leicester, Leics. 162, 163, 164, 165, 166, 167.
Linby, Notts. 49, 51, 53.
Little Bowden, Leics. 193, 195, 197.
Little Bowhill, Derby. 42, 44, 46.
Little Dalby, Leics. 151, 153, 155.
Little Eaton, Derby. 79, 81, 83.
Little Stretton, Leics. 180, 182, 184.
Lockington, Leics. 102, 104, 106.
Lockwell Hill, Notts. 37, 39, 41.
Loddington, Leics. 169, 171, 173.
Long Eaton, Derby. 103, 105, 107.
Long Whatton, Leics. 121, 123, 125.
Loscoe, Derby. 66, 68, 70.
Loughborough, Leics. 121, 123, 125.
Lowdham, Notts. 73, 75, 77.
Lubenham, Leics. 192, 194, 196.

Mackworth, Derby. 78, 80, 82.
Mansfield Woodhouse, Notts. 31, 33, 35.
Mansfield, Notts. 31, 33, 35.
Mapperley, Derby. 66, 68, 70.
Marefield, Leics. 169, 171, 173.
Market Harborough, Leics. 192, 194, 196.
Market Warsop, Notts. 18, 20, 22.
Markheaton, Derby. 78, 80, 82.
Markifield, Leics. 139, 141, 143.
Marston Trussell, Leics. 192, 194, 196.
Matlock, Derby. 24, 26, 28.
Medbourn, Leics. 193, 195, 197.
Melbourne, Derby. 115, 117, 119.
Melton Mowbray, Leics. 133, 135, 137.
Milford, Derby. 61, 63, 65.
Milton, Derby. 96, 98, 100.
Morley, Derby. 79, 81, 83.
Morton, Derby. 25, 27, 29.
Mountsorrel, Leics. 144, 146, 148.
Mowsley, Leics. 187, 189, 191.

Nailstone, Leics. 156, 158, 160.
Narborough, Leics. 174, 176, 178.
Nether Langwith, Notts. 13, 15, 17.
Netherfield, Notts. 91, 93, 95.
Newbold Verdon, Leics. 156, 158, 160.
Newbold, Leics. 115, 117, 119.
Newstead, Notts. 49, 51, 53.
Newton Harcourt, Leics. 175, 177, 179.
Newton Linford, Leics. 139, 141, 143.
Newton Unthank, Leics. 157, 159, 161.
Normanton upon Soar, Notts. 121, 123, 125.
Normanton, Derby. 97, 99, 101.
Norton, Notts. 18, 20, 22.
Nottingham, Notts. 72, 74, 76, 90, 92, 94.
Nuthall, Notts. 67, 69, 71.

Oadby, Leics. 175, 177, 179.
Ockbrook, Derby. 84, 86, 88.
Old Basford, Notts. 72, 74, 76.

Old Brampton, Derby. 6, 8, 10.
Old Dalby, Leics. 132, 134, 136.
Old Radford, Notts. 90, 92, 94.
Old Radley, Notts. 55, 57, 59
Old Tupton, Derby. 25, 27, 29.
Ollerton, Notts. 19, 21, 23.
Osbaston, Leics. 156, 158, 160.
Osgathorpe, Leics. 120, 122, 124.
Oxton, Notts. 55, 57, 59

Papplewick, Notts. 54, 56, 58.
Peatling Magna, Leics. 186, 188, 190.
Peatling Parva, Leics. 186, 188, 190.
Penrich, Derby. 43, 45, 47.
Perlethorpe, Notts. 19, 21, 23.
Pickwell, Leics. 151, 153, 155.
Pilsley, Derby. 30, 32, 34.
Pinxton, Derby. 48, 50, 52.
Pleasley, Derby. 31, 33, 35.
Plumtree, Notts. 109, 111, 113.
Prestwold, Leics. 126, 128, 130.
Pye Bridge, Derby. 48, 50, 52.

Quarndon, Derby. 78, 80, 82.
Queniborough, Leics. 145, 147, 149.
Quorndon, Leics. 144, 146, 148.

Radbourne, Derby. 78, 80, 82.
Radcliffe on Trent, Notts. 91, 93, 95.
Ragdale, Leics. 127, 129, 131.
Rainworth, Notts. 36, 38, 40.
Ratby, Leics. 157, 159, 161.
Ratcliffe on the Wreak, Leics. 145, 147, 149.
Ratcliffe upon Soar, Notts. 103, 105, 107.
Rearsby, Leics. 145, 147, 149.
Rempstone, Notts. 126, 128, 130.
Repton, Derby. 96, 98, 100.
Ripley, Derby. 43, 45, 47.
Risley, Derby. 84, 86, 88.
Robin-a-Tiptoe, Notts. 169, 171, 173.
Rolleston, Leics. 180, 182, 184.
Romford, Derby. 42, 44, 46.
Rotherby, Leics. 150, 152, 154.
Rothley, Leics. 144, 146, 148.
Ruddington, Notts. 108, 110, 112.
Rufford Abbey, Notts. 37, 39, 41.

Saddington, Leics. 187, 189, 191.
Sandiacre, Derby. 85, 87, 89.
Saxelby, Leics. 132, 134, 136.
Scalford, Leics. 133, 135, 137.
Scarcliffe, Derby. 13, 15, 17.
Seagrave, Leics. 127, 129, 131.
Selston, Notts. 48, 50, 52.
Scraptoft, Leics. 163, 165, 167.
Shangton, Leics. 180, 182, 184.
Shardlow, Derby. 102, 104, 106.
Shearsby, Leics. 187, 189, 191.

Shelford, Notts. 73, 75, 77.
Shepshed, Leics. 121, 123, 125.
Sherwood, Notts. 72, 74, 76.
Shipley, Derby. 66, 68, 70.
Shirebrook, Derby. 13, 15, 17.
Shoby, Leics. 132, 134, 136.
Shuttlewood, Derby. 12, 14, 16.
Sileby, Leics. 144, 146, 148.
Skeffington, Leics. 169, 171, 173.
Skegby, Notts. 31, 33, 35.
Slawston, Leics. 181, 183, 185.
Smeeton Westerby, Leics. 192, 194, 196.
Smisby, Derby. 115, 117, 119.
Somerby, Leics. 151, 153, 155.
Somercotes, Derby. 48, 50, 52.
Sookholme, Notts. 18, 20, 22.
South Croxton, Leics. 150, 152, 154.
South Normanton, Derby. 48, 50, 52.
South Wingfield, Derby. 43, 45, 47.
Spondon, Derby. 79, 81, 83.
Stanton by Bridge, Derby. 97, 99, 101.
Stanton by Dale, Derby. 84, 86, 88.
Stanton under Bardon, Leics. 138, 140, 142.
Stapleford, Notts. 85, 87, 89.
Stoke Bardolph, Notts. 73, 75, 77.
Stone Edge, Derby. 6, 8, 10.
Stonton Wyville, Leics. 181, 183, 185.
Stoughton, Leics. 163, 165, 167.
Stretton, Derby. 25, 27, 29.
Sutton Bassett, Northants. 193, 195, 197.
Sutton Bonington, Notts. 121, 123, 125.
Sutton in Ashfield, Notts. 31, 33, 35.
Swadlincote, Derby. 114, 116, 118.
Swannington, Leics. 138, 140, 142.
Swarkeston, Derby. 97, 99, 101.
Swithland, Leics. 144, 146, 148.
Sysonby, Leics. 133, 135, 137.
Syston, Leics. 145, 147, 149.

Tansley, Derby. 24, 26, 28.
Temple Normanton, Derby. 12, 14, 16.
Theddingworth, Leics. 187, 189, 191.
Thornton, Leics. 156, 158, 160.
Thorpe Acre, Leics. 121, 123, 125.
Thorpe Arnold, Leics. 133, 135, 137.
Thorpe Langton, Leics. 193, 195, 197.
Thorpe Satchville, Leics. 150, 152, 154.
Thringstone, Leics. 138, 140, 142.
Thrumpton, Notts. 103, 105, 107.

Thrussington, Leics. 145, 147, 149.
Thurcaston, Leics. 144, 146, 148.
Thurmaston, Leics. 163, 165, 167.
Tibshelf, Derby. 30, 32, 34.
Tickhall, Derby. 115, 117, 119.
Tilton, Leics. 169, 171, 173.
Tollerton, Notts. 91, 93, 95.
Tonge, Leics. 120, 122, 124.
Trowell, Notts. 85, 87, 89.
Tugby, Leics. 181, 183, 185.
Tur Langton, Leics. 180, 182, 184.
Turnditch, Derby. 60, 62, 64.
Twyford, Leics. 150, 152, 154.

Uppertown, Derby. 24, 26, 28.

Waltham on the Wolds, Leics. 133, 135, 137.
Walton on the Wolds, Leics. 126, 128, 130.
Wanlip, Leics. 144, 146, 148.
Welby, Leics. 132, 134, 136.
Welham, Leics. 193, 195, 197.
Wessington, Derby. 43, 45, 47.
West Bridgford, Notts. 90, 92, 94.
West Hallam, Derby. 84, 86, 88.
West Leake, Notts. 103, 105, 107.
West Thorpe, Notts. 127, 129, 131.
Weston by Welland, Northants. 193, 195, 197.
Weston Underwood, Derby. 60, 62, 64.
Weston upon Trent, Derby. 97, 99, 101.
Whetstone, Leics. 174, 176, 178.
Whitehill, Leics. 138, 140, 142.
Whitwick, Leics. 138, 140, 142.
Wigley, Derby. 6, 8, 10.
Wigston Magna, Leics. 175, 177, 179.
Wilford, Notts. 90, 92, 94.
Willington, Derby. 96, 98, 100.
Willoughby on the Wolds, Notts. 109, 111, 113.
Willoughby Waterless, Leics. 186, 188, 190.
Windley, Derby. 60, 62, 64.
Widmerpool, Notts. 109, 111, 113.
Wingerworth, Derby. 7, 9, 11.
Wirksworth, Derby. 42, 44, 46.
Wollaton, Notts. 85, 87, 89.
Woodborough, Notts. 73, 75, 77.
Woodhouse, Leics. 139, 141, 143.
Woodthorpe, Notts. 72, 74, 76.
Woodville, Derby. 114, 116, 118.
Worthington, Leics. 115, 117, 119.
Wymeswold, Leics. 127, 129, 131.
Wysall, Notts. 109, 111, 113.